The Construction of Exodus Identity in Ancient Israel

The Construction of Exodus Identity in Ancient Israel

A Social Identity Approach

Linda M. Stargel

◆PICKWICK *Publications* • Eugene, Oregon

THE CONSTRUCTION OF EXODUS IDENTITY IN ANCIENT ISRAEL
A Social Identity Approach

Copyright © 2018 Linda M. Stargel. All rights reserved. Except for brief quotations in critical publications or reviews, no part of this book may be reproduced in any manner without prior written permission from the publisher. Write: Permissions, Wipf and Stock Publishers, 199 W. 8th Ave., Suite 3, Eugene, OR 97401.

Pickwick Publications
An Imprint of Wipf and Stock Publishers
199 W. 8th Ave., Suite 3
Eugene, OR 97401

www.wipfandstock.com

PAPERBACK ISBN: 978-1-5326-4098-8
HARDCOVER ISBN: 978-1-5326-4099-5
EBOOK ISBN: 978-1-5326-4100-8

Cataloguing-in-Publication data:

Names: Stargel, Linda M., author.

Title: The construction of exodus identity in Ancient Israel : a social identity approach / Linda M. Stargel.

Description: Eugene, OR: Pickwick Publications, 2018 | Includes bibliographical references.

Identifiers: ISBN 978-1-5326-4098-8 (paperback) | ISBN 978-1-5326-4099-5 (hardcover) | ISBN 978-1-5326-4100-8 (ebook)

Subjects: LCSH: Bible. Exodus—Evidences, authority, etc. | Bible. Exodus—Criticism, interpretation, etc. | Exodus, The | Group identity | Israel—History |

Classification: BS1245.52 S76 2018 (print) | BS1245.52 (ebook)

Manufactured in the U.S.A.   05/15/18

Unless otherwise noted, all biblical references in English are taken from the New Revised Standard Version Bible: Catholic Edition, copyright © 1989, 1993 National Council of the Churches of Christ in the United States of America. Used by permission. All rights reserved.

All biblical references in Hebrew are from the *Biblia Hebraica Stuttgartensia,* © 1997 Deutsche Bibelgesellschaft. Used by permission. Verse designations will be based on the BHS.

Scripture quotations marked (NIV) are taken from the Holy Bible, New International Version®, NIV®. Copyright © 1973, 1978, 1984, 2011 by Biblica, Inc.™ Used by permission of Zondervan. All rights reserved worldwide. www.zondervan.com. The "NIV" and "New International Version" are trademarks registered in the United States Patent and Trademark Office by Biblica, Inc.™

Scripture quotations marked (NASB) are taken from the New American Standard Bible®, Copyright © 1960, 1962, 1963, 1968, 1971, 1972, 1973, 1975, 1977, 1995 by The Lockman Foundation. Used by permission. www.Lockman.org

Scripture quotations marked (JPS) are taken from the *Tanakh: A New Tranlation of the Holy Scriptures according to the Traditional Hebrew Text.* Copyright © 1985 by the Jewish Publication Society. All rights reserved.

Contents

Acknowledgements | ix
Abbreviations | xi
Introduction | xv

1 The Social Identity Approach | 1
2 The Application of the Social Identity Approach to Biblical Studies | 16
3 Social Identity Formations in the Primary Exodus Story | 32
4 Social Identity Formulations in Retold Exodus Stories: Pentateuch | 68
5 Social Identity Formulations in Retold Exodus Stories: Prophets and Writings | 93
6 The Significance of Exodus Identity for Ancient Israel | 124
7 Conclusion | 143

Appendix 1: Prior Research on Identity and Memory in Text | 155
Appendix 2: Direct References to Exodus in the Hebrew Bible | 157
Appendix 3: Three Translation Models for Exodus 15:13–18 | 159
Appendix 4: Methodology Worksheets | 160

Bibliography | 193

Acknowledgments

This study is a revised version of my dissertation, "The Construction of Exodus Identity in the Texts of Ancient Israel: A Social Identity Approach" completed in the spring of 2016 (University of Manchester/Nazarene Theological College, Manchester UK). Parts of the dissertation have been removed, reorganized, and rewritten.

I would like to express my gratitude to my PhD advisor Dr. Dwight Swanson for his tireless reviews and advice and to my second advisor Dr. Kent Brower for his insightful critiques. I am also grateful to the faculty and post-graduate students of the Nazarene Theological College for their positive feedback and constructive criticism. I owe a particular debt of gratitude to Dr. Svetlana Khobnya and her family for their warmth, encouragement, hospitality, and for including me in many family dinners and outings during my yearly sojourns in Manchester.

Finally, I want to thank my family for their tremendous flexibility and support: for my kids Nick and Bec who left their "Haiti home" so I could embark on a new educational endeavor lasting over a decade; and for my wonderful husband, Scott, who played both mom and dad during my annual residencies in England, who endured my passionate rants and lightbulb moments, who offered priceless editorial assistance, and who, in the homestretch, made excessive words disappear.

Abbreviations

AA	American Anthropologist
AB	The Anchor Bible
ACOT	Apollos Old Testament Commentary
Am Sociol Rev	*American Sociological Review*
AOAT	Alter Orient und Altes Testament
AOTC	Abingdon Old Testament Commentary
BibInt	*Biblical Interpretation*
BTB	Biblical Theology Bulletin
BZAW	Beihefte zur Zeitschrift für die alttestamentliche Wissenschaft
CBR	*Currents in Biblical Research*
CBQ	*Catholic Biblical Quarterly*
DBAT	*Dielheimer Blätter zum Alten Testament und seiner Rezeption in der Alten Kirche*
ECB	The Expositor's Bible Commentary
ECC	Eerdmans Critical Commentary
EJSP	*European Journal of Social Psychology*
FRLANT	Forschungen Zur Religion Und Literatur Des Alten Und Neuen Testaments
HBT	Horizons in Biblical Theology

HER	Hermeneia—A Critical and Historical Commentary on the Bible
IBC	Interpretation: A Biblical Commentary for Teaching and Preaching
JANER	*Journal of Ancient Near Eastern Religions*
JBL	*Journal of Biblical Literature*
JEMS	*Journal of Ethnic and Migration Studies*
JPS	Jewish Publication Society
JPSP	*Journal of Personality and Social Psychology*
JSOT	*Journal for the Study of the Old Testament*
LA	Liber annuus
LHBOTS	Library of Hebrew Bible/Old Testament Studies
LNTS	Library of New Testament Studies
NAC	New American Commentary
NAS	The New American Commentary
NCB	New Century Bible Commentary
NCBC	New Cambridge Bible Commentary
NEBAT	Die neue Echter-Bibel Kommentar zum Alten Testament
NIB	The New Interpreter's Bible
NIBCOT	New International Biblical Commentary on the Old Testament
NICOT	New International Commentary on the Old Testament
NTS	*New Testament Studies*
OTL	Old Testament Library
PEQ	*Palestine Exploration Quarterly*
SBL	Society of Biblical Literature
Sociol Q	*The Sociological Quarterly*
TBT	*The Bible Today*
TOTC	Tyndale Old Testament Commentaries
TWOT	*Theological Wordbook of the Old Testament*

TZ	*Theologische Zeitschrift*
VT	*Vetus Testamentum*
WBC	Word Biblical Commentary
WestBC	Westminster Bible Companion
WTJ	*Westminster Theological Journal*
WUNT	Wissenschaftliche Untersuchungen zum Neuen Testament
ZAW	*Zeitschrift für die alttestamentliche Wissenschaft*

Introduction

FANS FROM DIFFERENT CONTINENTS cheer for the same team, and soldiers on scattered battlefields fight for a common cause. Relief workers unknown to one another stand shoulder to shoulder pulling survivors from the rubble. Patriots, separated by generations, commemorate their fallen, and worshippers practice an age-old faith. These individuals, detached from one another by space, anonymity, or time, find themselves in a context in which individual self-orientation fades and is replaced by a collective self-concept. Competition, shared belief, tragedy, or a myriad of other factors may engender this collective identity. It may have fleeting, situational salience, or it may be long-lasting, central to a people's self-concept and pervasive of their reality.

How is the long-lasting and internalized type of collective identity created and maintained? The answer is complex and multidimensional. Literary and biblical studies have repeatedly demonstrated that narratives lie at the heart of collective identity formation.[1] An identity constructing narrative often appears as a story shared by a people, and it captures key understandings about what it means to be a member of that group. It can ultimately be reduced to something along the lines of "we are the people who . . . ,"[2] and it is often found in a condensed form as a group label.[3] Because people form them retrospectively, life narratives are able to show both continuity and causality and to give significance and closure to life events, thereby contributing to identity.[4] Shared stories both express the identity

---

1. See Appendix 1, section 1 for a list of these studies.
2. Cornell, "Story of Our Life," 42.
3. Ibid.
4. Lau, *Identity and Ethics in Ruth*, 40.

claims of their producers and shape the identity of their audiences.[5] They help to define, maintain, strengthen, and transmit social identity.

Not all narratives, though, create or reinforce identity. Some narratives function primarily to inform or to entertain. The principal objective of social memory narratives, however, is the concretion of group identity. Memories deemed constitutive of a group are constantly told and retold. Sociologist Maurice Halbwachs coined the term "collective memory"[6] to describe this type of memory. He shifted the study of memory from its traditional framework as an individual faculty of recollection to an examination of it as a social reality. His focus was primarily on orally communicated group memory, and he noted that individuals who were part of a group shared its collective memory without having personal experience of the events remembered.[7]

To have enduring significance, collective memory must eventually be inscribed in the form of texts, monuments, images, buildings, and other such concrete representations.[8] This inscribed collective memory consists of a particular set of dynamic, slowly evolving, meaningful images comprising a group's agreed upon version of the past into which its members are consciously and unconsciously socialized. Because group memory is selective, the memories brought forward in such a fixed form are those that have been deemed worthy of representing the group.

There exists a general consensus among social memory theorists that the function of inscribed collective memory is to bind individual members to the group, to orientate and shape the everyday experiences of the group members, and to stabilize the identity of the social group over time, making it visible to itself and, to some degree, others. "Today it is widely held that 'memory is a central, if not the central, medium through which identities are constituted' since identity is the sense of sameness over time that is derived from memory."[9]

Collective identity is what creates a sense of "us-ness" in people. People from collectivist cultures are less likely to perceive themselves as unique individuals and more likely to identify themselves entirely in terms of group membership. Pilch contends that "the vast majority of the people described in the Bible represent collectivist personality types. Individualist personality

---

5. Ibid., 41.
6. "Social memory" and "collective memory" are now used interchangeably.
7. Halbwachs, *On Collective Memory*, 52–53.
8. Assmann, "Collective Memory and Cultural Identity," 128–30.
9. Spaulding, *Commemorative Identities*, 8.

types are rather rare in the Bible and the Mediterranean culture in general."[10] For the purpose of this study, collective (or social) identity will be defined as a group's continually renegotiated awareness of who they are, their unity and peculiarity and their central understanding about what it means to be a member of the group.

The interest of this book is ancient Israel[11] and how certain narrative resources may have contributed to an enduring collective identity. It is well established that the Hebrew Bible consists of or contains ancient Israel's inscribed collective memory.[12] This study will show *how* specific examples of narrative collective memory in the Hebrew Bible may have functioned to construct and reinforce identity for hearers.

The memory of Israel's sojourn in and departure from Egypt has been chosen as the specific focus of analysis. Narratives of these particular events have a greater "mnemonic density"[13] in the Hebrew Scriptures than any other single narrative theme. They are often accompanied by the sense of obligation characteristic of collective memory.[14] This specific story will be referred to as the "exodus story," although elsewhere the same designation has been used to refer to the broader story encompassing Egyptian bondage, deliverance, wilderness wanderings, giving of the covenant, and entry into the land.[15] The narrower story of Israel's sojourn in and departure from Egypt meets Cornell's description of an identity narrative as an event-centered story of a group. Likewise, it can be condensed into a group label,[16] identifying Israel as "the people whom God brought out of Egypt."[17]

10. Pilch, "Individual? Or Stereotypes?," 71. See also Lau, *Identity and Ethics in Ruth*, 20–25. Scholars arguing that individualism, as a cultural phenomenon, did not appear until at least the sixteenth century include Esler, *Galatians*, 46–47; Marohl, *Faithfulness and Hebrews*, 86–87; Bell, *Cultural Contradictions of Capitalism*, 16; Cushman, *Constructing the Self, Constructing America*, 375; and Lieu, *Christian Identity*, 179.

11. Ancient Israel refers to the real, dynamic, and diverse collective extending from the Iron Age I though the Roman Period. It was this entity that created the literary, biblical Israel and that was informed and transformed by this self-creation.

12. See Appendix 1, section 2 for a list of key studies.

13. Zerubavel explains that while time is homogeneous, equal durations of time are remembered unequally. Some parts of history are essentially relegated to social oblivion while others are remembered intensely. The latter are said to have a greater "mnemonic density" or to occupy a greater "mnemonic space." Zerubavel, *Time Maps*, 25–31.

14. See Assmann, "Collective Memory and Cultural Identity," 131–32; and Hearon, "Woman who Anointed Jesus," 100. For a list of studies of the exodus as collective memory, see Appendix 1, section 3.

15. Frisch, "Exodus Motif in 1 Kings," 5; Coogan, "The Exodus," 209; and Zakovitch, *"You Shall Tell Your Son . . . "* 9.

16. Cornell, "Story of Our Life," 42.

17. See Exod 32:11, Lev 25:55; and Deut 9:26.

Bearing in mind that reality may be created through a text's literary and rhetorical design,[18] exodus stories will be examined to determine how, as narrative resources, they were capable of presenting hearers with and socializing them into a dominant, social identity. The tools used for analyzing the narratives of non-fictional peoples are not limited to those used for analyzing literary fiction. Therefore, a methodological tool based on the principles of the social identity approach (henceforth SIA) will be developed and outlined to assist in exposing identity construction at a rhetorical level. Since the Hebrew Bible took shape over a considerable period of time, its writers and editors likely adjusted stories to fit identities, resulting in variations in identity construction evident in the form and content of exodus narratives.

The Hebrew Bible contains over 120 direct references to the exodus as well as multiple echoes and allusions.[19] Because independent research, cited earlier in this chapter, has shown that it is the stories people tell, in particular, that are formative of group identity, this analysis will limit itself to the examination of exodus stories. Echoes, allusions, and other short references to exodus that do not take on a story form will not be considered.

Biblical stories are comprised of three basic elements: setting, plot, and character.[20] Since echoes, allusions, and other short references to exodus may also embrace elements of setting and characterization, it is the presence of plot that is most helpful in identifying exodus stories. A plot is formed when situations or events are linked to one another in causal, sequential, or associational ways.[21] This implies the presence of at least two such elements.

As stated, this book will examine stories of Israel's sojourn in and departure from Egypt. It will examine both the "primary exodus story" and multiple "retold stories of exodus." The primary exodus story or narrative begins with the summary of the descent of the sons of Israel into Egypt and ends with the Song of the Sea (Exod 1:1—15:21). This literary unit, designated as such by both Childs and Brueggemann,[22] comprises a story with a beginning and an end. While new stories proceed from it, this narrowly defined exodus story is frequently recalled as a historical watershed and means of measuring the passage of time within other stories (beginning with Exo-

---

18. Bal, *Death & Dissymmetry*, 3.

19. Appendix 2 categorizes direct references to exodus according to their apparent function. Echoes of and indirect allusions to exodus are a more subjective endeavor, and therefore no comprehensive list is attempted.

20. Ryken, *Words of Delight*, 19.

21. Cornell, "Story of Our Life," 43.

22. Childs, *Introduction to Old Testament*, 170; Brueggemann, "Book of Exodus," 690–804.

dus 16:1).²³ Although it is widely accepted that various elements of the story, such as the plague narratives, had an independent compositional origin, they are represented in the finished form as part of the exodus story that must be retold to subsequent generations of Israel (Exod 10:2).

The literary unit of Exodus 1:1—15:21 will be referred to as the "primary exodus story" for two reasons. Firstly, it presents itself as an omniscient, eyewitness narration of events. While not historically verifiable (i.e., with respect to the supernatural events reported), or even possible (i.e., in terms of the human knowledge of internal motives and musings), this is nevertheless the implicit claim of the text on the hearer. Secondly, this narrative is designated "primary" because it presents itself as the dominant voice of Israel's sojourn in and departure from Egypt. It comprises the most explicit and extensive treatment of the exodus found in the Hebrew Scriptures. It densely communicates many of the expressions and images of exodus found throughout the rest of Scripture. The designation "primary," however, does not imply that this is developmentally the first and oldest exodus story.

Three broad plot elements characterize the language and imagery of the primary exodus story. There is an initial situation of adversity. This is variously described in terms of oppression or affliction (derivatives of ענה), being enslaved (derivatives of עבד), being mistreated (רעע), as well as in the expressions of groaning and crying out. This first element primarily characterizes Exodus 1:1–2:23, although it is rehearsed throughout the story.²⁴ The second element is the supernatural intervention of God in response to the initial situation. This extends from 2:24—12:30 and is described with expressions such as "strong hand" (יד חזקה), "outstretched arm" (זרע נטויה), "signs" (אות) and "wonders" (מופת). While other short references use these terms to refer broadly to exodus, Martens demonstrates that they refer specifically to God's power to cause plagues and diseases rather than to military power.²⁵ These terms, therefore, primarily bolster the second plot element—the supernatural response of God to a prior situation of adversity. The final plot element in the story is the bringing of Israel out of Egypt and broadly characterizes 12:31—15:21. Terms describing this include the hiphil forms of נצל, ישע, and יצא, as well as the narration of the crossing of the sea. In addition to these three major²⁶ elements of plot, there are two minor ones,

---

23. See references in Appendix 2, section 3d.

24. See for example 3:7, 9, 17; 4:31; 5:6–21; 6:5–6; 13:3, 14.

25. Martens, "Strong Hand and Outstretched Arm," 123–41.

26. This is based on the mnemonic space they occupy in the narrative, not on any evaluation of their significance.

namely, the ancestors' descent into Egypt (1:1–6) on one end of the story and the entry into the land on the other (15:13–17).

In addition to the primary exodus story, this book will examine various "retold exodus stories." These recurring stories represent Israel's departure from Egypt as being in the historical past, recalled from a variety of seemingly later vantage points. It is the resemblance of these retold stories to the dominant narrative that makes them recognizable as exodus stories, even though this may not represent the developmental direction of influence. Certain plot elements and vocabulary found in the primary narrative also characterize these retellings. The story-like character that narratively links together (or crafts a plot with) these various elements identifies the exodus retellings, regardless of whether the narrative is prose or poetic. This sets them apart from both short references to exodus and echoes of exodus.

Some retellings of exodus, such as Deuteronomy 26:5b–9 and Deuteronomy 6:20–24, not only include all three of the common plot elements of the primary narrative in the form of a concise story, but also impose an obligation on the hearer to retell the story. In this way, they explicitly highlight the storytelling act. The retellings in Psalm 78 and Psalm 105 also contain all three plot elements, although in a less succinct story format, as well as an obligation to retell the exodus story within the context of a broader story of God's acts. Deuteronomy 5:15, Joshua 24:2–7, 17, and Nehemiah 9:9–12, 36 also contain all three plot elements of the primary narrative and are, therefore, easily recognizable stories of Israel's sojourn in and departure from Egypt. Other retold exodus stories, distinguished by the presence of at least two of the common plot elements of the primary narrative arranged in story form, are catalogued in Appendix 2, section 2. Direct references to exodus that do not fit the definition of an exodus story will not be examined, nor will echoes and allusions to exodus, since prior research has demonstrated specifically that stories can be creative of collective identity.

The primary exodus story and retold exodus stories will be examined to determine *how* their literary and rhetorical design may have contributed to Israel's collective identity. This study will show how literary rhetoric supports particular constructions of collective identity. It will measure the persuasiveness of the rhetoric rather than its historical accuracy. While the latter may be important to faith and theology, it is not indispensable to identity claims. "What matters is not the validity of the representations but their effects: the degree to which the narrative and its component parts are understood—by group members or by outsiders—as illustrative or exemplary, as capturing something essential about the group in question."[27] In other

---

27. Cornell, "Story of Our Life," 44.

words, collective identities are authentic to the degree they are accepted as real and believed to be descriptive of self. The specific interest in this study is to show how the rhetoric and verbal images of exodus narratives have the potential to persuade unresisting hearers and socialize them into a particular group identity.

The focus of this thesis is on *how*, rather than *when*, exodus narratives constructed identity. Without speculating on the intentions of the producers or the *actual* historical role of the exodus motif in identity formation, the ensuing chapters examine the potential of these narratives, through their literary rhetoric, to create and maintain social identity for ancient Israel. They show that both a well-established, recognizable language of social identity and a narrative configuration that invites ongoing collective identification characterize exodus stories.

Sociological understandings of group identity formation and their recent applications to ancient texts provide a helpful foundation for this analysis. Chapter 1 explores the Social Identity Approach (SIA) and the recognizable elements that constitute collective identifications in both face-to-face relationships and textual constructions. Chapter 2 examines recent investigations that establish the SIA's applicability to ancient cultures and their narratives, including several specific applications of this approach to biblical texts. Then it presents a new tool that emerges from this examination. This tool will prove helpful for isolating rhetorical formulations of collective identity in narratives

Chapters 3 through 5 use the newly developed heuristic tool to expose the distinct identity-forming rhetoric of exodus narratives. This application reveals textual examples of cognitive, evaluative, emotional, behavioral, and temporal formulations of collective identity. Chapter 3 considers the primary exodus story and its prior literary context, while chapters 4 and 5 examine eighteen retold exodus stories. Chapter 6 provides an extensive comparative analysis and synthesis of chapters 3–5. It compares a dominant identity discourse with various other voices of exodus identity. Finally, chapter 7 evaluates the effectiveness of this new tool for analyzing narrative identity construction and it offers recommendations for further study.

1

The Social Identity Approach

SOCIAL IDENTITY WAS FIRST defined as "that part of an individual's self-concept which derives from his knowledge of his membership of a social group (or groups) together with the value and emotional significance attached to that membership."[1] That is to say, social identity was thought to include the following components:

> A cognitive component, in the sense of the knowledge that one belongs to a group; an evaluative one, in the sense that the notion of the group and/or of one's membership of it may have a positive or a negative value connotation; and an emotional component in the sense that the cognitive and evaluative aspects of the group and one's membership of it may be accompanied by emotions (such as love or hatred, like or dislike) directed towards one's own group and towards others which stand in certain relations to it.[2]

While this definition is still widely accepted, the term "social identity" has been used by a few to describe the gregarious aspect of individual identity. In response, some scholars have adopted the term "collective identity" to refer to group identity.[3] Although this newer term provides clarity, both "social identity" and "collective identity" will be used interchangeably in this book since the former is used by the Social Identity Theory (SIT) and the Self-Categorization Theory (SCT), which are central to our methodology.

Collective identity should not be equated with one's beliefs, values, language, culture, and so on. People *first* come to the realization they are a distinct people and *then* they define themselves in relation to certain

---

1. Tajfel, *Differentiation*, 28.
2. Ibid.
3. Thoits and Virshup, "Me's and We's," 106.

cultural indicia that change over time.[4] Collective identity tends to be a dynamic entity, and not something static forced on groups by others or by circumstances. Such a view acknowledges groups as active agents in the making and remaking of their identities over time. Collective identities are perceived as identities that people "accept, resist, choose, specify, invent, redefine, reject, actively defend, and so forth. They involve an active 'we' as well as a 'they.' They involve not only circumstances but also active responses to circumstances by individuals and groups, guided by their own preconceptions, dispositions, and agendas."[5] This constructionist view of collective identities is presumed here. The validity of the assumption will be confirmed by findings of variability in identity formulations in exodus narratives.[6]

The social identity approach (SIA) offers a well-established, theoretical, and empirical understanding of how groups construct collective identity in social contexts. It is an aggregate of various observations and theories of social identity. Its earliest proponents, Henri Tajfel and his colleagues in Britain in the 1960s and 1970s, recognized certain expressions of collective identity in face-to-face relationships. Two ensuing and related theories outlined the psychology and dynamics of groups. Tajfel's Social Identity Theory of Intergroup Behavior (SIT)[7] described the interactions that take place *between* distinct groups and the minimal conditions necessary for intergroup discrimination. Turner's Self-Categorization Theory (SCT)[8] described how a group emerges and what processes take place *within* it.

SIT and SCT grew, at least in part, out of the "master problem"[9] of social psychology: deciphering the relationship between individual and group behaviors. In the first half of the twentieth century, social psychology tended toward a reductionist approach, understanding groups simply in terms of the sum of individual and interpersonal processes. Social identity theories emerged as a critical response to such reductionism. The fundamental hypothesis shared by Tajfel, Turner, and others who further developed their theories,[10] is that individuals define themselves in terms of their

---

4. Esler, "Ezra–Nehemiah," 414.

5. Cornell and Hartmann, *Ethnicity and Race*, 81.

6. Other examples of the reshaping of social memory and identity can be found in Zerubavel, *Recovered Roots*; Schwartz, "Social Change and Collective Memory," 221–36; and Schwartz, "Collective Memory and History," 469–96.

7. Tajfel, *Differentiation*.

8. Turner et al., *Rediscovering the Social Group*.

9. Marohl, *Faithfulness and Hebrews*, 62.

10. Other early contributors to the theory include Hogg and Abrams (see subsequent note).

memberships in social groups, and group-defined self-perception produces psychologically distinctive effects on social behavior.[11]

For the SIA, groups are "processes" more than "things," determined by dynamic self-perception rather than static composition.[12] Group behaviors fall on an "interpersonal-intergroup" continuum. Social encounters defined primarily by personal relationships fall near the interpersonal end, while those defined by membership in different social categories fall near the intergroup end. The SIA is chiefly concerned with interactions near the intergroup end of the continuum.

While Tajfel and his colleagues primarily observed and analyzed various indications of collective identification in face-to-face relationships, later scholarship noted other more enduring representations. Rather than deliberating further on the SIA's historical and chronological development,[13] this chapter offers a comprehensive, categorical overview of the SIA's current understanding of the processes of collective identification. It examines each of these processes independently, while recognizing their integration within a social context.

This chapter not only examines the three dimensions of collective identity recognized by Tajfel—cognitive, evaluative, and emotional—but also the more recently probed behavioral and temporal dimensions.

Cognitive Dimension

The cognitive dimension of social identity is the self-awareness that one belongs to a group.[14] As the SIA developed, it became evident that such knowledge is conveyed in a variety of ways, including categorization, boundary formation, designations of prototypical group members and stereotyping.

Categorization and Boundary Formation

Humans simplify the seemingly infinite stimuli that daily bombard their senses to create a "more manageable number of distinct categories,"[15] a process called categorization. Social categorization happens as humans

---

11. Hogg and Abrams, *Social Identifications*, xiv.
12. Tajfel, *Social Identity and Intergroup Relations*, 485.
13. An example of this can be found in Esler, "Outline of Social Identity Theory," 13–39.
14. Ibid., 28.
15. Hogg and Abrams, *Social Identifications*, 18.

systematize and simplify their environment by grouping together similar people, objects, and events.[16] People may be sorted into named groups or categories or into a category represented by a plural pronoun such as "us" and "them." When encountering something novel, people tend to evaluate it based on one or more existing categories that make sense to them. Categorization also guides people's actions. Grouping similar situations and events based on one's past experience, along with previously tested responses, creates a more limited array of choices and a greater possibility of a positive outcome. Categorization of other people varies widely based on the context of the interaction.

Categorization leads to the creation and maintenance of boundaries, or boundary markers. Social boundaries are the criteria used to distinguish between group members and non-members.[17] The study of the interrelationship between boundaries and group identity originated with social anthropologist Fredrik Barth.[18] He reacts against the assumption that group identity persists because of geographic or social isolation. Instead, he posits that identity exists in the midst of social interaction due to the creation and maintenance of boundaries. Recently, scholars have integrated Barth's approach to identity and boundary formation into social identity research.[19]

Barth rightly notes that boundaries comprise only those features that the members themselves regard as significant, rather than all the objective differences that may exist between groups.[20] Group boundaries may be situational and fluid, adapting to the needs of the group. They are always dialectical. The group generates the boundary and not the reverse. One such boundary, examined in this book, is "the people whom Yahweh brought up out of Egypt." It creates a means of distinguishing Israel from not-Israel. However, neither this boundary nor a historical exodus event created Israel per se. Instead, Israel, who regarded this distinction as significant, selectively emphasized it in her narratives as an act of social identification.

Boundaries affect the processes of exclusion and incorporation but they do not necessarily prevent social interaction. They range in nature from rigid—making it impossible or difficult for individuals to move from one group to another—to flexible—permitting individual social mobility.

16. Tajfel, *Differentiation*, 61.

17. Tajfel introduces the idea of social boundaries to SIT, though he expounds little on this concept. Tajfel, *Differentiation*, 27–60.

18. Barth, *Ethnic Groups and Boundaries*.

19. See for example Esler, "Ezra–Nehemiah," 413–26; Esler, *Conflict and Identity in Romans*; Esler, *Galatians*; and Baker, "Social Identity Theory and Biblical Interpretation," 131.

20. Barth, *Ethnic Groups and Boundaries*, 14.

Individuals may cross group boundaries by natural means, such as marriage or adoption, or by fabricated approaches, such as re-actualizing a past event[21] or creating "fictive kinship" ties[22] and myths of common origin.[23] The latter examples serve to unify group members across time, and they fit more appropriately into the temporal dimensions of social identity.

Social psychologist Daniel Bar-Tal argued that some groups came into existence and persisted because of a perception of shared beliefs among individuals, not just because of social categorization.[24] Group beliefs could be in the form of values, goals, norms, or ideology. The willingness to accept those beliefs determines one's inclusion in or exclusion from the group. Distinguishing group members from non-members based on shared beliefs, however, should be viewed as a type of boundary formation. The significance of particular beliefs may change over time, while a sense of being a distinct group remains.

Boundaries provide meaning and significance to social categorization and often are the basis of evaluative differentiation of one's group (the ingroup) from others (the outgroups).[25] Negative effects of cognitive processes on group behavior, however, may motivate a group to redefine itself. To reduce bias or discrimination, for example, a group may redraw is boundaries to be more inclusive.

Prior to the formation of the SIA, a social psychologist named Sherif examined intergroup conflict. He found that he could reduce bias and hostility by introducing mutual goals into a situation of conflict between groups.[26] From these observations, contemporary social identity theorists developed recategorization models that encourage members of conflicting groups to regard themselves as belonging to a common overarching group that is inclusive of both memberships.[27] Thus, "when members of two groups or subgroups are incorporated within a superordinate group, they will treat one

---

21. Nasuti and Childs do not speak about boundary crossing (in the language of SIT) but they do talk about taking on the identity of others through actualization. Nasuti, "Historical Narrative and Identity," 132–53; Childs, *Memory and Tradition*, 53–89.

22. Miller, "Ethnicity and the Hebrew Bible," 174.

23. Smith, *Myths and Memories*, 57–89.

24. Bar-Tal, "Group Beliefs," 94–101.

25. The terms ingroup and outgroup were coined by Sumner, who intimated that preference for and attachment to one's own group (ingroup) rather than the other-group (outgroup) may be a universal feature of human social life. Sumner, *Folkways*, 12–13.

26. Sherif et al., *Intergroup Conflict and Cooperation*, 160–88.

27. Gaertner and Dovidio, *Reducing Intergroup Bias*, 33.

another favorably as ingroup members rather than engage in the practices of stereotyping and antipathy accorded to outgroups."[28]

Prototypes and Stereotypes

For groups, information about a social category is aggregated into a prototype, an actual or idealized member of the group who "is believed to capture the central tendency of a social category."[29] The prototype, then, represents the group: its character, its values, its goals, its beliefs, and its norms, and those who conform more closely to the prototypes tend to have enhanced esteem and status within the group.[30] Changing situations and recategorization processes require prototypes that are dynamic and adaptable.[31]

Similarly, categorization is moderated by the use of stereotyping, an "accentuation effect" that emphasizes the similarities between the units of a particular category—people, events, concepts, etc.—while minimizing their differences. People may not fully understand every unit of a category, so they streamline them to include only those attributes shared by most of the category's members. As a result, members tend to define both ingroups and outgroups homogeneously or stereotypically. Hakola notes:

> The central hypothesis for group behavior is that, as shared social identity becomes salient, individual self-perception tends to become depersonalized. This means that when we experience ourselves as identical with a certain class of people and in contrast to some other classes, we tend to stereotype not only the members of outgroups, but also ourselves as a member of our own ingroup.[32]

That is to say, people may perceive and interact with others on the basis of their categorical assignment rather than as unique individuals.

The creation of prototypes and stereotypes are interrelated. According to Hogg, "When we categorize others as ingroup or outgroup members we

---

28. Esler, *Conflict and Identity in Romans*, 142.

29. Marohl, *Faithfulness and Hebrews*, 133. Some scholars distinguish between "prototypes" and "exemplars" based on whether the idealized member is a past group member or a present one (Smith and Zarate, "Exemplar and Prototype Use," 243–62) or an imaginary group member or real one (Esler and Piper, *Lazarus, Mary and Martha*, 33). In this book, the term "prototype" is used for any ideal representative of a social group.

30. Roitto, "Behaving like a Christ-Believer," 109.

31. Baker, "Social Identity Theory and Biblical Interpretation," 132.

32. Hakola, "Burden of Ambiguity," 447.

accentuate their similarity to the relevant prototype—thus perceiving them stereotypically and ethnocentrically. When we categorize ourselves, we define, perceive, and evaluate ourselves in terms of our ingroup prototype, and behave in accordance with that prototype."[33] The depersonalization process that occurs as a result of categorization, stereotyping and the creation of prototypes guides group perception and behavior. Tajfel contends that the depersonalization process is so indispensable to group identity that categorical distinctions are maintained even when they are not completely rational or reasonable.[34]

Evaluative Dimension

Categories, boundaries, prototypes, and stereotypes are all shared realities among members of a group. Once constituted, self-aware groups and their members tend to act on the basis of those formulations: comparing, differentiating, and making value judgments about themselves, their members, and others. These evaluative processes act in concert with the cognitive processes.

The evaluative dimension of social identity has to do with one's positive or negative evaluation of a group and its membership.[35] It applies to the ingroup's assessment of itself and of others. Evaluative components often include a group's positive evaluation of itself, and its acts of differentiation from and devaluation of others.

Differentiation

A self-aware group with defined categories tends to differentiate itself from other groups. An outgroup or "other" is "[a] person or group of people symbolically constructed as foreign or alien so as to serve as a definitional boundary for the self or for one's own group."[36] The differentiation (or social comparison) contrasts the ingroup both to this other and to how the ingroup *thinks* the other perceives it. The formation of collective identity is, thus, a relational process. Often, the "other" is not radically different, especially in the case of the "proximate other," which is why it becomes

---

33. Hogg, "Social Identity Theory," 559.
34. Tajfel, *Human Groups and Social Categories*, 132–33.
35. Tajfel, *Differentiation*, 28.
36. Newsom, "God's Other," 34.

necessary to create distinctions between the two groups.[37] "It is often the perceived similarity between groups that threatens the distinctiveness of the group and triggers intergroup conflict."[38]

Hinkle and Brown observed that not all groups engage in this intergroup differentiation. In one study, only nine of fourteen groups showed comparative inclinations. The authors determined that groups are more likely to engage in intergroup comparison if 1) the social setting is more collective than individualistic and 2) the group exhibits a comparative outlook.[39] The SIA is an appropriate tool for analyzing the identification processes of groups, but especially for the collective-comparative groups. Members of such groups tend to evaluate themselves closely with respect to a prototypical ingroup representative.[40] Likewise, they view others as exemplified by a perceived outgroup prototype. Differences between the ingroup and the outgroup, therefore, tend to be exaggerated and polarized.[41] This need for social differentiation, according to Tajfel, "is fulfilled through the creation of intergroup differences when such differences do not in fact exist, or the attribution of value to, and the enhancement of, whatever differences that do exist."[42] While categorization and differentiation accentuate the differences *between* groups, they also maximize similarities and minimizing differences *within* the group.

Positive Evaluation of the Ingroup

Groups engage in differentiation to create a positive identity by making comparisons that favor the ingroup in relation to the outgroup. It is a selective process in which positive characteristics are enhanced and negative aspects minimized or selectively eliminated. At the same time, the outgroup's negative features tend to be exaggerated and their positive qualities minimized. These distinctions are generalized to the whole group. Thus, "while categorization produced the search for distinguishing features, social

---

37. Smith, "What a Difference a Difference Makes," 5.
38. Hakola, "Social Identities and Group Phenomen," 264.
39. Hinkle and Brown, "Intergroup Comparison and Social Identity," 67–68. A collective orientation emphasizes cooperation within the group, collective achievements, and close ties with ingroup members rather than interpersonal competition, individual achievement, and separation from the ingroup. Comparative ideologies may be based on the nature of the group or the specific group context.
40. Turner, "Social Identity Perspective," 11.
41. Hakola, "Social Identity and a Stereotype in the Making," 132.
42. Tajfel, *Human Groups and Social Categories*, 276.

comparison and the need for positive identity promote selective accentuation of intergroup differences that favor the in-group."[43]

Social comparison results in both positive esteem for the ingroup and in behavior favoring the ingroup and discriminating against outgroups. Tajfel's social identity research was prompted, in part, by a series of studies conducted by social psychologist Muzafer Sherif.[44] Sherif studied boys of similar ages and backgrounds who did not know each other prior to attending a summer camp. They were randomly separated into two groups. After each group built social attachments within its ranks, they were pitted against each other in a series of competitive games. Sherif observed that the competitions became increasingly aggressive. He documented hostility, inter-group bias and discrimination. He then made various attempts to reduce tension between the groups. The most successful was the introduction of common, superordinate goals, which could not be achieved apart from the cooperation of both groups.

Building on Sherif's study, in the 1970s Tajfel conducted experiments designed to determine the minimal requirements needed to cause individuals to create perceptions of group belonging, to think in terms of "us" and "them," and to sanction intergroup discrimination.[45] Sherif had shown that differentiation occurred in situations where 1) group members anticipated future interaction between groups, 2) group members thought their responses would benefit their own interests, or 3) there were previous attitudes of hostility. Tajfel eliminated these factors along with the face-to-face encounters between participants. Individuals still were noted to discriminate against an imaginary outgroup. That is to say, individuals developed an ingroup identity and showed favoritism toward it with respect to a *symbolic* outgroup. Thus, Tajfel demonstrated that even a small act of categorization was enough to produce intergroup behavior aimed at fostering a positive social identity.

Devaluation of the "Other"

While groups tend to emphasize and enhance their own favorable characteristics in order to promote positive self-esteem, social identity theorists have observed that groups achieve the same outcome by devaluing or denouncing an outgroup. An outgroup's negative characteristics are emphasized and exaggerated. Devaluation takes many forms: mocking,

---

43. Abrams and Hogg, *Social Identity Theory*, 3.
44. Sherif et al., *Intergroup Conflict and Cooperation*.
45. Tajfel et al., "Social Categorization and Intergroup Behavior," 149–78.

pronouncements of curses, announcements of doom, ironic reversals, political satire, and so on. In extreme forms, devaluation gives rise to violence and even to dehumanization of the "other."

Emotional Dimension

Emotional responses of a group's members toward themselves and others often accompany the above-mentioned cognitive and evaluative aspects of their social identity.[46] This emotional dimension, however, has received little attention by SIA theorists.

Positive emotions linked to group membership may include feelings of attachment and belonging, a sense of interdependence, and the perception of a shared fate. Negative emotions may include feelings of hostility and conflict toward an outgroup. Hogg argues that this affective dimension is the outcome and not the basis of ingroup identification.[47] This coincides with Turner's earlier contention that "social categorization per se should cause individuals to perceive their interests as cooperatively linked within groups and competitively linked between groups."[48]

Members of social groups tend to possess some degree of emotional involvement or closeness with one another, which results in feelings of group attachment and belonging. These in turn reinforce the positive esteem of the ingroup,[49] and may lead to affective ties toward symbolic representations of the group, such as flags, cities, buildings, and land.[50]

The more a group positively perceives itself as interdependent and having a shared fate, the greater their attachment is to one another. Interdependence is "a functional relationship in which one's own outcomes depend instrumentally on the actions of the other and the other's outcomes depend on one's own behavior."[51] The perception of a shared fate is the sense of "being together in the same situation facing the same problems"[52] or "sharing the same positive or negative outcomes."[53] Theorists from Sherif to

---

46. Tajfel, *Differentiation*, 28.

47. Hogg, "Social Identity and Group Cohesiveness," 102; and Hogg and Abrams, *Social Identifications*, 100.

48. Turner, "Experimental Social Psychology," 98.

49. See also Brown and Capozza, "Motivational, Emotional, and Cultural Influences," 4.

50. Ashmore, Deaux and McLaughlin-Volpe, "An Organizing Framework," 90.

51. Turner, "Social Identity, Interdependence and the Social Group," 38.

52. Turner et al., *Rediscovering the Social Group*, 34.

53. Turner, "Social Identity, Interdependence and the Social Group," 38.

Korostelina have demonstrated, however, that strong identification with an ingroup often leads to antagonism, antipathy and conflict with others.[54] Recategorization of two disparate groups into a superordinate group, in turn, may reduce such negative emotional aspects.

Behavioral Dimension

The behavioral dimension of social identity—also referred to as "group identity norms" and "identity descriptors"[55]—has recently received increased attention by scholars. Social psychologist Rupert Brown defines group norms as "a scale of values that defines a range of acceptable (and unacceptable) attitudes and behaviors for members of a social unit."[56] Group norms, in essence, guide members into how to behave appropriately in order to remain part of the group. Thus, group norms act as a further means of ingroup/outgroup differentiation.

Norms serve several functions relevant to the creation and maintenance of collective identity. They create cohesion as well as visible displays of group identity in social interactions. They bring order and predictability to new situations by narrowing the number of appropriate moral choices. Likewise, the acceptance of group norms helps to instill a group's particular vision of reality into the hearts and minds of its members, thus helping the group achieve its goals.[57]

Temporal Dimension

The temporal dimension of social identity is the latest to be brought to light and formulated. Early social identity theorists did not significantly address the question of how a group might maintain a sense of "us-ness" over time. Recent works by Condor and Cinnirella address this deficit.[58]

---

54. Sherif et al., *Intergroup Conflict and Cooperation*. Korostelina, *Social Identity and Conflict*.
55. Esler, "Social Identity, Virtues, and Good Life," 55.
56. Brown, *Group Processes*, 56.
57. Esler, "Social Identity, Virtues, and Good Life," 54–55.
58. Condor, "Social Identity," 285–315; Cinnirella, "Temporal Aspects," 227–48.

Transmission and Translation of Social Identity over Time

In a Festschrift honoring Tajfel, Condor acknowledges his inaugural contributions toward viewing social groups as temporal processes. She underlines several of his brief descriptions of social identification as dynamic and variable.[59] She astutely notes, however, that Tajfel did not develop this idea to any significant extent in his empirical research that regards social perceptions and identifications as relatively enduring. In examining Turner's SCT, Condor notes that while he, by contrast, empirically demonstrates social identifications as flexible and context-dependent, he does not account for the temporal continuity of social identities, stereotypes, categories, and groups over time.

Condor argues that social groups, as processes, must be viewed as both dynamic and enduring. The key to a social group's endurance is having "successive social actors." Each of these social actors will effectively "'translate' (drop, transfer, corrupt, modify, add to or appropriate) [certain] practices in the course of taking them up and passing them on."[60] With respect to social identity, the translation over time and the dispersal over space create the perception of an ontological continuity encompassing successive generations.[61] In this way, social identity may be experienced as a serial connectedness with other ingroup members.[62] "This sequence extends beyond the boundaries of my life, both into the past before my birth and into the future after my death.... The *we* with whose experience the individual identifies can both pre-date and survive the individuals that make it up."[63]

Condor recognizes that a social identity's coherency over time or space is dependent upon boundaries that are flexible enough to allow the inclusion of new social actors. "Translated" identities and manipulations of a group's past and possible future are essential to the maintenance of social identity over time. Otherwise, a social identity would be limited to a particular group of people at a particular time in a particular place. Condor demonstrates that a temporal understanding of social identity is simultaneously enduring and malleable.

---

59. Condor, "Social Identity," 288.
60. Ibid., 291.
61. Ibid., 305–6.
62. Ibid., 306.
63. Ibid.

Possible Social Identities and Shared Life Stories

Cinnirella further develops the under-researched temporal dimension of social identity. Extending Markus and Nurius's "possible selves" perspective (unconnected with the SIA),[64] he creates the concept of "possible social identities"—all potential group memberships that a group imagines as possible or desirable.[65] These possible social selves are influenced by social representations of a group's past and of their possible future. They are also molded by group efforts to seek coherence among these past, present, and future identities.

Cinnirella is particularly concerned with the effect of past social identities. He maintains that social groups predominately oriented to the past tend to re-discover and re-activate past-oriented prototypes, stereotypes, and social identities in order to construct their own present identity.[66] He also contends that possible social identities associated with large social groups are especially subject to negotiation, manipulation, and contestation. They tend to be widely and visibly distributed in order to persuade both ingroupers and outgroupers to endorse the desired possible social identities of the ingroup.[67]

One means of socializing members into possible social identities is through shared "life stories." These are broad and ongoing narratives created by social groups to integrate the contemporary hearers with those of the past and the predicted future in order to create a sense of "us-ness" that will endure over time. The re-tellings and re-casting of these life stories promote a cohesive group identity.[68] This allows a group to see its identity over time as a coherent, perhaps gradually unfolding, story.

Carr's findings are consistent with Cinnirella's "shared life stories." According to Carr, all human reality, including experience and memory, is inherently temporal, and therefore inherently narrative. In other words, life is best understood as story, and "narration, as the unity of story, story-teller,

---

64. Marcus and Nurius, "Possible Selves," 954–69. The authors maintain that "possible selves" represent one's ideas of what he/she might become, would like to become or is afraid of becoming. The pool of possible selves derives from representations of the self in one's sociocultural and historical context and from models, images, and symbols provided by social experiences and mass communication. "Possible selves thus have the potential to reveal the inventive and constructive nature of the self but they also reflect the extent to which the self is socially determined and constrained" (954).

65. Cinnirella, "Temporal Aspects," 227–48.

66. The truth of this claim is demonstrated in Friedman, "The Past in the Future," 837–59.

67. Cinnirella, "Temporal Aspects," 235.

68. Ibid.

audience, and protagonist is what constitutes the community, its activities, and its coherence in the first place."[69] For Carr, there is no separation between a community and its constitutive narrative. "A community exists where a narrative account exists of a *we* which persists through its experiences and actions. Such an account exists when it gets articulated or formulated—perhaps by only one or a few of the group's members—by reference to the *we* and is accepted or subscribed to by others."[70] That is to say, a group is defined, composed and maintained by the stories it lives and tells.[71] Linde asserts that there exists within a social group the obligation to tell and participate in the group's shared life story.[72]

Cornell and Hartmann argue that the construction of social identities involves the use of symbolic resources to communicate meaning.[73] These symbolic resources "establish or reinforce the sense among group members of sharing something special—a history, a way of being, a particular set of beliefs—that captures the essence of their peoplehood."[74] Stories, celebrations, and other symbols condense and capture the meaning of a group's social identity, or at least its desired meaning. For Cornell, stories become most salient in constructing social identities in periods of "rupture" when "the taken-for-grantedness that characterizes most collective identities is disturbed."[75]

> When people take on, create, or assign an ethnic identity, part of what they do—intentionally or not—is to take on, create, or assign a story, a narrative of some sort that captures central understandings about what it means to be a member of the group. It is a story that can be told in many ways, but ultimately it can be reduced to something along the lines of "we are the people who ..." (alternatively: "they are the people who ..."), in which the lacuna becomes a tale of some sort, a record of events,... the things the group does or did or will do or has done to it.... [The] narrative is an event-centered conception of the group. The label group members carry or assign to others is a referent or symbol, in effect a condensation of that narrative.[76]

69. Carr, "Narrative and the Real World," 128.
70. Ibid., 130.
71. See also Linde, *Working the Past*; and Cornell, "Story of Our Life."
72. Linde, *Working the Past*, 72–195.
73. Cornell and Hartmann, *Ethnicity and Race*, 236–37.
74. Ibid., 237.
75. Cornell, "Story of Our Life," 42.
76. Ibid.

In other words, one of the most common ways for social groups to identify themselves is by telling stories of who they are in relation to significant events. This is what is meant by a shared life story.

Cinnirella, Carr, Linde, and Cornell all demonstrate the crucial role stories play in the shaping of a group's collective identity over time. The shared life story model is essential to understanding the temporal dimension of social identity construction in face-to-face relationships.

Myths of Common Descent

Studies of ethnic identity have developed independently from the SIA. One of the first efforts to incorporate findings into SIA from these studies was Esler's application of Barth's ethnic boundaries. The concept of boundaries is now well integrated into SIA. Lacking, though, is the integration of the conception of *myths of common descent* into social identity studies. Smith recognizes the important role of myths in social movements, including their potentialities for group identity and collective action. He differentiates between *genealogical* and *cultural-ideological* myths. The former traces descent biologically from a common ancestor and the latter rests on a spiritual kinship, cultural affinity, or ideological "fit" with a previous group. Smith posits that myths of common descent are vital for national solidarity.[77] In this book, I will show that they are applicable to the more comprehensive category of social identity as well, serving as temporal expressions of group identity.

This overview of the theoretical expressions of collective identity comprising the Social Identity Approach has integrated relevant research and presented it in coherent categories. The identification processes it describes have been validated in controlled face-to-face experiments and real life social situations. This book, however, will also demonstrate how these identification processes are evident in the narratives of ancient cultures.

---

77. Smith, *Myths and Memories*, 57, 62. See also Zerubavel, *Time Maps*, 57–58.

2

The Application of the Social Identity Approach to Biblical Studies

As mentioned in chapter 1, previous empirical data has substantiated each dimension of the SIA. Additional longitudinal studies would broaden SIA's understanding of the temporal dimension, but such studies are complex and time consuming in nature. Thus, the retrospective study of social identity in the narratives of an ancient culture, as is undertaken by this analysis, will offer helpful insight into this particular dimension of social identity.

This chapter examines and validates the applicability of the SIA to ancient societies and their inscribed cultural memory, particularly as it relates to the study of ancient Israel and her narratives. It also presents a new methodological tool that is useful for discerning social identity formation in biblical narratives. Chapters 3–5 will apply this tool to exodus stories in order to gain insight into how they may have functioned as identity resources for ancient Israel.

Ancient Cultures and Social Identity

The SIA was developed within the British context of the 1970s and 1980s. Can its principles be applied to ancient cultures and their writings?

The SIA as a Universal Conception

Identity theories are descriptive rather than prescriptive. They were developed by examining how groups express collective identity in face-to-face relationships. The theories expanded and changed as subsequent observations conformed to or challenged previous descriptions of identity construction.

Newer research revealed that elements identifiable in narratives of the past were similar to the methods of identity construction found in the face-to-face contemporary relationships. Lieu, for example, demonstrates that the SIA's differentiation of "us" from "others" was present as early as the fifth century BCE.[1] Bosman found that identities are constructed and operate according to certain basic principles that are then customized to a particular group. He concludes that the SIA is a "universal" theory and, therefore, may be applied to ancient societies such as Israel.[2] Tellbe agrees saying, "Theories about the construction of social identity transcend time and history, at least at a general level."[3] Therefore, the relatively recent emergence of the language of "identity" and "identity construction" does not invalidate the application of identity models to ancient writings.

Cultural Dimensions and Social Identity

According to Hinkle and Brown, collectivist-comparative groups are by nature more likely to engage in social identification processes such as categorization and differentiation. Bosman shows that ancient Israel is an example of a collectivistic culture.[4] This is well established in biblical scholarship especially with respect to Israel's portrayal of herself in her sacred texts,[5] in cultural anthropological studies of the ancient Near East, the examination of biblical law and ideology and, in a limited way, through the findings of ethnoarchaeology. Coleman Baker points to the common scholarly understanding of Israel as a tribal coalition by the twelfth century BCE and to the unifying effect of covenant as further evidence of the collective orientation of ancient Israel.[6] While personal identity in Israelite society was present, it was a non-dominant component. Since the SIA is more appropriate for evaluating processes of collectivist groups, it is a relevant tool to use in the study of ancient Israel.

---

1. Lieu, *Christian Identity*, 17.
2. Bosman, *Social Identity in Nahum*, 84.
3. Tellbe, *Christ-Believers in Ephesus*, 138.
4. Bosman, *Social Identity in Nahum*, 86. Triandis describes four traits of collective cultures: 1) the definition of the self as interdependent; 2) the primacy of ingroup goals; 3) the primary emphasis on group norms as the determinant of behavior; and 4) the importance of communal relationships. Triandis, "Individualism and Collectivism," 36.
5. Lau, *Identity and Ethics in Ruth*, 39; and Meyers, "The Family in Early Israel," 21.
6. Baker, "New Covenant, New Identity," 5.4–5.6.

Not only was ancient Israel collective in nature,[7] but her scriptures reflect a comparative ideology, at least on the part of the producers. Even a cursory examination of the Hebrew Bible reveals a portrayal of Israel as distinct from the wider ancient Near Eastern societies, of the elect over against the non-elect.[8] This is to be expected, as research shows that collectivist cultures tend to be comparative and competitive, directing great loyalty and commitment toward the ingroup, while treating outgroup members with hostility and contempt.[9]

Ancient Narratives and Social Identity

While the previous sections show that the SIA is applicable to ancient cultures such as Israel, the question remains as to whether this approach may be properly applied to narratives and not just to the people who might compose them.

Assimilation of Collective Memory and Social Identity

Although social identity concepts were first developed by examining real or imagined social interactions, newer studies suggest that temporal dimensions of social identity are created or sustained by means of collective memory. For social identity to be translated over time and dispersed over space, retroactive and proactive memory is required.[10] Shared life stories are one possible means of how this translation occurs.[11] These stories may subsequently be reinterpreted or reconstructed in order to maintain the continuity of a group's identity over time. Groups that have an orientation to the past will mobilize these shared stories to "tell itself who it is in the present."[12]

Social Memory Theory, developed independently of SIA, explores the ways that social groups and their members reconstruct, commemorate, and transmit their pasts. Social memory, also called collective memory, is defined as "recollections of the past that have been shaped and formed by and for a

---

7. Even if the Hebrew Bible were a literary invention that did not reflect the reality of the early history of Israel, its portrayal of a group characterized by a collective orientation would reflect the time of its composition.
8. Kaminsky, "Israel's Election and the Other," 18.
9. Marohl, *Faithfulness and Hebrews*, 89.
10. Condor, "Social Identity," 303–5.
11. Cinnirella, "Temporal Aspects," 235.
12. Esler, "Collective Memory and Hebrews 11," 158.

corporate group."[13] Groups selectively construct their collective memory "in ways that provide them with collective self-esteem, distinctiveness, continuity over time, self-efficacy and group cohesion."[14] These memories may be transmitted orally for several generations until the person-to-person links weaken with time. Long-term memory, however, especially in contexts of cultural or political instability, must be preserved in other ways such as by ritual reenactment, commemoration, or inscribing practices.[15]

Kirk and Thatcher compiled research on significant analytic approaches to the operations of inscribed social memory among ancient peoples, assessing their effects. They show that through social memory "a group continually reconstitutes itself as a coherent community."[16] As mentioned in chapter 1, it is now widely recognized that collective memory is the central medium through which group identities are constructed. When Assmann expanded collective memory to include cultural memory in the form of texts, images, rituals, and so on, he argued that such a crystallized memory has the same constructive effect on group identity.[17] Studies of inscribed collective memory have proven this to be true.

Esler shows how the SIA is helpful for augmenting the collective memory model.[18] The growing field of collective memory studies easily assimilates recent interest in the temporal dimension of the SIA.[19] Both domains are concerned with how a group deals with the past for the sake of the present and future. The collective memory of the one approximates the shared life stories of the other, and both of these have been shown to be fundamental to the construction and reinforcement of collective identity.

Shared life stories are not the only point in which the temporal dimension of the SIA intersects social memory theory. According to social memory theories, the collective memory of a group is stored in—and mobilized by an appeal to—idealized figures from a group's past.[20] A recent book examines how particular figures from the Hebrew Scriptures provided Yehud and Judean diasporic communities with a sense of a shared past and a common identity.[21] The SIA similarly recognizes that group prototypes

13. Spaulding, *Commemorative Identities*, 6.
14. Bikmen, "History, Memory, and Identity," 21.
15. Blenkinsopp, "Memory, Tradition, and the Construction of the Past," 77–78.
16. Kirk, "Social and Cultural Memory," 5.
17. Assmann, "Collective Memory and Cultural Identity," 128–30.
18. Esler, "Collective Memory and Hebrews 11," 157.
19. Esler and Piper, *Lazarus, Mary and Martha*, 4.
20. Ibid., 37.
21. Edelman and Zvi, *Remembering Biblical Figures*.

"must be remembered and commemorated in various ways for their prototypical status to remain effective."[22] Prototypical figures from the past are offered as "possible social identities" for a contemporary group.[23]

The temporal dimension of the SIA, therefore, overlaps with Social Memory Theory at a minimum of two points: the use of prototypical figures from the past as possible social identities for a group's present and the use of shared life stories to define group identity. Since the application of Social Memory Theory to biblical studies is broadly supported, its integration with the SIA reinforces the applicability of the latter to ancient narratives as well.

Prior Research on Ancient Texts and Social Identity

Not only is the SIA theoretically suitable for examining the collective memory of ancient texts, but prior research in the field of biblical studies has demonstrated its practical applicability.

Applications of the SIA to the Christian Testament and Qumran Texts.

Esler was the pioneer of this type of application in studies of the Christian Testament.[24] He reveals the presence of various components of the SIA in the rhetoric of these ancient texts. His early works focus on the narrative use of social identification processes either to create and maintain distinct group identities or to reduce the resulting intergroup conflict.[25] He explores each of the three dimensions of social identity recognized by Tajfel—cognitive, evaluative, and emotional—and cites specific examples of each found in the texts. He then introduces the fourth dimension of collective identity—behavioral.[26] These dimensions are shown to define and maintain a

---

22. Baker, "Social Identity Theory and Biblical Interpretation," 132.

23. Esler, "Collective Memory and Hebrews 11," 163.

24. Esler's first published work on the extended use of the SIA in the Christian Testament was "Group Boundaries and Intergroup Conflict in Galatians." An earlier essay on the Beatitudes had been presented by Esler at a 1994 British New Testament Conference in Nottingham. This was eventually published in 2014 as Esler, "Group Norms and Prototypes," 147–71.

25. Esler, "Group Boundaries and Intergroup Conflict in Galatians"; Esler, *Galatians*; Esler, "Keeping it in the Family," 145–84; Esler, "Jesus and the Reduction of Intergroup Conflict," 325–57; Esler, *Conflict and Identity in Romans*; and Esler, "Social Identity, Virtues, and Good Life."

26. Although this is introduced briefly in Esler, "Group Boundaries and Intergroup

new identity for Christ-followers that is distinct from those of Gentiles and Israelites. Esler further shows how social identification processes such as recategorization are used in the text to widen the scope of the Christian group identity and to reduce conflict among hearers.[27]

In three later works, Esler examines the more recently articulated temporal dimension of social identity.[28] He demonstrates how narratives reconstruct the Israelite past to create a shared story that is formative of Christian identity in the present with "a trajectory trailing into the future," as well as how prototypes, not only in their cognitive dimension but as possible selves, have the potential to sustain identity over time.[29] Paul is given as a prototype of the Christ-movement[30]—a real person from the historical past characteristic of its identity—as are Lazarus, Mary, and Martha.[31]

Esler demonstrates how narrative rhetoric is employed to create and maintain group identity among listeners. His application, however, is limited to small literary units and to the use of the SIA to "make sense of the meanings biblical texts communicated to their original audiences."[32] He interprets texts as windows into a particular past. He does not explore how they communicated identity to a broader audience over time, but he paves the way for such discussion by advancing the temporal dimension of social identity. In total, his writings lay the foundation for the systematic exploration of how the rhetoric of ancient texts encompasses a wide range of social identity formulations. Several dozen recent studies are built upon this foundation, including scholarly applications of the SIA to the Christian Testament and Qumran writings.

The most common dimensions of social identity examined in Christian Testament and Qumran texts are cognitive and evaluative formulations. Emotional formulations are only examined in depth by Tellbe.[33] Behavioral formulations are developed extensively by several of Esler's writings[34] as

---

conflict in Galatians," 228–29; and Esler, *Galatians*, 45; its first extensive treatment is in Esler, "Social Identity, Virtues, and Good Life," 53–61.

27. Esler, "Jesus and the Reduction of Intergroup Conflict," 347–49 (recategorization); and Esler, *Conflict and Identity in Romans*, 30–32 (common ingroup identity).

28. Esler, "Collective Memory and Hebrews 11"; Esler, "Remember My Fetters"; and Esler and Piper, *Lazarus, Mary and Martha*.

29. Esler, "Remember My Fetters," 163, 171.

30. Ibid., 239.

31. Esler and Piper, *Lazarus, Mary and Martha*, 75–103.

32. Esler, "Remember My Fetters," 235.

33. Tellbe, *Christ Believers in Ephesus*.

34. Esler, "Group Boundaries and Intergroup conflict in Galatians"; Esler, *Conflict and Identity in Romans*; and Esler, "Group Norms and Prototypes," 147–71.

well as those of Ukwuegbu, Tellbe, and Roitto.³⁵ The temporal formulation of shared life stories is examined by Tellbe, Marohl, and Esler,³⁶ while the examination of past figures as prototypes or "possible social selves" for later hearers is found in writings by Esler, Marohl, Baker, and Carter.³⁷ The most noteworthy applications of the SIA to the rhetoric of Christian Testament texts (after Esler) are those of Marohl and Tellbe,³⁸ but their treatments are far from comprehensive or systematic.

The application of the SIA is not limited to a particular time or context, and, as a heuristic device, it "can help interpreters to pay attention to social aspects and processes of identity formation in the texts." ³⁹ Scholars vary, however, in their estimation of the usefulness of textual formulations for also reconstructing the history and social world of the producers of the text or their audiences. Many, like Esler, see the processes of social identification in the text as a reflection of processes occurring within the historical context.⁴⁰ Marohl, for example, asserts that the text of Hebrews employs social categorization in the form of us/them to compare the faithfulness of the ingroup with the unfaithfulness of the symbolic outgroups. As a result, Marohl identifies the addressees of Hebrews as a distinct social group whose "dominant identity descriptor" was "faithfulness." The weakness of Marohl's argument is the assumption that the text reflects the social context of the addressees, while it is equally likely to reflect the ideal, polemical world of its creators. In other words, the addressees may not have categorized the world into "faithful" and "unfaithful," thus prompting the writers to generate such a process of social identification.

Hakola cautions against assuming a direct correlation between textual rhetoric and existing socio-historical context.⁴¹ He judiciously notes that social identification processes should be understood as the product of

---

35. Ukwuegbu, "Paraenesis, Identity-defining Norms, or Both?," 538–59; Tellbe, *Christ Believers in Ephesus*; and Roitto, "Act as a Christ-Believer," 141–61.

36. Tellbe, *Christ Believers in Ephesus*; Marohl, *Faithfulness and Hebrews*; and Esler, "Collective Memory and Hebrews 11."

37. Esler, "Collective Memory and Hebrews 11"; Esler, "Remember My Fetters"; Marohl, *Faithfulness and Hebrews*; Baker, *Identity, Memory, and Narrative in early Christianity*; and Carter, "Social Identities, Subgroups, and John's Gospel," 235–51.

38. Marohl, *Faithfulness and Hebrews*; Tellbe, *Christ Believers in Ephesus*.

39. Tellbe, *Christ Believers in Ephesus*, 138.

40. See Roitto, "Act as a Christ Believer," 153, for an explicit example. Nebreda also uses the SIA "to get as close as possible to the social context of Philippians." Nebreda, *Christ Identity*, 35.

41. This argument is made throughout Hakola's writings, including his most recently published book: Hakola, *Reconsidering Johannine Christianity*.

efforts to construct and clearly define ingroup social identity.[42] In his essay applying the SIA to Qumran writings, for example, Hakola examines the polemic against the Pharisee. He concludes that it was more a reflection of social differentiation against a proximate other that threatened the distinction of the Qumran community than it was a representation of an existing, real world distinction. Analyzing texts with a social identity hermeneutic may illuminate the processes of social identification, therefore, without revealing the actual socio-historical world of the original audience.

Baker's narrative-identity model highlights how narratives affect the identities of their audiences.[43] He builds on Ricoeur's understanding of the emergence of identity as hearers of narrative are engaged in a three-fold process of prefiguration, configuration, and refiguration.[44] Firstly, an audience brings to their hearing of the text information, experiences, memories, and an initial identity (prefiguration). Then an interaction occurs between this audience and the narrative (configuration). Finally, this interaction results in either the reinforcement of the initial identity and memory or the reformation of identity and memory (refiguration). Baker's model is invaluable to any discussion of texts as identity-shaping resources, reminding scholars that identity formation takes place in dialogue between active agents and textual identity rhetoric. Although Baker, like Esler, is concerned with the authorial audience, his model is applicable to subsequent hearers of the text. The methodological question might be, "how might the identity-shaping processes evident in a text interact with a particular audience's pre-existing identity to reinforce or transform it?"

The applications of the SIA to Christian Testament and Qumran texts not only serve as examples for a similar application to the Hebrew Bible, but they provide essential cautions about inferring a direct relationship between identity rhetoric and actual socio-historical situations.

Applications of the SIA to the Hebrew Bible.

In contrast to the multiple works applying the SIA to the Christian Testament, comparatively few studies have specifically employed the SIA in the study of the Hebrew Bible. Bosman's 2005 doctoral dissertation[45] offers the first explicit and extensive application of SIA to the Hebrew Bible. He focuses

42. Hakola, "Burden of Ambiguity," 453.
43. Baker, *Identity, Memory, and Narrative in early Christianity*, 28–30.
44. Ricoeur, *Time and Narrative*, 1:52–83, 2:157–79.
45. This dissertation was published in book form as Bosman, *Social Identity in Nahum*. Citations are from the book.

on how the social identity of ancient Israel is constructed *in* and *through* the Oracles Concerning the Nations found in Nahum. He posits that "groups create their social identity by constructing textual identities."[46] Not only do texts reflect the collective identities of their composers, but, he asserts, these same texts present a possible social identity to their hearers. Thus, the identity formulations present in the biblical text "have a hermeneutical effect on the way readers (old and new) of these oracles interpret their own lives and construct their own identity."[47] Similarly, a group's possible social identities are limited by the resources available to it at any given point in time.[48]

Bosman insists that *social* identity, rather than another specific category of identity—religious, ethnic, national, etc.—represents an integrated approach to understanding Israel's identity. Bosman argues that the SIT and the SCT (referred to together in this book as the SIA) provide the best instruments for describing ancient Israel's collective identity construction. He notes that while other approaches may be able to describe a group's identity, the SIA is best able to describe the *process* and *dynamics* of identity construction.[49]

Bosman specifically applies many of the social identity principles delineated in the previous chapter to the text of Nahum. He demonstrates how the text defines homogeneous, stereotypical outgroups, how prototypes are created in the process of categorization, how certain rhetorical methods are used to devalue the outgroup, and how group norms affect identity construction.

Two years after Bosman's dissertation, Jonker's applied the SIA to Chronicles, comparing its account of Hezekiah's reign to that of Kings. He found that the Chronicler recasts the narrative to shift the focus from the Deuteronomist's emphasis on political events to an emphasis on cultic events. As part of an identity reforming process, this retelling supports Israel's new identity not as an independent political entity but as the Persian province of Yehud.[50] Jonker cites Bosman's use of the SIA in Nahum and agrees that it is the appropriate method to describe the processes of identity construction in Chronicles. Jonker especially applauds Bosman's understanding of and application of "textual identities." He adds, "Texts that are the products of reinterpretation, allusion and rephrasing, are therefore not merely a reflection of social identities, but the process of construction of

---

46. Ibid., 89.
47. Ibid., 16.
48. Ibid., 89.
49. Ibid., 84.
50. Jonker, "Reforming History," 26.

these texts in itself contributes to the process of identity formation during their time of origin."[51]

Jonker also applies the SIA to a study of rhetorical differences between the accounts of Jehoram's reign in Chronicles and Kings.[52] In the omissions, additions, and changes found in the Chronicles text, Jonker observes a "blurring of the lines" between Judah and Israel consistent with the condition of post-exilic Yehud in which boundaries between north and south were no longer clearly defined. The formerly divided kingdoms now endured a common political fate under Persian rule which motivated them to remember their shared past.[53] On the other hand, the portrayal of Jehoram turning from the ways of the kings of Judah to the ways of the kings of Israel, challenges the people of Jerusalem to differentiate themselves from the *religious* behaviors of the north.[54] Thus, assimilation and differentiation are held in tension with respect to Yehud's "blood brothers" to the north. Foreigners are also displayed ambiguously, both as different and as useful tools of judgment in the hands of Yehud's God.

Jonker summarizes his research, "historical traditions were repeated not for the sake of reconstructing the past but for the sake of self-categorization in a new present."[55] Chronicles reflects the identity work of the post-exilic Jerusalemite composers and functions as a resource for a community negotiating its identity. Jonker discerns many social identity components in his analyzes, including categorization, boundaries, differentiation, positive evaluation of the ingroup, shared fate, and of the coherence of the group over time.

Baker purposes to employ the SIA as a heuristic tool for understanding the treatment of the New Covenant in Jeremiah.[56] He summarizes the SIA and defends its applicability to ancient Israel as a collective and competitive culture. He argues that 31:31–34 should be understood as an attempt to create a new common in-group identity for the collective category consisting of both the House of Israel and the House of Judah in the post-exilic Israelite

---

51. Ibid., 33.
52. Jonker, "Textual Identities in Chronicles," 197–217.
53. Ibid., 211.
54. Ibid., 212.
55. Ibid., 214.
56. Baker, "New Covenant, New Identity." For bibliographical purposes, it should be noted that this biblical scholar was previously known as Jr. Coleman Baker, J. Coleman Baker or J. C. Baker. Following the completion of his PhD studies and the death of his father, he has been referred to as Coleman A. Baker.

community.⁵⁷ He does not succeed in applying any specific principles of the SIA to his textual analysis.

In contrast to Baker, Finitsis explicitly applies the SIA to a consideration of "the Other" in Haggai and Zechariah 1–8. He shows that the polarized portrayal of Israel's identity, characteristic of the late postexilic period and reflected in the text of Ezra–Nehemiah, is atypical of the early postexilic period. The prophecies of Haggai and Zechariah are shown to adopt a more conciliatory approach, formulating a new cohesive group identity for the people of Yehud.⁵⁸ Avoiding Ezra–Nehemiah's distinction between returnees and "remainees," Finitsis underscores Haggai's rhetorical representation of his audience as all the people who came out of Egypt (2:4–5a). In other words, he unifies his audience by associating them with the exodus tradition, invoking the shared, foundational story to help achieve the rebirth of the nation.⁵⁹

Haggai also uses exodus imagery to construct the outgroup as "the oppressing enemy and the wealthy neighbor"⁶⁰ (cf. 2:21b–22; 2:6b–8). According to Finitsis, Haggai's re-purposing of the exodus motif allows him to avoid casting the "other" as merely a part of the former self. This representation establishes cohesion for the ingroup and a commitment to rebuilding the Temple together.⁶¹ This is in keeping with Brown's contention that "biased intergroup attitudes may be functional in assisting the group to achieve its objective."⁶² Further, the use of exodus imagery creates a sense of continuity between the contemporary group and the past generation of exodus, building a sense of certainty that a future deliverance is coming.⁶³

For Finitsis, Proto-Zechariah paints a more complex portrait of self and Other than Haggai. Like Haggai, the ingroup comprises all the people of Yehud. By using the designation "your ancestors" in every verse of his introduction and by presenting a common heritage, Zechariah connects his audience with the past of pre-exilic Israel and connects the returnees to those who stayed behind.⁶⁴ At the same time, Zechariah creates categories for inclusion and group behavior. The people should shun the practices that led to their ancestors' demise because membership in the community is not automatic

---

57. Ibid., 5.1.
58. Finitsis, "The Other in Haggai and Zechariah 1–8," 117.
59. Ibid., 120.
60. Ibid., 120–22.
61. Ibid., 122.
62. Brown, *Group Processes*, 260.
63. Finitsis, "The Other in Haggai and Zechariah 1–8," 121.
64. Ibid., 123.

or unconditional but based on superior, ethical behavior. Group boundaries are flexible enough, though, to include others, beyond the residents of Yehud, including the diasporic remnant who will one day be gathered to Jerusalem.[65] Zechariah's vision of the community may encourage further returns among the diaspora as well as motivate Israelites abroad to financially support the restoration project, something Haggai does not envision.

Proto-Zechariah's boundary between self and Other is less rigid that Haggai's. Although the nations that inflicted exile on the Israelites must be punished, once the balance is restored the prophet opens the door for outsiders to join Yahweh's people. Proto-Zechariah presents Israel's group identity as enviable even to outsiders, making it even more valuable to the ingroup.[66] Finitsis identifies specific formulations that contribute to group identity: defining an "other," delineation of boundaries, emotional imagery of belonging and conflict, interdependence and shared fate, identity norms, images of the group as coherent over time, and a sense of common heritage.

Lau also applies the SIA to the Hebrew Bible. His heuristic approach to the Ruth narrative, analyzes the behavior of the text's protagonists to show how literary devices might have promoted group identity norms in ancient Israel. Ruth's presence as a virtuous foreigner, for example, promotes the value of tolerance towards outsiders, and it challenges their reader to broaden their conception of membership in Israel to include choice and quality of character rather than simple genetic descent.[67] Likewise, Boaz is portrayed as an ideal Israelite, presenting חסד to the reader as an identity norm that exceeds the minimal prescriptions of the law.

Lau highlights various aspects of social identity including a prototypical group member (Boaz), stereotyping of the outgroup (Ruth the Moabite), and emotional images of attachment, belonging, interdependence, and shared fate. In addition to exposing the text as a potential identity resource, Lau posits that the pressing social identity concerns of the text help to establish its provenance in the Persian Period. Finally, Lau defends the use of this methodology against charges of reductionism and determinism, and shows how these pitfalls might be avoided.[68]

---

65. Ibid., 124–25.
66. Ibid., 131.
67. Lau, *Identity and Ethics in Ruth*, 115–18.
68. The charge of reductionism is that viewing the biblical text through a particular lens, such as SIA, flattens the inherent contours of a text by concentrating attention on only a specific aspect of the text. This is true of every analytical method and can only be avoided by recognizing the multidimensional character of the biblical text and supplementing social scientific approaches with other methods of critical interpretation (7–8). The charge of determinism is that the use of a method such as SIA "leads

The five applications of the SIA to the Hebrew Bible considered here[69] do not focus on reconstructing the past through their textual analysis but rather on questioning how the identity rhetoric of their particular literary unit may have functioned to negotiate a new identity for Israel in the post-exilic period. They recognize the persuasive potential of these texts, regardless of their provenance, during a "period of rupture" when ancient Israel's collective identity was questioned and contested.[70] There is wide agreement that most of the books of the Hebrew Bible were read together and came to be seen as a coherent collection in the late Persian or early Hellenistic period.[71] Thus, the potential identity-forming function of any one of these literary units might best be discerned and understood in conversation with the others. A study that places a larger cross-section of texts in conversation with one another will add to the understanding of the potential effect of textual resources as a whole on identity formation.

The applications of the SIA to the Hebrew Bible examined thus far illuminate social identification processes closely resembling those observed in face-to-face relationships by Tajfel and others. Such evidence provides sound argument for the applicability of the SIA as a heuristic tool for understanding Israel's sacred texts.

A Methodological Tool for Discerning Social Identity Formation in Biblical Texts

The applications of the SIA to the Hebrew Bible, cited above, show that the dimensions of social identity recognized in face-to-face relationships are also discernible in the rhetoric and images of ancient texts. Dimensions of collective identity construction that are often internal and invisible in face-to-face relationships, become visible, audible, and even exaggerated in their narrative formulation. This allows them to be deeply internalized and personalized by the hearers of the text.

By integrating the SIA's five dimensions of social identification explored in the first section of this chapter with prior scholarship recognizing

---

the interpreter to view the biblical evidence in a certain way, or assume that a particular pattern of conduct must be present" (8). Lau maintains that the use of models as heuristic tools, prompting the search for patterns, correlations, and coherency among masses of material in a comparative process, is central to the avoidance of determinism (9). Lau, *Identity and Ethics in Ruth*, 7–9

69. Baker's work has been excluded for not making specific application of the SIA.
70. Cornell, "Story of Our Life," 42.
71. Edelman and Zvi, *Remembering Biblical Figures*, xi–xii.

their textual formulation, a valid methodological tool for discerning the expression of social identity in biblical texts has been devised (see Table 1). This multidimensional heuristic tool follows the systematic organization of the processes seen in face-to-face relationships and presents a matrix of verbal and imaginal representations of social identity that might be expressed in narrative. When placed alongside of a biblical text, the heuristic tool will help to pinpoint the consciously or unconsciously crafted narrative formulations of social identity. These formulations not only represent collective identification processes present in narratives but they have the potential to mediate social identity to hearers. Combined with the recognition that social identity is "not an essence but a positioning,"[72] this tool will assist in analyzing exodus narratives and exposing their possible impact on ancient Israel's collective identity.

Israel's foundational story, preserved in sacred text, is centered on a major event, the exodus, and is condensed in the label "we are a people whom God brought up out of Egypt, out of the land of slavery." As such, it is constructed in the manner and with the ingredients previously described by Cornell as characterizing an identity story. The aim of the remainder of this book is not to further prove the validity of a social identity approach to ancient texts, but rather to utilize the newly developed methodological tool to illuminate social identification processes at work in exodus narratives. The primary exodus story will first be examined for language and images reflecting the five dimensions of social identity formation. Then eighteen retold exodus stories will be examined in the same way.

This study will show how a collective exodus identity was broadened through literary formulations to incorporate previous and subsequent social actors who were not initially included in the category of "the people whom Yahweh brought up out of Egypt." Such representations (possibly even "manipulations") of a group's past and possible future were essential to the maintenance of social identity over time. In this way, the exodus generation and exodus event become prototypical of all Israel and her experience.

---

72. Hall, "Cultural Identity and Diaspora," 237.

THE CONSTRUCTION OF EXODUS IDENTITY IN ANCIENT ISRAEL

Table 1: Rhetorical Formulations of Social Identity

Verbal or Imaginal Representations	Definition or Example
Cognitive Formulations	
Categorization	
Named Group (group name or label)	General names, e.g. "people of God," "foreigners" as well as specific, proper names, e.g. "Israel," "Egyptians," "Philistines"
Plural Pronouns	The placement of self or others in a category represented by plural pronoun, e.g. "Us," "You (plural)," "Them"
Boundaries	Features of the group that its members consider significant or defining, e.g. "Those who worship Yahweh," "those who keep covenant," "descendants of Abraham," "circumcised," "one who had turned from idols to God"
Shared Beliefs	Values, goals, norms, or ideology characteristic of the group
Prototypes	A member who typifies the group or is depicted in an idealized way to represent the group
Stereotypes	A selection of one or more characteristics of a group as representative of the entire group, e.g. "And all Israel heard the news that Saul had smitten the garrison of the Philistines, and also that Israel had become odious to the Philistines." Both Israel and the Philistines are stereotyped here as homogeneous groups, acting corporately.
Evaluative Formulations	
Differentiation	Distinctions made between the self and the "other"
Positive Evaluation of the Ingroup	Emphasizes or accentuates positive traits of ingroup
Devaluation of the "Other"	Mocking, pronouncing of curses, announcements of doom, ironic reversals, political satire

Verbal or Imaginal Representations	Definition or Example
Emotional Formulations	
Inter-Group Conflict	*Expressions of struggle or opposition*
Attachment and Belonging	*Expressions of closeness and solidarity*
Interdependence	*Terms involving cooperation and reliance*
Shared Fate	*"My fate and my future are bound up with that of all Israel"*
Behavioral Formulations	
Identity Norms	*Defining acceptable group behavior and attitudes*
Temporal Formulations	
Coherency Over Time	*The group is perceived as a unified whole over time*
Possible Social Identities	*Identity a group believes it has had in the past, often embodied in a real or imagined person, which becomes prototypical of its identity in the present or for the future.*
Myths of Common Descent	*Trace a group's origins back to common place, ancestor, event, etc.*
Genealogical	*Traces the group's descent biologically to a common ancestor*
Cultural-Ideological	*Traces descent by means of spiritual kinship, cultural affinity, or ideological "fit" to presumed ancestors*
Shared Life Stories	
Obligation to Tell	*Israel was to tell the story of the invasion of locusts to her children (Joel 1:3)*
Actualization	*Summons to enter into the group, often by re-enacting their story*

3

Social Identity Formations in the Primary Exodus Story

CHAPTERS 1–2 INTRODUCED THE social identity approach (SIA), established its applicability to ancient texts, and proposed a methodological tool for recognizing and distinguishing rhetorical formulations of identity in biblical narratives. The next three chapters employ this heuristic tool to search for consciously or unconsciously crafted narrative formulations of social identity in the primary exodus story and retold exodus stories.[1] Narrative examples of the cognitive, evaluative, emotional, behavioral, and temporal formulations of collective identity are analyzed both separately and in conversation with each other.

This chapter will examine, in particular, how the primary exodus story (Exodus 1:1—15:21) and its prologue construct and maintain Israel's identity using social identity formulations. In his survey of the book of Exodus, Johnston maintains that

> The narrative itself is not a sober historiographical analysis and reconstruction, seeking merely to satisfy the antiquarian interest of the intellect, but an artistic work which seeks also to appeal to the imagination and win the commitment of readers or hearers of all ages and abilities. It employs suitable devices of narrative art to capture and intrigue the audience.[2]

Johnstone may not have had in view literary formulations of social identity when he asserted that the book of Exodus employed "suitable devices of narrative art," but it is just such formulations which stand out in the story of the exodus and which may have captured the imagination and commitment of the hearers of the text.

1. See Appendix 4 for methodology worksheets.
2. Johnstone, *Exodus*, 31–32.

Prologue to the Primary Exodus Story
(Genesis 12:1—50:26)

The "prologue" to the primary story (Genesis 12:1—50:26) contains two proto-exoduses: Abram's sojourn in and departure from Egypt (12:10-20) and Jacob's descent (46:1—47:12), promise of being brought out (46:4), and post-mortem exodus from Egypt (50:7-14). Also included are two "prequels" to exodus: God's revelation to Abraham of the eventual descent of his posterity into an unnamed foreign land, bondage, and exodus (15:13-16), and Joseph's prediction of Israel's departure from Egypt and his request for his bones to be taken with her (50:24).[3] The identity formulations found in this literary prologue will help illuminate those found in the primary exodus story.

Cognitive Formulations

In Genesis it is common for collective peoples to be categorized into named groups. Examples include the Hittites, Canaanites, and Perizzites (23:7 and 34:30). However, with the exception of an anachronistic comment found in 32:33, references to בני ישראל in Genesis refer to the patriarch and his fixed set of sons rather than to a community of people. The use of בני ישראל as the named group of a community or society of people commences in the book of Exodus. The singular עבר is used once to describe Abraham (14:13) and three times in reference to Joseph (39:14; 39:17; 41:12). The plural עברים occurs twice (40:15; 43:32) as an ethnic designation for proto-Israelites.[4] This dearth of collective labels alerts the hearer[5] that Israel's collective identity has not yet taken a definitive shape. Whether this reflects a socio-historical reality or an ideological claim is unknown. It is, nevertheless, what is communicated to the hearers of the text.

---

3. It is unclear in Gen 50:24-25 whether Joseph is speaking about the exodus of the Israelites from Egypt after a period of bondage (as claimed by the Christian Testament in Heb 11:22) or simply referring to God's abbreviated promise to Jacob in Gen 46:3-4. The narrative claims that the latter was explicitly transmitted to Joseph in Gen 48:21, but there is no explicit indication that God's plan revealed to Abraham—of bondage and deliverance (Gen 15:13-16)—was transmitted ultimately to Joseph or that he recognized his situation as a preliminary enactment of this scenario. Nevertheless, Gen 50:24-25 would be heard as a "preview of exodus" by those who hear these stories in juxtaposition.

4. Freedman and Willoughby, "עברי," 431.

5. As this primary exodus story belongs to Israel's sacred text, the earliest and most regular hearer would be ancient Israel.

While cognitive formulations of social identity are rare, subtle evaluative formulations of collective identity begin to appear in these texts.

Evaluative Formulations

One might expect the defining of Israel as a collective people to begin with rhetorical differentiation of her from others. Instead, the texts of Genesis reveal conflicting images of a relationship between Israel[6] and Egypt. Discordant images of Egypt's valuation are seen. In a positive light, Egypt is seen as a place of nourishment, refuge, and enrichment. In 13:10, for example, she is grouped together with the well-watered plain of the Jordan and the garden of Yahweh. In contrast, Egypt is also depicted negatively, as a place of fear, deception, assimilation, and death. These discordant images of Egypt are found throughout the Abraham and Joseph cycles of Genesis.[7]

In addition to conflicting images of Egypt as an entity, the text of Genesis vacillates in its presentation of Israel's integration with and separation from Egypt. Literary images of integration include the following: Abram takes an Egyptian concubine as a wife (16:1ff); Joseph engages in Egyptian government (41.41—50:25), speaks Egyptian (42:23), takes an Egyptian name (41:45), and marries the daughter of an Egyptian priest (41:45); all Israel comes to dwell in Egypt during the famine (46:5-34); Jacob blesses Pharaoh (47:7); Jacob blesses Joseph's half-Egyptian sons as if they were his own (48:1-21); Egyptian dignitaries accompany Joseph and his family to Jacob's burial (50:7-9); Canaanites label the entire funerary group "Egyptian" because they apparently cannot distinguish one group from the other; and generations of Israel are found in Egypt long after the famine has apparently ended (50:22-23). Offsetting these images of integration are portrayals of separation: Abram's Egyptian son is excluded from the lineage that would become Israel (21:8-12); a subtle undercurrent of Hebrew superiority is seen in Joseph's sexual restraint compared to his Egyptian mistress and in his pre-eminence as a dream interpreter and government administrator[8] (39:7—41:45); Joseph dines separately from the Egyptians (43:32); Israel acquires property and prospers while the Egyptians are reduced to servitude

---

6. The claim of the narrative is that Israel came into existence in Egypt. The use of the designation prior to that time is admittedly anachronistic.

7. The details of these contrasting images of Egypt in the Abraham and Joseph cycles are well illustrated in Greifenhagen, *Egypt on the Pentateuch's Ideological Map*, 28–42.

8. Ibid., 35.

(47:20–27); and Jacob and Joseph reject Egypt as a proper resting place for their bones (49:29–30; 50:24–25).

The strongest image of separateness in the midst of integration, however, is Israel living in Goshen, separate from the rest of Egypt (46:34; 47:1), purportedly because "all shepherds are abhorrent to the Egyptians" (46:34). Because of this separation, Israel will later escape God's plagues (Exod 8:22; 9:26). Goshen, however, contrasts with other images of Israel receiving Pharaoh's promised benefits from *all* of the land (47:18, 20), of potentially taking charge of Pharaoh's own livestock (47:6), and of receiving post-mortem care from Egypt's physicians (50:2). Following the story of Joseph's own near assimilation, Goshen symbolically serves as a means of establishing a distinct identity for Israel, thereby preserving an illusion of segregation. Greifenhagen is justified in his interpretation of the discrepancy, "Perhaps here the concept of a 'mental map' may be used to interpret Goshen less as an actual location and more as an ideological construct that seeks to maintain the separateness of Israel while in Egypt."[9] The conflicting images of Israel as both integrated into and separate from Egypt foreshadow an imminent identity crisis.

In these pre-exodus narratives, a people begins to emerge from an unnamed, undifferentiated collective with ill-defined boundaries. Proto-Israel's differentiation and positive evaluation, however, is attenuated by her integration and assimilation with Egypt. Devaluation of the "other" is diluted by positive evaluations of Egypt.

Emotional Formulations

Emotional formulations of identity in Genesis contribute little to the portrayal of Israel as a collective people. Only two explicit images are found of the attachment and belonging of individuals to a collective larger than a family group. A company of the dead is represented in 25:8, 17; 35:29; and 49:33, and a broadly inclusive circumcision group is portrayed in Genesis 17. A living and distinct collective with a shared fate—first of oppression then of deliverance—is projected only as a future entity in 15:13–15, 46:3, and possibly in the shadows of 50:24–25.

---

9. Ibid., 40.

Behavioral Formulations

Behavioral formulations of identity are absent in the literary prologue to exodus. This is to be expected as, unlike the other formulations of identity, behavioral formulations tend to sustain rather than create collective identity. They define acceptable attitudes and behaviors for a collective and assure coherence and visibility in social interactions. Such formulations will proliferate in the retellings of exodus, but they do not exist at this initial stage of group identification.

Temporal Formulations

In contrast to the absence of behavioral formulations of identity in the prologue to the primary exodus story, temporal formulations abound. The first is God's revelation to Abraham that his descendants will one day constitute a continuous, coherent, identifiable group (15:13–16). Then Joseph, Abraham's grandson, looks backward and insists that the fate of his brothers is tied to the promise made to this predecessor (50:24). These projective and retrojective visions together portray connectedness and coherence over time between individual members of proto-Israel.

Genesis 12–50 constructs a genealogical myth of common descent, tying a future Israel and her fate to Abraham, Isaac, and Jacob. This myth purportedly motivates Joseph's petition in 50:24–25. Yet the exodus story that follows portrays this myth of shared ancestry with Abraham as offering no comfort or assurance to Israel in the midst of bondage (Exod 6:5–9). The narrative claim is that this genealogical myth of descent did not create a strong sense of collective identity in that people.

In addition to the myth of genealogical descent connecting the ancestors of the prologue to the exodus generation of the primary exodus story, significant literary artistry has been used to link the patriarchal narratives to the stories of Israel's sojourn in and departure from Egypt. Greifenhagen depicts these efforts as forming bookends, beginning with Abram's sojourn in Egypt and ending with Jacob's burial outside of Egypt and Joseph's request to have his bones carried out from there.[10]

Cassuto, Fishbane, and Zakovitch[11] have discussed in detail the parallels, both verbal and imaginal, between Abram's sojourn in Egypt (12:10–20)

---

10. Ibid., 44.

11. Cassuto, *Commentary on Genesis*, 135–36; Fishbane, *Biblical Interpretation*, 375–76; Zakovitch, "*You Shall Tell Your Son . . .*" 18–20, 46–47. See also Fretheim, "Genesis," 669; Brodie, *Genesis as Dialogue*, 415; and Wenham, *Genesis 16–50*, 492.

and the exodus story. Similarities include the descent into Egypt due to famine, the murderous Egyptians who kill males and spare females, the acquisition of riches from Egypt, God's wrath poured out in the form of plagues upon the "other," and Pharaoh's command to leave Egypt. At the other end of the patriarchal stories of Genesis is Jacob's burial outside of Egypt with its similarities to the exodus story: requests made to Pharaoh to let the people go, the presence of chariots and charioteers (Gen 50:9; cf. Exod 14), and the people's circuitous route to Canaan.[12]

After the narrative of Jacob's burial, the text of Genesis condenses the remainder of Joseph's life into a few verses, ending with Joseph's deathbed request that his bones be taken up out of Egypt when Israel departs the land. He then dies, is embalmed, and is placed in a coffin "in Egypt," the final words of the Hebrew text of Genesis. While the pattern of "entry into and exodus from Egypt" is accomplished in the stories of Abraham and Jacob, it is left incomplete in the account of Joseph.[13]

Scholars vary widely in their interpretation of the purpose of this recurring "entry into and exodus from Egypt" pattern. De Pury views it as the literary glue that allows three independent legends of the origin of Israel to be joined together,[14] though he offers no reason why this particular motif was selected. For some, the stories of Abraham and Jacob prefigure or foreshadow the exodus.[15] Others regard them as typologies or pre-enactments of exodus.[16] The consensus is that these parallels connect the patriarchs to the exodus, but to what end?

Cassuto claims that the parallels teach Israel that bondage in Egypt was part of the long-range divine plan.[17] Zakovitch expands on this didactic purpose, saying,

> The impression of repetition or even periodicity in history is created to teach that the world is not governed by chance but by a well-defined plan, discernible in patterns set by divine providence.... The Chronicles of the patriarchs are thus like a detailed table of contents; they are an overview at the beginning of the book of the history of Israel. Just as Abraham entered Egypt safely and left it safely, so did his children, and so the children

12. Alter, *Genesis*, 304; Arnold, *Genesis*, 387.
13. Greifenhagen, *Egypt on the Pentateuch's Ideological Map*, 44.
14. De Pury, "Le choix de l'ancêtre," 105-14.
15. Fretheim, "Genesis," 429; Alter, *Genesis*, 52; Greifenhagen, *Egypt on the Pentateuch's Ideological Map*, 44; and Mathews, *Genesis 11:27—50:26*, 123.
16. Brettler, *Creation of History*, 48-53; Cassuto, *Commentary on Genesis*, 326-27; Wenham, *Genesis 16-50*, 292.
17. Cassuto, *Commentary on Genesis*, 337.

of Israel will survive other calamities awaiting them, such as the Babylonian exile.[18]

For Zakovitch, the familiar pattern generates confidence. Brettler concurs, "By creating an exodus-liberation pattern in Genesis that then gets repeated in Exodus (and still later in Deutero-Isaiah), the community, even when in a state of subjugation, will feel that the cycle is about to turn, that liberation is again around the corner."[19]

While agreeing with Zakovitch on the positive psychological effect of the exodus literary pattern in Genesis 12:10–12, Brettler offers a more comprehensive explanation for the overall exodus pattern found in the Hebrew Bible. He sees exodus as such a seminal event in Israel's collective memory that imposing it on earlier events became a way of fulfilling the injunction to remember their departure from Egypt all the days of their life (cf. Deut 16:3).[20] In other words, when the producers of the text integrated exodus into many of Israel's stories, even those whose literary position preceded the exodus account, it was, in effect, being *remembered*.

While the patriarchal stories do appear to have been redacted in light of the exodus story,[21] the exodus story, on the other hand, does not demonstrate the same strong connections to the patriarchal traditions. For example, according to Exodus 3, the land to which Israel would journey after her rescue from Egypt was unknown, the home of foreign nations. There is no mention of the patriarchs having lived there or that it was promised as a permanent possession.[22] Similarly, it is only in the light of the exodus narratives that the full import of the proto-exodus element is grasped. Only in the exodus narratives does the Jacob/Israel who hears about Egypt in Genesis become a people.[23] The primary exodus story, which for all intents and purposes excludes the patriarchs from what it means to be Israel, exists *"in einer Kohabitation"*[24] in the final form of the Hebrew Bible with texts depicting the patriarchs as descending into and coming out of Egypt, in an exodus-like pattern. The placement of Abraham's[25] exodus near the beginning of

---

18. Zakovitch, *"You Shall Tell Your Son . . ."* 20.
19. Brettler, *Creation of History*, 54.
20. Ibid.
21. Römer, "Exodusmotive und Exoduspolemik," 6–7.
22. Rendtorff, *Das überlieferungsgeschichtliche Problem des Pentateuch*, 66.
23. Carr, "What is Required?," 167. The contention that Israel's collective identity is forged in Egypt will be further described in the analysis of the primary exodus story.
24. Römer, "Exodusmotive und Exoduspolemik," 16.
25. Abraham was still referred to as Abram at this point of the Genesis narrative.

the patriarchal narratives and Jacob's exodus near the end forms a literary *inclusio*, unifying Genesis 12–50.

Seemingly two different origin traditions[26]—genealogical and cultural-ideological—coexist in Israel's narratives, rather than being seamlessly integrated into a hybrid. The genealogical tradition of common descent portrays Israel as a relatively old people, descending from Abraham, Isaac, and Jacob. The stronger cultural-ideological myth will portray her as a people united together through the cultural kinship of bondage and exodus. The redacting of several patriarch stories with an exodus-like overlay does not collapse the differences between these two origin myths. Both harmony and dissonance are evident in the superimposing of the exodus pattern on the patriarchal narratives. The proto-exoduses of Abraham and Jacob do not fit well into the definition of exodus stories outlined in chapter 1. In Abraham's story, the minor plot element of the descent into Egypt due to famine bears a close resemblance to that of the primary exodus story. The first major plot element, however, is absent or infinitesimal. There is no initial situation of adversity described in terms of oppression or affliction, groaning or crying out. On the contrary, Abraham is treated well in Egypt (Gen 12:16). There is only an enigmatic reference to Sarai being "taken into Pharaoh's house," with no explicit description of enslavement or mistreatment. Nevertheless, it is this situation apparently that inspires the supernatural response of God (second major plot element), bringing plagues upon Egypt (cf. Exod 11:1). Like in the primary exodus story, this results in Abraham coming out of Egypt. The vocabulary of this third plot element, however, is dissonant. Abraham is not brought out using the common language of exodus stories (hiphil form of יצא) or even the uncommon language of Joshua 24:17's retold exodus story (hiphil form of עלה).[27] He simply comes up out of Egypt (qal form of עלה).

Jacob's proto-exodus is an even more imperfect fit with respect to our definition of exodus stories despite the repetition of the "entry into and exodus from Egypt" pattern. The minor plot element of his descent into Egypt because of famine is not unique. This is the same corporate descent of the primary exodus story. Again, there is no description of adversity in Egypt and, in this case, no supernatural intervention. And it is Joseph who comes up out of Egypt (qal form of עלה), bringing along Jacob's embalmed body.

---

26. See Schmid, *Erzväter und Exodus*; and Van Seters, "The Patriarchs and the Exodus," 1–15. It should be noted that these authors are concerned primarily with when and by whom the two traditions were combined rather than the literary purpose or effect of this joining.

27. The use of עלה rather than יצא in Josh 24:17 will be discussed in the analysis of this passage in chap. 5.

In contrast to the more successful effect of the primary exodus story and the retold exodus stories in incorporating other non-exodus generations into the exodus experience,[28] the proto-exodus stories do not neatly fit the patriarchs into this story. In contrast to both Gertz—who sees the Genesis stories as an attempt to "reclaim the exodus tradition for the patriarchs"—and Carr—who rejects this intent[29]—this analysis emphasizes the possible effect on hearers rather than the authorial motive behind the text. Hearers of the proto-exoduses would see both the parallels to the exodus story in terminology and theme and the uneasy fit of the patriarchs in the exodus story.

Summary of Findings

While the prologue to the primary exodus story portrays a nameless, indistinct proto-Israel, the image of a collective begins to take on a vague shape through the rhetoric of differentiation (evaluative formulations). Proto-Israel is ambivalent in her identity with respect to Egypt, the proximate other, yet it is out of this contiguity that a more distinct people will emerge. A myth of genealogical descent connects the patriarchs to the soon-so-be-examined-people of the primary exodus story, but the narrative imagination of these ancestors' proto-exoduses does not allow them to fit flawlessly into the latter's exodus story. Other retold exodus stories, however, will be shown to incorporate the patriarchs more successfully as "participants" in exodus.[30]

Primary Exodus Story (Exodus 1:1—15:21)

The rhetorical formulations of collective identity—and the lack of them—in Genesis 12–50 add perspective to the consideration of identity formation in Exodus 1:1—15:21, the primary exodus story. The latter augments the evaluative and temporal formulations of identity found in the texts of Genesis. Likewise, it adds cognitive formulations, as well as the emotional formulations of both shared fate and intergroup conflict.

---

28. This will be examined in the section and chapters to follow.
29. Carr, "What is Required?," 167.
30. See the examination of Deut 26:5–9; Neh 9:9–12; and Ps 105:23–39 in chaps. 4 and 5.

Cognitive Formulations

Categorization, boundary formation, and prototypes—all of which are cognitive formulations of collective identity—are identifiable in the primary exodus story.

Categorization

Thirteen uses of the named group עברי are found in the primary exodus story.[31] Six of these refer to the "God of the Hebrews,"[32] an expression that appears only 12 times in the remainder of the Hebrew Bible.[33] By and large, "Israel" displaces "Hebrews" as the designation for this collective people, and that process begins in the book of Exodus. Compared to just six uses of בני ישראל in the prologue—referring to Israel's sons[34]—this expression is employed 51 times in the primary exodus story[35]—referring to a collective people. It is then commonly used throughout the remainder of the Hebrew Bible.

In the primary exodus story, בני ישראל first appears in the mouth of Pharaoh in 1:9. It is also used by the narrator, God, and Moses. God refers to Israel both as העם and עמי with a preference for the latter, while Pharaoh and the narrator refer to Israel simply as העם. By contrast, Pharaoh refers to his own people three times as עמי.[36]

In the wording of the fifth plague, God affirms that he will make a distinction between the livestock of *Israel* and that of *Egypt* (9:4). This is the beginning of the use of these labels in the primary exodus story, and initially their use is limited to the divine voice, his mouthpiece Moses, and the narrator. In Exodus 12, the collective designation עדת־ישראל is used twice by God. It is not until Pharaoh summons Moses and Aaron after the death of the firstborn that he makes a clear verbal categorization of the two people groups living under his reign saying, "Rise up, go away from עמי, both you

---

31. Exod 1:15, 16, 19; 2:6, 7, 11, 13; 3:18; 5:3; 7:16; 9:1, 13; 10:3.

32. Exod 3:18; 5:3; 7:16; 9:1, 13; 10:3.

33. Deut 15:12; 1 Sam 4:6; 4:9; 13:3; 13:7; 13:19; 14:11; 14:21; 29:3; Jer 34:9, 14; and Jonah 1:9. Both Deut 15:12 and Jer 34:9 include separate gender specific terms to designate male and female Hebrews.

34. The exception, as previously mentioned, is the anachronistic mention of a future collective in Gen 32:33.

35. This does not include the appearance of this term in 1:1 where it refers to individual sons of Israel rather than to a collective body.

36. Exod 8:8; 9:27; 12:31.

and בני ישראל"! (12:31). As the Egyptians struggle in the midst of the Sea, they too make the distinction between "Israel" and "Egypt" (14:25).

This increased use of collective labels (e.g., בני ישראל), designating a community of people (rather than a fixed set of individuals), in the primary exodus story, compared to their minimal use in the prologue of Genesis, is of particular significance. It informs the hearer that Israel's collective identity is taking on definitive shape during her sojourn in Egypt. That is to say, בני ישראל as a group of 12 sons is portrayed as conceived in Canaan but בני ישראל as a collective is depicted as conceived in Egypt and born in exodus. This does not mean that the concept of common ancestry does not exist in the primary exodus story or that it was immaterial to this collective. Genealogical links may exist between individuals without contributing significantly to their self-conscious sense of peoplehood. The claim of the text to unresisting hearers, however, is that it was the corporate experiences of Egypt and exodus that took individuals with a common ancestry and forged them into a people.

Boundaries

The primary exodus story does not delineate a qualitative boundary of meaningful features that defined Israel and separated her from Egypt. The closest approximation may be the representation of Israel as a people capable of worshiping Yahweh, compared to Egyptians who found such practices detestable (8:25–26). Another type of real or imagined boundary, however, continues to define and differentiate Israel, namely, the borders of Goshen. This boundary, ambiguous in nature, is significant enough to protect the Israelites from the decimation caused by the plagues, but so inconsequential that it both permits Israel to ask her Egyptian neighbors for spoils (12:35–36) and prevents her from offering sacrifices for fear of offending these neighbors (8:25–26). Greifenhagen fittingly interprets Goshen as an ideological construct necessary for the composition of Israel's distinct identity.[37] That is to say, settling in Goshen allows the narrative to show that Israel clearly lived in Egypt, while ideologically remaining separate from her.

Although a qualitative boundary separating Israel from Egypt is lacking, the text is unmistakably concerned with the question of boundaries. Boundaries not only differentiate between peoples, but they define membership within a social group, expressed often as "we are this . . . "[38] or "we

---

37. Greifenhagen, *Egypt on the Pentateuch's Ideological Map*, 40.
38. Assmann, "Collective Memory and Cultural Identity," 130.

are a people who … "³⁹ So, while the ideological-physical boundary of Goshen attempts to distinguish ingroup from outgroup, it is the resolution of the primary exodus story that ultimately constructs the ingroup as "the people whom God brought up out of Egypt."⁴⁰ This ingroup is portrayed as exceedingly large, with the adult, male Israelites leaving Egypt totaling about 600,000 (12:37). This figure has resulted in estimations of the entire exodus group (including women, children, and the "mixed multitude") totaling between 2 and 3 million.⁴¹ Critical scholars balk at such a large number, citing the impossibility of such a huge increase in population in a span of several hundred years, the inconceivability of a comparable food and water supply, or the lack of a physical imprint from such a tremendous group.⁴² Among those who reject this figure as a literal statistic, various interpretations have been offered. The gematria approach postulates that the 600,000 number resulted from the Hebrew letters in בני ישראל being given a numerical interpretation.⁴³ Another common explanation insists that, before military units were patterned after the monarchical 1000/unit, אלף in certain contexts (such as Numbers 1:16 and Judges 6:15) represented not 1000 individuals but a smaller, family-sized military unit.⁴⁴ This interpretation of אלף does not fit in other contexts, however, such as in Exodus 38:26 where individual men are indicated as being counted.⁴⁵ Similarly, the two later censuses referred to in Numbers 1 and 26, recording population figures comparable to that of Exodus 12:37, do not suggest the counting of groups. In addition, אלף as a family-sized unit was an expression used early in Israel's history. Even if this were the original intent of the term in Exodus 12:37, such an interpretation would not have been common by post-exilic times.⁴⁶ By the time of the final editing a less ambivalent translation likely would have been possible if "family unit" had been intended.

The gematria and "family-group" approaches just discussed assume that a factual, and more plausible, measurement was actually intended by the narrative. By offering explanations for such and, thereby, diminishing

---

39. Cornell, "Story of Our Life," 42–45.

40. This designation is implicit in the primary exodus story but is not used explicitly until later, as in Exod 32:11, Lev 25:55, Deut 9:26, Amos 3:1, and 1 Chr 17:21.

41. Knight, *Theology as Narration*, 94; and Beer, *Exodus*, 68–69, respectively.

42. Lucas, "Number of Israelites at Exodus," 164–68; and Longman, *How to Read Exodus*.

43. Beer, *Exodus*, 69.

44. This was originally proposed by Petrie and then refined by Mendenhall. Petrie, *Egypt and Israel*, 42–47. Mendenhall, "Census Lists," 52–66.

45. Bruckner, *Exodus*, 119.

46. Durham, *Exodus*, 72.

the impact of the narrative claim, they disregard obvious literary efforts to expand the grandiosity of this ingroup with the addition of each phrase in 12:37–38: ויצאן ובקר מקנה כבד מאד and וגם־ערב רב, הגברים לבד מטף. Similar literary attempts to expand the dimensions of Israel even in the face of oppression and persecution were also evident in Exodus 1:12 and 1:20.[47] Meyers, therefore, interprets the 600,000 as hyperbole, "as such round figures often are in the literary mode of the Hebrew Bible," and she asserts that this hyperbole "functions here to echo the assertion of 1:7 that the Israelites became so numerous that they filled the land."[48] Such views focus on the literary function of the claim. They recognize 600,000 not as a corrupted historical representation but as another example of meaningful editorial freedom similar to that used in redacting the patriarch stories with the "entry into and exodus from Egypt" pattern. They recognize that 600,000 would certainly have been an accurate representation of the Israelite fighting men during the time of Solomon, and possibly during the time period when the finished text was produced.[49] The use of the figure in this verse, then, may represent a "retrojective attempt to include that population as a delivered people"[50] or "a theological statement that all later Israelites have a share in the exodus from Egypt, even if they were not literally there."[51] Even if the inclusion of later Israel was not the intention of the producers, it would have been the effect of this measurement on later hearers. This inordinately large number, similar to the population of Solomon's time, expands the boundary of the exodus people and apprehends all Israel who hears the finished text. For the hearer of the text in exilic or post-exilic Israel, the narrative creatively suggests that all Israel was present at exodus. This interpretation is consistent with other, sometimes imperfect, literary attempts to include previous and subsequent generations in the experience of exodus. Such literary attempts will be examined throughout this book.

The delineation of the boundary of the "people whom God brought out of Egypt" is also evident in Exodus 12:38, which asserts that those who came out of Egypt included more than just ethnic Israelites. Among those leaving Egypt was ערב רב a "large motley group"[52] or "a mixed multitude."[53]

47. Utzschneider and Oswald, *Exodus 1–15*, 258.

48. Meyers, *Exodus*, 100.

49. Janzen, *Exodus*, 163; Sarna, *Exodus*, 62; Fretheim, *Exodus*, 144; and Durham, *Exodus*, 172.

50. Bruckner, *Exodus*, 119.

51. Janzen, *Exodus*, 163.

52. Durham, *Exodus*, 172.

53. Sarna, *Exodus*, 62. See also KJV translation; Cassuto, *Commentary on Exodus*, 147; Noth, *Exodus*, 99; Hyatt, *Exodus*, 139.

Some scholars suggest it comprised the slaves of the Israelites, kindred Semitic groups, or other non-Israelite forced laborers who took advantage of Israel's departure as a chance to escape their own bondage.[54] Others have suggested that they were Egyptian slaves,[55] spouses from intermarriages,[56] or mercenaries.[57] Regardless of their makeup, they have also been equated with the "rabble" mentioned in Numbers 11:4.[58]

Whoever comprised the ערב רב, they too shared the boundary of ones "brought out of Egypt" and served the literary function of augmenting the perceived magnitude of this group. Although distinct from the Israelites mentioned in 12:37 and 12:15, the mixed multitude's inclusion in this narrative memory portrays "the people whom God brought out of Egypt" as both diverse and as characterized by a sense of solidarity. Inclusion and exclusion are bundled together, and the hearer must wait until the next narrative to see how this is clarified. While only ethnic Israelites celebrated the first Passover (Exod 12:1–28), subsequent celebrations must account for, at a minimum, the ערב רב who exited Egypt with Israel, making "the issue of the non-Israelite role an acute one."[59] Exodus 12:43–49 is therefore significant, as it identifies precisely who may participate in the ritual commemorating the exodus. Clearly, this is the language of boundaries.

Rituals and commemorative celebrations tend to promote inclusion. They comprise language and images of attachment and belonging, connecting participants to the shared past and thereby heightening and preserving a sense of corporate identity.[60] According to 12:47, כל-ישראל is to celebrate Passover.[61] Meyers argues that while this term ordinarily

---

54. Noth, *Exodus*, 99; Fretheim, *Exodus*, 143; Sarna, *Exodus*, 62.

55. See, for example Hyatt, *Exodus*, 139.

56. See Cole, *Exodus*, 53–54.

57. This and other arguments are summarized by Bar, "Who Were the 'Mixed Multitude'?," 27–39.

58. See Sarna, *Exodus*, 62; Bar, "Mixed Multitude," 31; and Gaebelian, *Genesis-Numbers*, 379.

59. Childs, *Book of Exodus*, 202.

60. See Turner, "Rites of Communitas," 98; and Meyers, *Exodus*, 95. Lamoreaux maintains that rituals and symbols are often used in social groups to allow new members to cross group boundaries and be incorporated into a group; Lamoreaux, "Social Identity, Boundary Breaking, and Ritual," 125–27.

61. The annual "re-performance" of exodus is so essential to what it means to be an Israelite that, in the further development of Passover in Num 9:1–14, the Israelites are told that if they should find themselves in a state of uncleanness on Passover, rather than being completely excluded from the celebration, they may delay their observance for a month. On the other hand, anyone who is able to observe Passover but fails to do so will be cut off from the people of Israel (Num 9:13).

refers to the assembly of adult males, here it appears to be age and gender inclusive, as indicated by the involvement of households and families.[62] Exodus 12:19 made it clear that "the whole congregation of Israel" includes both the אזרח and the גר. In 12:44, the עבד is included as well.[63] Those excluded are תושב, כל־בן־נכר , and שכיר, who apparently are only loosely attached to Israel[64] and do not ratify God's lordship through circumcision.[65] Circumcision is not intended to exclude but to integrate the experience of freedom with the confession of faith in the God who frees.[66] Clearly, Passover "provides identity, shared values, and thus group cohesiveness to those who celebrate it"[67] and "form[s] a community around the historical deliverance of God's people,"[68] but the significance of the second Passover narrative 12:43–49 is its implicit claim that it is possible for outsiders to cross group boundaries and become part of the faith community. The experience of deliverance along with the profession of faith in the God of that deliverance defines the boundary of "the people whom God brought out of Egypt" or "the exodus people."

62. Meyers, *Exodus*, 95.

63. The Hebrew גר has been variously translated "sojourner" (Cassuto, *Exodus*, 150), "alien" or "alien resident" (Meyers, *Exodus*, 89 and 95), and "newcomer" (Durham, *Exodus*, 156). (Child's translates it as "foreigner" but then also translates נכר as "foreigner"—Childs, *Exodus*, 179–80.) The גר is a permanent resident of the community and was treated as a protected citizen and largely regarded as a proselyte (Stigers, "[330a] גר [gēr] sojourner," 156. Thus, the גר enjoyed many of the same rights as the native (אזרח) and was expected to show fidelity to Yahweh. The עבד (slave or servant) was also joined permanently to the community of Israel. Circumcision was the sign that the אזרח, the גר, and the עבד were joined to the faith community.

64. The נכר (foreigner) in the Hebrew Bible frequently refers to those who worship other gods (Bruckner, *Exodus*, 120). Sarna contends that the נכר "does not profess the religion of Israel and does not identify with the community's historical experiences" (Sarna, *Exodus*, 63). The תושב was a temporary, landless wage earner (Kaiser, "[922d] תושב [tôshāb] sojourner," 412) who didn't plan on being associated with the believing community very long (Bruckner, *Exodus*, 120), and the שכיר worked for wages and was only associated with the community for monetary purposes (ibid.).

65. Hamilton argues convincingly that circumcision was not a cognition sign. It did not identify Israelites to non-Israelites—many of whom also practiced circumcision as a social (rather than religious) rite—since the mark was ordinarily concealed. Similarly, he contends that circumcision should not be understood as a mnemonic sign for Israel or for God because it lacks the clause explaining the purpose of the sign characteristic of mnemonic signs found in scripture. Instead, circumcision is a confirmation sign—a means by which people ratify God's lordship over them. See Hamilton, *Book of Genesis*, 470–72.

66. Fretheim, *Exodus*, 143.

67. Meyers, *Exodus*, 92.

68. Bruckner, *Exodus*, 119.

Several conclusions may be drawn with respect to the ערב רב. Firstly, social categories are neither fixed nor singular. Those who would otherwise be considered outsiders, may be recategorized. In this case, the exodus people is both coterminous with Israel and representative of a superordinate category that allows those once classified as "other" to be regarded in this particular social context in a more positive light. Secondly, although such outsiders may be viewed more positively, this does not necessarily mean that they become insiders.[69] Those permitted to celebrate Passover are not identical to "Israel," though they are part of the larger group of exodus people, and they legitimatize Israel's identity as the ones whom God delivered. The category "exodus people" is more flexible than would be possible if it were defined based solely on genealogy.

The inextricable linking of exodus and Passover will keep the reality of redemption alive in the community over time.[70] The dominant identity descriptor of Israel—"the people whom God brought up out of Egypt"—defines commonality not in ethnic terms but in the language of a shared experience. This will become the cultural-ideological myth of common descent unifying later generations of Israel with this exodus generation.[71] Prior to considering other types of identity formulations present in the primary exodus story, however, one final type of cognitive identity formulation—the literary depiction of a prototypical Israelite—will be examined.

Prototypes

Moses and Aaron are the only visible members of the ingroup. The people, who are becoming Israel, remain in the background. Moses and Aaron are notable in the primary exodus story for their obedience; they do just as the Lord commands. Because their obedience is repeated many times over, it becomes characteristic of these prototypical ingroup members.[72] Thus when Israel finally emerges as a people at the first Passover, their characterization is identical to that of Moses and Aaron, they "did just as the Lord had commanded" (12:28).[73]

69. Hakola, "'Friendly' Pharisees," 198–99.

70. Fretheim, *Exodus*, 143.

71. See temporal formulations for further development.

72. Exodus 7:10 and 20 use the actual phrase כאשר צוה יהוה; Exod 8:6, 17, 9:10, 23, 10:3, 13, and 22 simply show Moses and Aaron carrying out the specific thing that was commanded by God in the preceding narrative.

73. Israel is again characterized as doing כאשר צוה יהוה after the giving of the ongoing Passover regulations (12:50).

Similar to Israel, the people of Egypt are inconspicuous in the primary exodus story. The shadowy images that are presented of them are not entirely negative. For instance, the Egyptians, suffering from the lack of potable water, anxiously dig for drinking water, in contrast to Pharaoh who is immovable and unconcerned (7:22–24). Egyptians who fear the word of God are interspersed with those who ignore it (9:20). Pharaoh's officials encourage Pharaoh to relent and let Israel go (10:7). The Egyptians are favorably disposed toward Moses and the Israelites (11:3; 12:36). Even near the end of the narrative, caught in the confusion at the Sea, the Egyptians cry out, "Let us flee from the Israelites, for the LORD is fighting for them against Egypt" (14:25).

Social identification, however, depends on categorization and differentiation, particularly the sorting into categories of "us" and "them" and the distinguishing of the ingroup from the "other." Normally, social identification would be impeded by a positive, or even ambiguous, perception of Egypt. The depiction of Pharaoh as the prototype of Egypt surmounts this obstacle. In contrast to the favorable, though infrequent, images of the Egyptian people, the portrayals of Pharaoh are numerous and unambiguous: he is arrogant, obdurate, and recalcitrant; he opposes the legitimate governance of God.[74] He is a diametric opposite to the prototypes of Israel—Moses and Aaron—who do just as Yahweh commands. It is he, not the Egyptians per se, who embodies the outgroup in the intergroup conflict depicted in the narrative. Pharaoh's wise men, sorcerers, and magicians make an initial appearance in the conflict, but by the third plague, they admit, "This is the finger of God!" (8:15). They appear one last time after the fifth plague strikes, only to admit they could no longer stand before Moses (9:11). Pharaoh, by contrast, is the epitome of callousness. He is, from first to last, the stereotypical embodiment of Egypt as the "other." The ingroup's perception of this "other" is not based on geography or ethnicity. Instead, it is the qualities of Pharaoh that define Egypt's boundary. Here—and in the retold exodus stories—the metaphoric or symbolic nature of the outgrouper is one who is resistant or opposed to God.

---

74. This refers specifically to the image of Pharaoh in the primary exodus story. Previous Pharaohs in the Abram and Joseph cycles were partially favorable like the current image of the Egyptian people.

Evaluative Formulations

Evaluative formulations of collective identity, which were weak and unstable in the Genesis prologue, grow in frequency, force, and clarity in the primary exodus story.

Differentiation

Like the Genesis narratives, the early sections of the primary exodus story reveal conflicting images of Israel's relationship with Egypt. At times, the narrative depicts Israel's integration with Egypt: generations of Israelites remained in Egypt even after the famine apparently ended (1:6–8, cf. Gen 50:22–23); Moses was mistaken for an Egyptian (2:19); Israel dwelt so closely to the Egyptians that at their departure they demanded spoils from their neighbors (3:22);[75] and, finally, the Israelites called themselves servants of Pharaoh (5:15–16). The strongest image of separation in the midst of this integration is the sustained depiction of Israel living in Goshen, separate from the rest of Egypt (8:18, 9:26).

Moses is also portrayed as a conflicted individual. The linguistic blending of his name, with roots both in Egyptian ("child of") and Hebrew ("to draw out") is not evidence of a "dual identity" or of "the youth's membership in two communities," as Carol Meyer suggests.[76] Such a positive estimation is not supported by the literary context. Instead, Moses has a confused identity. Like Israel, Moses's origins are outside of Egypt. Assimilated into Egypt, both Moses and Israel are content with their apparent integration until their distinction from Egypt turns into victimization. Even then, both Moses and Israel are apprehensive and insecure when faced with God's plan of separation. As Greifenhagen notes, "Moses's ambiguous identity mirrors that of Israel itself."[77] That is to say, Moses's and Israel's stories are to be heard in conjunction. It is this crisis of identity that the subsequent narratives will attempt to resolve.

The conflicting representations of Israel's integration with and separation from Egypt, prominent in the literary prologue and in the opening sections of the primary exodus story, begin to give way as the narrative draws lines of distinction between Israel and Egypt. The first occurs in Exodus 1:9, ויאמר אל־עמו הנה עם בני ישראל רב ועצום ממנו. The story casts Pharaoh as the first to utter words of differentiation, distinguishing rhetorically between

---

75. The context indicates the neighbor is Egyptian.
76. Meyers, *Exodus*, 44.
77. Greifenhagen, *Egypt on the Pentateuch's Ideological Map*, 59.

עמו (his people) and עם בני ישראל (the Israelite people). This is immediately followed by physical acts of discrimination and victimization (1:10ff).

In spite of Pharaoh's ruthless efforts to abase the Israelites, the narrative highlights their positive distinctiveness: "But the more they were oppressed, the more they multiplied and spread, so that the Egyptians came to dread the Israelites" (1:12). Pharaoh escalates the differentiation, charging the midwives to kill Hebrew boys. When they fail to do so, their rhetoric of self-preservation, intentionally or unintentionally, emphasizes Israel's positive distinctiveness: "The Hebrew women are not like the Egyptian women; for they are vigorous and give birth before the midwife comes to them" (1:19). Undeterred, Pharaoh again orders a distinction event—the drowning of all male babies (1:22).[78] Pharaoh's daughter, finding the baby Moses, makes a distinction—"This must be one of the Hebrews' children" (2:6)—but, like the midwives, she refrains from victimizing the perceived "other." Moses, when grown, also makes a distinction, between איש מצרי and איש־עברי מאחיו, with this distinction resulting in violence (2:11).

Following Moses's flight from Egypt, the old Pharaoh dies, and a new Pharaoh comes to power (2:23). The language of transition is so smooth and imperceptible that the hearer is apt to regard these two unnamed Pharaohs as one in the same. The new Pharaoh continues the inequitable treatment of Israel, further differentiating Egypt and Israel. The minimizing of distinctions between the two Pharaohs has a stereotyping effect, and "Pharaoh," as mentioned earlier, becomes the prototype of the arrogant outsider who opposes God.

Soon after the new Pharaoh appears, the narrative voice of distinction changes. God is portrayed as the one differentiating his people from Egypt (6:6–8). This change is carried forward in the narrative up to Israel's departure from Egypt. Israel, by comparison, is depicted as unable or unwilling to have a voice in the differentiation. In 5:16, the Israelite foremen respond to Israel's harsh treatment saying, והנה עבדיך מכים וחטאת עמך. The abstruseness of וחטאת עמך has generated two different translations based on corrections to the text: "you sin against your own people" and "the fault is with your own people."[79] The first interpretation places עמך and עבדיך in a synonymous relationship, and Israel's assimilation is visible (Pharaoh's servants="your own people"). The second translation distinguishes between two groups, with עבדיך referring to the Israelites and עמך to Egyptians, though the difference is minimal since both groups belong to Pharaoh. The obscurity of

---

78. The Masoretic text simply reads כל־הב ן הילוד. The Samaritan Pentateuch, Septuagint, and Targums add "to the Hebrews" to clarify the implied meaning.

79. Durham offers a good overview of the textual difficulty in *Exodus*, 67.

the narrative as it appears is indicative of the ambiguity of Israel's perceived identity. Unclear with respect to her distinction or assimilation, the words of her foreman rhetorically represent Israel's identity crisis.

From an unnamed, undifferentiated people with ill-defined boundaries found in the literary prologue and the ambiguousness of Israel's identity in the early sections of the primary exodus story, a distinct people begins to emerge. The plague stories continue the differentiation of Israel from Egypt, inflating and embellishing it. At least nine of the ten plagues presumably strike only the Egyptians.[80] In the first, second, sixth, and eighth plagues, where Israel is not included in the list of those affected, the implication is that only the "other" suffered. That is to say, the plague narratives clearly differentiate between two peoples.

In the fourth, fifth, seventh, ninth, and tenth plagues, the distinction is explicit. In three of these five, the narrative claims the distinction arises from God's willful intent. The verb פלה is used to convey the idea of either being separate or distinct (niphal) or making separate or distinct (hiphil).[81] Differentiation is most clearly seen in 8:22–23, the plague of flies, where God announces that he will "set apart" Goshen (differentiation) thus making "a distinction between my people [עמי] and your people [עמך]" (categorization). The language of differentiation—"setting apart"—also characterizes the story of the plague of livestock (9:1–7). Here, God "make[s] a distinction" between the livestock of ישראל and the livestock of מצרים (v. 4). The results are categorical: "*all* the livestock of the Egyptians died ... of the Israelites *not one* died" (v. 6).

The narrative of the final plague, the death of the firstborn, dramatically demonstrates strategic differentiation, as God once again declares his intention to "make a distinction between Egypt and Israel" (11:7). "Egypt" is inclusive of not just humans and animals, but their gods as well (12:12). This is the first explicit inclusion of the gods of Egypt in the category of "other" threatened with conflict and judgment. This is also the first time that the terms of distinction require action on the part of the Israelites, painting their doorframes with lamb's blood. Exodus identity is not portrayed as *ascribed* to Israel; it is *achieved*.[82] The narrative implies that ethnic descent

---

80. The third plague, the plague of gnats, is unusually short in length and fails to mention who bore the effects of the scourge.

81. See Exod 8:22, 9:4, and 11:7. The verb פלה is not used in 8:19, however, where God says ושמתי פדת בין עמי ובין עמך. Both the contrast between "my people" and "your people" and the context here requires that the noun פדות be translated "a distinction" even though in all other occurrences it is translated "a ransom."

82. Deaux et al. distinguish between "ascribed identity," in which a person does nothing to gain membership, and "achieved identity," which requires some act of

will not prevent one from being counted as "Egyptian" (12:13, 23 cf. Exod 15:26) by the destroyer. Personal involvement becomes a necessary component of exodus identity. In chapter 5, it will be shown that new members will also achieve this exodus identity by personal involvement, namely, the appropriation of and participation in the group's shared life story.

The exaggerated differentiation between Israel and Egypt is depicted in vivid and poignant images. It is reinforced and framed by the unremitting demand, "let my people go." The refrain underscores unambiguously that a collective group now exists—"my people"—which is more highly esteemed by God and readily distinguishable from Egypt. This evaluative formulation of identity leads to another, perhaps the strongest formulation found in the primary exodus story, the devaluation of the "other" through the subtle but unequivocal mocking and fall of the outgroup.

Devaluation of the "Other"—Mocking the Outgroup

The SIA recognizes that groups often construct social identity through the devaluation of an outgroup. While the plague narratives may represent either a "progressive disordering of creation"[83] or a subtle mocking of the Egyptian pantheon (Nile, frogs, cows, and sun)[84] and the professed divinity of the Pharaoh,[85] an overt outcome is in view: the Israelites will be able to tell their children and grandchildren "how I made a mockery of the Egyptians" (10:2, NASB and JPS).[86]

Mockery of Egyptian Power

The first image of mockery in the primary exodus story is that of staffs becoming snakes (7:8–13). By imitating Aaron and throwing down their staffs,

---

attainment. Deaux et al., "Parameters of Social Identity," 282.

83. Greifenhagen, *Egypt on the Pentateuch's Ideological Map*, 101.

84. See Bonnet, Reallexikon der ägyptischen Religionsgeschichte, 198–202. Also, Sarna, *Exodus*, 39–56; Cassuto, *Commentary on Exodus*, 97–129; Dozeman, *Exodus*, 216–47; Davis, *Moses and the Gods of Egypt*, 79–129.

85. Davis, *Moses and the Gods of Egypt*, 89.

86. The verb here is עלל in the hithpael form. Its use varies with context and has elsewhere been translated as "to deal severely with" or "to abuse." In Num 22:29, Balaam accuses his donkey saying, כי התעללת בי ("you have made a fool of me"). Here as in Exod 10:2 the idea of making a mockery of or mocking someone is most fitting to the context. In both of these uses, the Septuagint also translates this verb as ἐμπαίζω meaning to ridicule, make fun of or mock. Images of mockery throughout the narrative also support this interpretation.

the Egyptian magicians do not remove the threat of a snake, but farcically add to the problem, as will also happen in the plagues of blood and of frogs. Not only is their wisdom satirized, but, when their staffs are subsequently swallowed up by Aaron's, their power is discredited. Greifenhagen notes that the context becomes "a means of delimiting the boundary of identity between Israel and Egypt by ridiculing what is seen as the illusionary pretensions of 'them' in contrast to the authentic power and wisdom of 'us.'"[87] The use of the verb בלע in 7:12 and again in the swallowing of the Egyptians at the Sea (15:12) ties the beginning of Pharaoh's demise to his ultimate defeat. The hyperbolic images of frogs invading not only the palace, bedrooms, and beds, but also ovens and kneading bowls adds to the derision of Egyptian wisdom and power.[88] "God chose not only to inflict a punishment upon the Egyptians, but to expose them to mockery by its ignominious nature."[89] When Pharaoh requests that Moses intervene in prayer, Moses responds, "Kindly tell me when I am to pray for you and for your officials and for your people" (8:5), an answer that sounds like Moses is "toying with Pharaoh."[90] After the magicians exit the story, the mockery loses, temporarily, its laughable quality. The devaluation of Egypt, however, continues as Pharaoh is belittled both generally—feigning unfaltering resoluteness in the face of hyperbolized calamity—and more specifically—bartering with Moses on the conditions of Israel's religious journey (8:21, 24; 10:8–11, 24).

Mockery of Pharaoh's authority.

Another depiction of devaluation, though subtle, is found when Pharaoh reverses his command forbidding Moses to return to his presence (10:28), and summons him once more (12:31–32). Following a series of six imperatives[91] in which he feigns sovereignty, Pharaoh reduces himself to a position of supplication by begging for a blessing, וברכתם גם־אתי. As an added insult, the next verse, 12:33, portrays "the Egyptians"—the whole outgroup—in the same deferential posture, begging the Israelites to hasten their departure. The mocking continues and is amplified in 12:35–36 where Israel is portrayed as a victorious militia, taking spoils from a defeated army.[92] The

---

87. Greifenhagen, *Egypt on the Pentateuch's Ideological Map*, 101.
88. Ibid., 98–102.
89. Calvin, *Commentaries on Four Last Books of Moses*, 159.
90. Brueggemann, "Book of Exodus," 745.
91. קומו צאו מתוך עמי . . . ולכו עבדו את־יהוה . . . קחו . . . ולכו.
92. Childs, *Book of Exodus*, 177.

image of spoils is doubly ironic: there was no military battle, and the spoils are taken before the coming non-battle at the sea.

Just as Egypt is devaluated, the valuation of Israel is conversely enhanced. "Their status has now changed; they leave Egypt 'dressed out,' not as slaves, but as persons who have been raised to a new level of life by their God. Their raiment and jewelry are those of persons no longer bound but free."[93] That is to say, the Israelites are not pictured as slinking out of Egypt; they depart with a very positive sense of self, like a conquering army.[94] Even the Egyptians are said to look with favor upon them (12:36).

Mockery of Pharaoh's judgment.

The narrative derides Pharaoh as stubborn (13:15), gullible (14:3), and indecisive (14:5). At the climactic non-battle at the sea, the narrative depicts Pharaoh and his troops as, at best, unreasonable or, at worst, completely mad as they pursue the Israelites into the sea (14:23–25). Favoring the latter, Durham says, "the effect of their madness is heightened by the repetition of their ranks: Pharaoh, horses, chariots, riders—they all went."[95] In other words, no one had the sense of mind to halt the pursuit. The scorn turns humorous in verse 24 as the already-lacking-in-reason Egyptians are *suddenly* thrown into confusion, and it continues, in a comical bit of understatement, as they have "difficulty driving" their wheel-less chariots (v. 25 NIV).

The narrative mocking of the outgroup continues, even as the story switches to a poetic version of events in chapter 15. The Egyptians are portrayed as being tossed into the sea like toys (15:1, 4).[96] They are shattered by God's right hand (15:6). They are thrown down and consumed like stubble (15:7). Egypt is mocked as "a cocky, bloody despoiler of Israel" who is "humbled and sunk in the depths of the sea" (15:9–10).[97]

Mocking Egypt is explicit in the primary exodus story, and in keeping with principles of the SIA the devaluation of the "other" is rhetorically

---

93. Fretheim, *Exodus*, 142.

94. Although Exod 12:39 claims that Israel was "driven out of Egypt," this does not conflict with the image of the positive elevation of Israel. גרשׁ typically communicates the physical removal of a person or group, often resulting in a lack in possessions or resources on the part of one who is driven out (as in Gen 3:24 and Gen 4:14). In Exod 12:39, there is no mention of Israel's physical removal by another party, nor are they left destitute as with other banished people. The context indicates that גרשׁ is employed here simply to emphasize the suddenness of Israel's departure.

95. Durham, *Exodus*, 196.

96. Hauser, "Two Songs of Victory," 273.

97. Ibid., 274.

designed both to augment Israel's esteem and to further define her collective identity.

Devaluation of the "Other"—Fall of the Outgroup

Another way the narrative rhetoric devalues the outgroup is by rehearsing or celebrating its downfall. In Exodus 15, the "fall of the outgroup" motif is literally seen as the Egyptian army sinks into the waters (15:5, 10) and falls into an abyss (15:12). Hauser posits that this "final iteration of the fall motif . . . no doubt symboliz[es] not only the defeat of the Egyptians but also their descent into the underworld."[98] Although it may be an overstatement to interpret the image of fallen Egypt as correspondent to her damnation, the representation is undeniably a portrayal of obliteration, not just defeat. As Greifenhagen notes, ambiguity and blurred boundaries are characteristics of the human world, while narratives have the potential to do away with such uncertainties. The primary exodus story depicts a God who not only insists on making a clear distinction between Israel and Egypt, but who must destroy Egypt for Israel (and its God) to exist.[99]

From a SIA perspective, this devaluation rhetoric directly contributes to the formation of Israel's corporate identity. By employing the fall motif, the producers of the narrative show Israel coming *up* out of Egypt (both geographically and in positive evaluation) while Egypt is going *down*, literarily and in negative evaluation.

* * *

The evaluative formulations of collective identity found in the primary exodus story will influence unresisting hearers of the narrative to align themselves with the protagonist, Israel. The abstractness of Israel's object of derision, the Egyptians, will allow them to apply the concept of Egypt symbolically to the arrogant "other" of their present circumstances. The exodus story they hear has the potential to become their story.

Emotional Formulations

Emotional formulations of collective identity did not contribute in any significant way to the portrayal of Israel as a collective people in the literary prologue. By contrast, the evaluative formulations of differentiation

98. Ibid., 278.
99. Greifenhagen, *Egypt on the Pentateuch's Ideological Map*, 116.

and distinction examined in the primary exodus story result in emotional formulations of identity that assiduously paint Israel as a collective people who belong to God.

Emotional formulations tend to cause individuals to perceive their interests either as cooperatively linked within a group or as competitively linked between groups.[100] Both of these are evident in the primary exodus story. The first explicit expression of group attachment is found in Exodus 1:9–22, apparently produced as a side-effect of the Israelite/Egyptian differentiation. Israel's cognizance of solidarity in oppression grows until she collectively groans and cries out (2:23). The story repeatedly depicts her shared fate of bondage (3:7, 9, 17; 6:9) and the bitter suffering of a collective people (1:13–14; 2:23–25; 6:9). The unresisting reader "is led by the narrative to be hostile to the Egyptians and to sympathize with the Israelites."[101]

The narrative not only conveys emotional formulations of bondage and bitter suffering, but it also predicts an impending change in Israel's collective experience (3:8, 20–22; 6:1–8; 7:3–5). God will hear the cry of Israel, and he will act on behalf of this collective whom he identifies as "my people." The use of עמי conveys images of both belonging *to God* and attachment *to one another*. The change of Israel's shared fate is described in poignant, sweeping terms: brought up out of misery, freed from slavery, redeemed, taken as God's own people, brought to and given the land promised. Through it all, God affectionately refers to Israel as עמי (3:7, 10; 7:4).

Multiple images of both God and Moses's attachment to Israel are evident in the narrative as they tirelessly campaign for Israel's freedom despite conflicts with the wise men, sorcerers, and especially Pharaoh, the prototypical "other." Emotional images of inter-group conflict appear in both the plague stories and in the conflict at the sea. The narrative concludes with Israel's new shared fate of collective rejoicing.

Behavioral Formulations

Behavioral formulations of identity develop from and sustain Israel's exodus identity. These will be more apparent in the retold exodus stories considered in the next two chapters. In the primary exodus story, however, there are three behavioral norms that emerge from Israel's newly forming collection identity: the explicit expectations that "all Israel" will commemorate the exodus (12:14–20) and retell the story (10:2; 12:25–27) and the implicit expectation that she will participate in the Song of Deliverance

---

100. Turner, "Experimental Social Psychology," 98.
101. Greifenhagen, *Egypt on the Pentateuch's Ideological Map*, 55.

(15:1–21). As each of these has noteworthy temporal components, they will be explored in the next section.

Temporal Formulations

Representations of evaluative and temporal formulations are by far the most common literary formulations of social identity found in the primary exodus story.

Temporal Coherence

Social identities cannot endure over time without being taken up by successive "social actors."[102] To be taken up, identities must have flexible enough boundaries to allow the inclusion of new members into the ingroup. Examples have already been given of how previous *and* subsequent generations are incorporated into the exodus story. This integration is evident in both the content and the form of narratives.

With respect to content, the narratives of Genesis 12–50 revealed the subtle, and admittedly imperfect, incorporation of Abraham and Jacob into exodus. Likewise the 600,000 men who purportedly participated in exodus (12:37) may represent the anachronistic incorporation of subsequent generations into the exodus. Joseph is posthumously incorporated into the exodus, as one who descended into Egypt as a slave but was brought up from there as part of a victorious army (13:19).

Various portions of the primary exodus narrative also create temporal continuity between the patriarchs of old and the people of the narrative present. In Exodus 1:1–7, a family of individual actors—known literally as בני ישראל (v.1)—gives way to an emerging people—represented by the group name בני ישראל (v. 7). The identity claim of the narrative is that Israel had her origins outside of Egypt but emerged as a people in Egypt.[103]

Other examples of temporal continuity between Abraham, Isaac, and Jacob of old and the growing people of Israel in Egypt are articulated in 3:6, 15–16; 4:5, and 6:2–8. The patriarchs are established as the אבות of all Israel. The explicit emphasis of these verses, however, is the assertion that the patriarch's God is one and the same as the God now acting on Israel's behalf. "The tradition wants to affirm the full continuity of God in the exodus

---

102. Condor, "Social Identity," 285–315; Cinnirella, "Temporal Aspects," 235–37.
103. Greifenhagen, *Egypt on the Pentateuch's Ideological Map*, 49.

narration with God in the ancestral tales of Genesis."[104] Thus, Exodus 3:6 claims the God of Abraham, Isaac, and Jacob is Moses's God (i.e., "the God of your [singular] father"). Then in 3:15–16 and 4:5, Moses is portrayed as being given the task of convincing a potentially resistant Israel that the God of the patriarchal triad is also her God.

The form of the narrative also conveys the ongoing participation of Israel in exodus. Actors in the narrative present are tied to those in the narrative past, creating a continuous and coherent group over time. This is seen in Exodus 2:24–25's portrayal of God engaged in four actions:

וישמע אלהים את־נאקתם 24

ויזכר אלהים את־בריתו את־אברהם את־יצחק ואת־יעקב

וירא אלהים את־בני ישראל 25

וידע אלהים

The first, third, and fourth actions are in relation to the Israelites: God heard their cries (2:24a), then, after an intervening action (2:24b), God saw the Israelites (2:25a), and God knew (2:25b).[105] The second action, God remembering his covenant with the patriarchs apparently stems from his hearing and results in his seeing and knowing. According to Brueggemann, "God connects present slaves and old promises. God has one eye on the old covenant oaths in Genesis. The other eye, however, is on the present circumstance of Israel in bondage.... God knew that promises were yet to be kept."[106] Brueggemann, however, does not state the obvious, that God connects two groups of people: one was *given* the promise, the other *received* it. The Israelites implicated in the first and last actions of the above verses enclose the patriarchs in the narrative construct, implying again that all their fates are joined together. Unless the two groups are part of one collective, the covenant oaths given to the one in the past would not be applicable to the other in the present. That is to say, covenant promises to ancestors presume the coherence of the group over time.

Exodus 6:2–8 offers another example of present Israel's relationship to social actors in the past. As in 2:24–25, it is the covenant promises that link the patriarchs to the collective group. While God promised the land of Canaan to Abraham, Isaac, and Jacob (6:4), God will keep this promise by

---

104. Brueggemann, "Book of Exodus," 733.

105. This may also be translated "knew them" (as in the Vulgate) or "he became known to them" (as in the Septuagint). The choice of interpretation does not alter the fact that God and Israel are linked in the action.

106. Brueggemann, "Book of Exodus," 706.

bringing the Israelites out of Egypt and into the land (6:8). In other words, "It is God's memory of promises to the ancestors in Genesis that operates in Exodus for liberation."[107]

The voice of continuity evident in this narrative, however, is accompanied by an equally audible voice of discontinuity with the past. Firstly, Abraham, Isaac, and Jacob are not explicitly referred to as Israel's אבות (as in Exodus 3:15–16 and 4:5). Also, present Israel's acquaintance with God is contrasted with that of the patriarchs (v. 3). Whether the claim of the narrative is that the patriarchs did not know the name יהוה (but only אל שדי),[108] had not experienced the full meaning or revelation of that name,[109] or had not encountered God in a specific "I am Yahweh" moment,[110] is immaterial to the identity claim of the narrative. The assertion of the narrative is that there is something unique about the Israelites in Egypt that is discontinuous with Abraham, Isaac, and Jacob. Finally, a unique relationship between Yahweh and the present collective is implied in the narrative of Exodus 6:7. God promises that he will take Israel as his people and become their God. Greifenhagen posits that "the language here suggests adoption or marriage or taking possession, language that presumes the beginning of a new relationship rather than the continuation of an old one."[111]

Continuity and discontinuity between the Israelites of Egypt and the patriarchs of the Genesis traditions intermingle in Exodus 6:2–8. Two perspectives of Israel's origins—one from outside Egypt and one from within—coexist without being fully integrated. It is impossible to ascertain whether this reflects two competing historical perspectives of Israel's origins[112] or simply the persuasive claim of the narrative upon unresisting hearers.

Some of the clearest examples of the use of the narrative form to convey the image of a present Israel as coherent with a future one are in Exodus 12–13. The narrative of the first Passover (12:1–13, 21–30) is split in two with instructions for its perpetual, cultic re-performance (12:14–20) in the middle. The consecration of the firstborn (13:1–2) is fused with that of the Feast of Unleavened Bread (13:3–4) and the narrative of their initial commemoration is immediately followed by directives for their

---

107. Ibid., 733.

108. This would imply the Genesis references to יהוה were anachronistic. Moberly, *Old Testament of the Old Testament*, 30–37.

109. Cassuto, *Commentary on Exodus*, 76–78. Sarna, *Exodus*, 31. Brueggemann, "Book of Exodus," 733–34. Janzen, *Exodus*, 51–52.

110. Hood, "I Appeared as El Shaddai," 174–88.

111. Greifenhagen, *Egypt on the Pentateuch's Ideological Map*, 93.

112. See discussion and notes on p. 71; and Greifenhagen, *Egypt on the Pentateuch's Ideological Map*, 97–98.

perpetual, ritualistic re-performance (13:5–16). Passover, the consecration of the firstborn, and the Feast of Unleavened Bread are all grounded in the "exodus formula," which says, in essence, "Do this . . . because the Lord brought you up out of Egypt."[113] The construction of the narrative ignores historical sequencing in favor of emphasizing how the events of the first night would be celebrated later.[114] Undoubtedly, interrupting the temporal flow draws out the storyline in a way that heightens the dramatic interest.[115] More significantly, however, the placement of the instructions to commemorate, remember, and tell[116] before the narrative of the exodus event itself highlights the primary importance of the persistent, ongoing experience over the punctiliar occurrence. All Israel is being integrated into the redemptive events from the start.

Broadening the boundaries of exodus social identity to incorporate previous and subsequent social actors into the category of "the people whom God brought up out of Egypt" is essential to the maintenance of that social identity over time. Through content and form, the narrative accomplishes this expansion; exodus identity is not restricted to a certain people of a specific time.

Myth of Common Descent

Contrary to de Pury's claim that "la légende d'origine fondée sur l'exode est une tradition foncièrement antitribale et antigénéalogique,"[117] the genealogical myth of Israel's descent from the patriarchs is not absent in the primary exodus story. This myth, however, does not appear to contribute greatly to Israel's emerging corporate personality. The Israelites are depicted as voicing their solidarity in the mutuality of their suffering, while needing to be schooled in their unity with patriarchs and promises. A cultural-ideological myth begins to define Israel, articulating her self-consciousness peoplehood through cultural kinship. She is defined by her suffering and bondage. Ancient hearers of the narrative could not miss the portrayal of "all Israel" as slaves in Egypt, bitterly suffering a shared fate. If they had experiential knowledge of social and political subjugation to a powerful "other," they would comprehend Israel's cultural-ideological myth of com-

---

113. Childs, *Book of Exodus*, 203.

114. Ibid., 199.

115. Meyers, *Exodus*, 92.

116. The obligation to remember and retell exodus will be examined in the next section.

117. De Pury, "Le cycle de Jacob," 91.

mon descent and might experience solidarity with this people. After the narration of Israel's exodus from Egypt is complete, a different, stronger myth of cultural-ideological descent predominates in the Hebrew Bible: one of mutual deliverance from Egypt.

Shared Life Story—Obligation to Tell

The primary exodus story opens the way to incorporate all Israel, regardless of their placement in time, into the exodus event. This section will examine what it means for all Israel to participate in exodus.

Scattered throughout the primary exodus story, hearers encounter various charges that are to be carried out after the exodus event. Children and grandchildren who did not witness the miraculous signs and wonders are to be told of them and their meaning (10:2). Children who ask about the meaning of the Passover during annual re-performances are to be told of the original Passover and its meaning (12:25–27). Israel is to remember the day she came out of Egypt by celebrating the Feast of Unleavened Bread (13:3) and by telling her children why she celebrates it (13:8). "When in the future" children ask why the firstborn are consecrated, they are to be told that it was because God delivered them from slavery (13:14–15). To aid in this future process of remembering and telling, Israel is instructed to set up זכרון (12:14; 13:9).

The Hebrew concept of remembering, communicated by both the verb זכר and the noun זכרון, is not limited simply to recalling the past. For Childs, "to remember [זכר] was to actualize the past, to bridge the gap of time and to form a solidarity with the fathers . . . זכון reactivates the original event in Egypt."[118] Thus, the producers of the narrative are "concerned, not only that the tradition be passed on to subsequent generations, but that the tradition be experienced . . . in an ongoing experiential appropriation."[119] Accordingly, Sarna notes not only that "Israel's liberation from Egypt is to be an event that is indelibly imprinted upon its memory, individually and collectively" but that "a set of symbols is created to actualize the experiences."[120] Durham also agrees with Childs, saying that the single purpose of Israel's exodus remembrances was "to make the parents' exodus also the children's exodus."[121] Remembering, telling, and

---

118. Childs, *Memory and Tradition*, 74, 69.
119. Childs, *Book of Exodus*, 203–4.
120. Sarna, *Exodus*, 65.
121. Durham, *Exodus*, 176–77.

establishing memorials function to maintain and transmit the memory of exodus, and, more importantly, to actualize it.

The social identification process, however, involves more than just acts of remembering and telling, and the SIA clarifies how collective identity is created and reinforced. The desire for continuity over time motivates the creation of a particular object of memory—the shared life story,[122] which is essential to the temporal maintenance of social identity. A shared life story is inclusive, incorporating past, present, and future generations. It is exemplified by the primary exodus story, which joins the exodus generation to prior and future generations who proleptically experience, tell, commemorate, and ritually re-enact it. Desired possible identities are disseminated through shared life stories because "ingroup members are concerned to persuade both other ingroupers *and also outgroupers* to endorse desired possible social identities of the ingroup."[123] It is not surprising that the obligation to tell the shared life story is often part of the story itself.

The first example of the obligation to tell the story found within the primary exodus story is in 10:2. Even before God's miracles and signs occur, Israel is obligated to transmit the collective memory of them from generation to generation.[124] This obligation is part of Israel's shared life story. Other examples of the "obligation to tell" are found in 12:27, 13:8, and 13:14.[125] Intentionally or not, the producers of the narrative are creating and transmitting a shared life story that is constructive of social identity, specifically exodus identity. The ultimate production of the text also exemplifies compliance with the obligation to tell.

Shared Life Story—Actualization

Israel's obligation is not just to tell the shared life story of exodus; she is summoned to enter into it. This is clearly illustrated in 15:1–21, and becomes the premise of the retold exodus stories examined in the next two chapters.

---

122. Cinnirella, "Temporal Aspects," 236.

123. Ibid., 235.

124. While the first verb תספר is second person singular, many scholars agree that this injunction was meant not just for Moses but for all Israel. For example Durham contends that Moses would begin the practice of recounting which would then be carried from generation to generation (Durham, *Exodus*, 135). Sarna maintains, "the singular form of the verb shows that Moses is addressed as the personification of the people of Israel, for whom the message is really intended" (Sarna, *Exodus*, 48). See also Cassuto, *Commentary on Exodus*, 123.

125. Similar examples of this obligation to tell the exodus story will be examined later in the study of Deut 6:20–23 and Ps 78.

Exodus 15:1–21 represents the only lengthy poetic narrative in the book of Exodus.[126] This in itself is indicative of its functional importance: "The Song marks a pause in the action and invites the audience of the text to participate."[127] Exploring this narrative using the SIA will draw attention specifically to how its form and content maintain and transmit exodus identity by inviting hearers to participate in the exodus story.

A prose introduction precedes the Song: "Then Moses and the Israelites sang this song to the Lord" (15:1a). The ensuing poem is framed by the literary *inclusio* in 1b and 21. The only difference between the two verses is the change in verb conjugation: first person singular cohortative—"let me sing"—and the second person plural imperative—"sing!" The introduction interprets the first person in 1b as Israel, a personified, singular collective. The implicit claim is that all Israel participated in the celebratory song. The imperative in verse 21 serves as a closing charge for the hearer to join in the song. The form of the song and its emotive, expressive language invites participation.

Several aspects of the form and content of Exodus 15 communicate a sense of temporal inclusiveness, allowing all Israel to take up this song, creating an exodus paradigm through which all Israel can interpret their experience.

A peculiar use of verbs in Exodus 15 offers the first example of how the form of this narrative contributes to its temporal inclusiveness. In verses 5–12, imperfect and perfect verbs alternate in phrases that seemingly refer to the same incident. While such non-standard use of verbs[128] is not uncharacteristic of Hebrew poetry, the context usually helps to determine an appropriate translation.[129] Thus, the majority of scholars including Childs, Cassuto, Sarna, Meyers, and Durham interpret the imperfect verbs in these verses as describing the same events as the perfect verbs, having the same force and describing complete action in the past time.[130] In verses 13–17,

---

126. This statement is based on the final unity of the text. Most scholars agree that two developmentally independent songs have been joined together by the prose insertion in 15:19–21a.

127. Russell, *Song of the Sea*, 48.

128. Perfect verbs generally reflect completed action, mostly in past time. Imperfect verbs generally reflect incomplete action in present or, more commonly, future time. When either of these verb forms is preceded by the conjunction ו (i.e., the *vav*-consecutive form), the reverse is usually true of both forms: perfect verbs suggest incomplete action in the present or future time and imperfect verbs indicate completed action in past time. Freedman, "Moses and Miriam," 73.

129. Craigie, *Psalms 1–50*, 111.

130. Childs, *Book of Exodus*, 240–41. Cassuto, *Commentary on Exodus*, 174–76. Sarna, *Exodus*, 79–80. Meyers, *Exodus*, 108–9. Durham, *Exodus*, 198–200.

however, problematic perfect verbs do not lend themselves to the same contextual approach. This results in a multiplicity of translations (see Appendix 3).[131] After a careful analysis of the finite Hebrew verbs and the strengths and weaknesses of each translation model, Shrekhise concludes that possibilities and problems are apparent with each model and no one interpretation is entirely satisfactory.[132] While all three translation models interpret the imperfect in verse 18 as incomplete action, David Freedman argues for the omnitemporal interpretation of the verb ימלך and suggests the following translation: "As for Yahweh, he has reigned, continues to reign, and will reign from most ancient times on into the endless future."[133] Although such a translation fails to reflect the terseness and rhythm of Hebrew poetry, it communicates well the essence of the Hebrew verbs, not only in verse 18, but throughout the song. This verbal ambiguity resulting in interpretive variability may have been present with the ancient hearer as it is with the contemporary one. Such an omnitemporal character of verbs would have contributed to the Song's repeatability.

In addition to the omnitemporal character of finite verbs, another structural aspect of Exodus 15 that contributes to its temporal inclusiveness is the violation in the temporal sequencing of the story line. Instead of providing a chronological narration, the story reflects backward on the earlier intentions of the enemy in verse 9 and infinitely forward in time in verse 18. Also reflected in the Song are multiple narrations of throwing adversaries into the sea and their subsequent drowning (15:1, 4–5, 7, 10, 12, 19, 21). Seven times the hearer is brought back to reflect on an "event" that only "happened" once.

The three content aspects of Exodus 15:1–21 that remove the song from a particular historical context and summon all Israel to participate in it are the unnamed Pharaoh, the exaltation of a timeless hero, and the application of the exodus deliverance to a new temporal perspective in verses 13–18.

Firstly, it is unlikely that the failure to name the Pharaoh in the song—and throughout the book of Exodus—resulted from inadvertent, unmotivated amnesia. Instead, "the blank of Pharaoh's identity may . . . function as a strategic feature of the tradition, providing a movable boundary of inclusion for those who shared this memory. . . . By leaving the name of Pharaoh a blank, the memory of Egyptian oppression could extend to all who had

---

131. Meyers, *Exodus*, 109–10; Sarna, *Exodus*, 80–82; Childs, *Book of Exodus*, 241–42; Cassuto, *Commentary on Exodus*, 176–77; Durham, *Exodus*, 200–201; Dozeman, *Exodus*, 319–20.

132. Shreckhise, "Problem of Finite Verb Translation," 287–310.

133. Freedman, "Moses and Miriam," 83.

felt the oppression of Pharaoh at any time in the remembered past."[134] By not identifying the Pharaoh and by avoiding specific references to time, the song is able to cross temporal boundaries.

The second content aspect that contributes to the Song's temporal inclusiveness, is its extolment of God alone, rather than of Moses or the fighting men of Israel. This allows for the Song's repeatability since the action is not tied to any particular human heroes of the past.

The third and strongest feature facilitating inclusion is the application of the deliverance at the Reed Sea to an altogether new set of circumstances in 15:13-18. As previously noted, exegetes and translators struggle over whether to interpret the events as anticipatory or as having already taken place. The uncertainty results both from ambiguous verb forms and from the content of the verses. After five rehearsals of God's destruction of the Egyptians, and without transition, God becomes Israel's guide and strikes the surrounding nations with terror. A broad listing of Israel's enemies adds a timeless note to the Song. Even more noteworthy is the inherent tension seen in the poem's abruptness. It creates an "illusion of simultaneity" as if the Canaanite nations instantly hear of the demise of the Egyptians and are panic stricken, years before the actual arrival of the Israelites.[135] The people are poetically transported from the shores of the Reed Sea to the "mountain of God's inheritance" amidst trembling nations, a temporal illusion augmented by the ambiguous use of the verb עבר[136] that could be heard as an allusion to the crossing of the Jordan.[137]

134. Hendel, "Exodus in Biblical Memory," 604-5.

135. Alter, *Art of Biblical Poetry*, 54.

136. Verse 16 claims that terror fell upon the nations as the people of Yahweh "passed." This verb may be translated as "passed by," "passed through," or "passed over," depending on the context. It may refer to the crossing of the Reed Sea, the crossing of the Jordan River, or the passing through the land in the Conquest. Here the context does not offer any clue to support one particular interpretation, thus giving it an ambiguous or atemporal nature. Multiple interpretations are possible for the unnamed mountain and sanctuary of v. 17 as well.

137. Many modern translations fail to reflect the temporal illusion, or they try to resolve the tension by simply translating these verses in the future tense. Grammatically speaking, this is irresponsible. The perfects in v. 13 set the tone for understanding the events as already completed. The two imperfects found in vv. 14-15 speak of the same event (the terror of the nations) as the perfects which surround them, compelling one to view them as completed action. One must do likewise with the imperfects in v. 16 which reflect the further reactions and responses of the nations. Verse 17 causes the greatest degree of uncertainty in terms of the "tense" and aspect of the two imperfect verbs. Here, however, one must agree with Freedman and translate them as having past time and completed action: "Up to this point, all of the imperfect verbs have been interpreted as having past time and completed action, owing in good part to their close association with perfect verbs referring to the same incidents and covering the same

While some simply interpret these verses as proleptic,[138] they should not be interpreted as "prophesying events still to come; it is a celebration of YHWH's victories, past and future, seeing them all encapsulated in the victory by the Reed Sea."[139] Within the song itself, other experiences are being viewed through the lens of the victory of exodus.

The song of God's victory by the sea invites the participation of all Israel. Its omnitemporal nature is appropriate to this paradigmatic function. Hearers of the Song, not present at the sea, become witnesses to God's act of salvation, thus joining the celebration from their own temporal perspective.[140] The past is appropriated, and common memory is created.

Two different but related effects are produced for the hearers of the narrative. Firstly, the Song's rehearsal provides a means through which all Israel, by her participation, may unite with the exodus generation. Secondly, the Song offers a paradigm of how God consistently acts on behalf of his people, delivering them from oppression and establishing them in relation to himself. The event at the sea becomes a paradigm through which hearers may reimagine and relive their own experiences.[141] Thus, the appropriation of the narrative would unify Israel's past and present both by identifying the hearers with the exodus generation and by actualizing the exodus and its meaning for the hearer.[142] Deliverance is not experienced simply by standing in the flow of observable events but also through participation in the poetic reading of reality. It is not just the artistry of the poem but particular social identity formulations that capture and absorb the hearers of the story. As Israel takes up the song, it creates Israel as a collective people, "the people whom God brought up out of Egypt."

---

territory. So there should be a predisposition to interpret these verbs in the same way, an indication supported by the presence of two perfect verbs in the same verse" (Freedman, "Moses and Miriam," 78).

138. See for example Stuart, *Exodus*, 356; Russell, *Song of the Sea*, 17.

139. Watts, "Song and Ancient Reader," 143.

140. Watts maintains that the text itself, especially vv. 12–18, facilitates this inclusion of the later reader: "The psalm moves from the temporal perspective of the narrative, in which the land's settlement lies in the future, to that of the readers, for whom it is in the past. The effect of the move is to allow the readers to join in the celebration at the sea from their own temporal perspective" ("Song and Ancient Reader," 143–44).

141. Brueggemann, "Psalms in Narrative Performance," 16. It should be noted that Brueggemann is speaking here specifically about the re-performance of Psalms.

142. Brueggemann, "Response to the 'Song of Miriam,'" 299.

Conclusion

The application of the SIA to the primary exodus story has brought to light specific social identity dimensions of the narrative that might otherwise have been overlooked. This elucidates it potential impact on unresisting hearers.

The narrative makes the case that Israel was constituted as a people in Egypt, in a context of oppression and misery. It persuades hearers to acknowledge that this was their initial fate too, the basis of their solidarity with all Israel. It convinces them of the disorientation and confusion of assimilation and the necessity of separation from the "other." It challenges them to do just as Yahweh commands. That is to say, these unresisting hearers are impelled to oppose any "Egypt" that would defy the legitimate governance of Yahweh. Further, they are to acknowledge that Yahweh is their deliverer and that he has placed them into a superordinate collective identity of the "people whom Yahweh brought up out of Egypt," an identity that also comprises the exodus generation of Israel, the mixed multitude, and the patriarchs. The narrative raises their own positive valuation and sense of attachment and belonging as it draws them into the collective "us" of Israel. Most importantly, though, the hearers are persuaded that this identity is now achieved not by painting doorframes but by retelling the story, commemorating the Passover, and singing the song. Through the rhetoric of the narrative, they sense a cultural affinity with all Israel, and they reimagine, relive, and re-experience their present situation through the paradigmatic lens of exodus.

The primary exodus story is the dominant voice of Israel's shared life story that becomes a narrative resource for subsequent hearers. Eighteen retold exodus stories, however, also add to the conversation and make identity claims on hearers. They will be examined next.

4

Social Identity Formations in Retold Exodus Stories: Pentateuch

Using the heuristic tool developed in chapter 2, the previous chapter exposed the literary formulations of social identity informing the design of the primary exodus story (Exod 1—15:21). It also acknowledged the persuasive potential of this rhetoric to capture the imagination and commitment of hearers of the narrative and to construct or reinforce their collective identity.

The primary exodus story was narrated from the perspective of one who was observing the events as they happened. Retold exodus stories, by contrast, portray exodus as a past event, told from other narrative perspectives. In the next two chapters, the social identity approach will be applied to these retellings.

According to Kirk, "genuine communities are communities of memory that constantly tell and retell their constitutive memories."[1] Ancient Israel qualifies as such, and the memory she tells and retells is the story of exodus. However, Israel was obligated to do more than simply retell the story; she was summoned to enter into it. The primary exodus story, presented as an eyewitness account, narrates the exodus generation's experience. In a limited way (e.g., Exod 12:14–20; 15:1–21), it also anachronistically calls future generations into the exodus experience. This summons, however, is the premise and purpose of the retold exodus stories.

The retold exodus stories are not as comprehensive or detailed as the primary narrative. They nevertheless include some key components of the story. This chapter and the next will show how certain rhetorical formulations found in retold stories also function to persuade hearers to enter into the shared exodus story and take up a collective exodus identity.

---

1. Kirk, "Social and Cultural Memory," 4. Kirk's work focuses specifically on the early Christian community.

Generally, the retold exodus stories depict the exodus generation as prototypical of all Israel. That is to say, they portray the exodus event as normative of all Israel's experience. Exodus becomes the shared life story defining Israel's collective identity. At times, however, these narratives offer a reinterpreted account of the exodus story in order to be relevant to new situations and to create a sense of commonality between the past and the present.

Of the eighteen retellings that meet the criteria outlined in the introduction for inclusion in this analysis, the ten from the Pentateuch will be considered in this chapter. These narratives would have been heard in juxtaposition with one another as they became available because, as Greifenhagen notes, these writings—encompassing the life of Moses with Genesis as a prologue—project themselves as a bounded literary entity.[2] The remaining eight retold stories will be considered in chapter 5.

The Scripture references used will identify the boundaries of the retold stories rather than the full literary units in which they appear. The surrounding literary contexts will be considered, however, in the analyses. Plot elements characterizing each story will be identified, as well as verbal and imaginal ties to the primary exodus story that link later generations to the exodus generation. This will be followed by a more detailed assessment of the identity constructing rhetoric found in each retold story. Brief observations will be made as to the possible effect of certain rhetoric on hearers of the narrative.

Numbers 20:14–16

Like the primary exodus story, the retold version found in Numbers 20 is prefaced by "our ancestors went down into Egypt." However, of the three major plot elements of the primary exodus story, only two are found in 20:14–16: an initial state of suffering and the bringing out of Egypt. There is no mention of the supernatural intervention of God in response to Israel's suffering. The emphasis is on their hardship, and this will be shown to play a significant role in the narrative construction of identity.

While the vocabulary used to describe Israel's affliction in the retold story is distinct from the primary exodus story, the term used for Israel's response of crying out, צעק, may be interpreted as parallel in meaning and a variant of זעק (Exod 2:23; cf. Deut 26:7).[3] Another interpretation, however, would be to recognize צעק as referring to Israel's cry at the Reed Sea

---

2. Greifenhagen, *Egypt on the Pentateuch's Ideological Map*, 21.
3. Wood, "(570a) זעקה ($z^{e\ʻ}āqâ$) cry, outcry," 248.

(Exod 14:10) followed by God's sending of a מלאך to bring Israel out (Exod 14:19). In either case, the shared images of hardship and shared vocabulary of crying out and being brought out (i.e., יצא and מצרים) tie this retold tale to the primary narrative.

The narrative context of this exodus story is one of increasing vulnerability[4] characterized by death and the intimation of death, lack of water and, most noteworthy, a *"mise en question par le peuple du projet exodique de Dieu"*[5] (i.e., Num 11:5 [18-20]; 14:2-4; 16:12-14; 20:4-5; 21:5 cf. Exod 14: 11-12; 16:3; 17:3). Expressions of nostalgia for Egypt immediately preceding the passage are subversions of the dominant exodus tradition.[6] While the producers of the narrative give voice to those who positively evaluate Egypt, they "make it a voice of complaint and rebellion against YHWH, thus negating its legitimacy."[7] Nostalgia for Egypt is also portrayed as characterizing only the exodus generation who will be excluded from the land.

Although, "the scroll of Numbers marks the transition from the generation of Israel that emerged from Egypt to a new generation birthed in the wilderness,"[8] Numbers 20:14-16 does not identify the characters in its story exclusively as a new generation of Israel. In fact, based on the literary design of Numbers, these verses capture the first and last retelling of exodus by the exodus generation. It is Numbers 25 and 26 that explicitly mark the transition from the Egypt-born generation of complaint and rebellion to a new generation of hope, respectively. Numbers 20, in its literary context of chapters 11-25, portrays the fate of the old generation, dominated by images of death. The last of this old generation presumably dies in the plague narrated in Numbers 25:9. By contrast, chapters 26-36 represent the fate of the new generation, and no Israelite death is recorded there (e.g., 31:49). It is this literary design that contradicts Alter's claim that the phrase "the whole community" at the beginning of the chapter (20:1), refers to the new generation of Israelites poised to enter the land.[9] Alter reads back into Numbers 20 the summary of Israel's journey in Numbers 33 that seemed to indicate that Israel's arrival at the border of Edom and Aaron's death marked the end of the original adult exodus generation. His conclusion, however, is based on an attempted historical reconstruction rather than on the literary context of the story.

4. Brodie, "Literary Unity of Numbers," 468.
5. Römer, "Exode et Anti-Exode," 171.
6. Ibid., 172. Greifenhagen, *Egypt on the Pentateuch's Ideological Map*, 178-84.
7. Greifenhagen, *Egypt on the Pentateuch's Ideological Map*, 178.
8. Ibid., 167. See also Olson, "Negotiating Boundaries," 229-40.
9. Alter, *Five Books of Moses*, 782. Alter holds to the view of Rashi and Ibn Ezra.

Thus, Moses sends a message to the King of Edom, purportedly from the Egyptian-born generation (20:14). The retelling does not elicit sympathy from Edom,[10] enlist a sense of Semitic ethnic solidarity against the non-Semitic Egyptian persecutors,[11] or persuade the king of Edom of the worthiness of Israel's journey.[12] This retold exodus story, nevertheless, contains various formulations of social identity. As the defining of self and others is closely integrated in this narrative with the making of value judgments about the ingroup and outgroup, cognitive and evaluative formulations will be examined together. The same will be done with respect to the blended emotional and temporal formulations. Behavioral formulations, however, are notably absent.

Cognitive and Evaluative Formulations

From the narrative perspective of this passage, Israel's exodus story was essential to her identity, to entry into the land, and to her future.[13] The story's placement after the introductory identifier of the speaker as "your brother Israel" alludes to its epithetical nature. The exodus story becomes the group label that should cognitively define Israel (i.e., "we are the people who . . . "[14]) and be central to her positive self-evaluation. As "seeing oneself" and "being seen" is what constitutes social identity,[15] the narrative makes the claim that Edom knows Israel and her story (20:14). Perhaps this is a nod to the primary exodus story, where Edom was among the nations that stood dismayed as Israel passed by, victoriously delivered from Egypt (Exod 15:14–16). However, this Edom is altogether different than the group that was "shaken to the core by the display of Yahweh's power."[16] She is unmoved by Israel's story and aggressively refuses the request for passage.

---

10. Olson, *Numbers*, 130; Milgrom, *Numbers*, 167; and Henry, *Matthew Henry's Commentary*, 217.

11. Alter, *Five Books of Moses*, 784.

12. Leveen, *Memory and Tradition in Numbers*, 1–2.

13. A contemporary example of this is offered in the opening paragraphs of Cornell's "Story of Our Life," 41. Cornell demonstrates how a representative from a Native American reservation prefaced his participation in an economic development dialogue with a summary of the history of his people. Cornell recognized that the man's historical digression was not merely informational. His people's identity, as contained in their shared life story, was of critical importance to the future of that nation and, consequently, was perceived as a necessary preface to the issue at hand.

14. Cornell, "Story of Our Life," 42.

15. Lieu, *Christian Identity*, 12, 102.

16. Meyers, *Exodus*, 120.

Although, in general, kinship language characterizes the Hebrew Bible's representation of the relationship between Israel and Edom,[17] Edom is, nevertheless, portrayed ambiguously, sometimes positively (i.e., Gen 33; 35:29–36:43; Deut 2:4; 23:8) and sometimes negatively (i.e., Gen 25; 27; Ezek 35:1–36:5; Obad 10–12; Amos 1:6, 9–12; Mal 1:4). The exodus retelling in Numbers advances a process of differentiation between the two peoples that is highlighted not only by Edom's refusal of Israel's request but by the ironic use of kinship terminology. Israel's request for safe passage through Edom is prefaced by, "Thus says your brother Israel" (20:14). This terminology does not reflect a claim by Israel that she and Edom have common ground and want similar things, as Bridge claims.[18] Furthermore, Edom's response to her sibling's request is not simply "impolite."[19] Her failure to "know" Israel's exodus story in any practical or functional way is a refusal to acknowledge Israel's identity. It is not merely rude; it is un-brotherly, effectively differentiating Edom and placing her in the category of "other." Failure to appropriate the story becomes the boundary that excludes Edom.[20]

The differentiation of Edom's "otherness" is also subtly insinuated in that Edom is not included in the "we" and "us" as it relates to the hardships and mistreatments of Egypt. Israel was the one oppressed and enslaved, prerequisites to the promise of land inheritance made to Abraham (Gen 15:13–16). Edom cannot make any claim to the land based solely on ancestry. Edom remained free, while Israel paid the debt of serfdom, giving her title to the land and the right to request passage.[21] The kinship label rings with irony rather than solidarity. This story not only evaluatively rehearses the us/them distinction between Israel and Egypt, but it differentiates, more subtly, between Israel and Edom. A further level of subtlety, however, is that the Egyptian-born Israel may be "other" as well, despite Moses's apparent claim that it is they who are telling the story. Their pro-Egyptian perspective calls into question their actual differentiation and their ability to construct their own identity over and against Egypt by the retelling of the story.

---

17. Anderson, "Edom in the Book of Numbers," 40.

18. Bridge, "Polite Israel and Impolite Edom," 83. Bridge's focus is on the language and strategies of politeness.

19. Ibid., 77–88.

20. In contrast, Deut 2:2–8 shows Israel passing through Edom without resistance as part of a narrative with the altogether different aim of vindicating God's provision during the forty years of wilderness wandering.

21. Leibowitz, *Studies in Bamidbar (Numbers)*, 252.

Emotional and Temporal Formulations

Numbers 20:15 alternates between past and present subjects, "our ancestors" and "us," with corresponding third person plural and first person plural verbs. For Noth, this alternation is insignificant and attributed to the author's variation or even carelessness.[22] Ashley, however, interprets this alternation as implicitly claiming that "harm to the fathers meant harm to the present generation."[23] Unresisting hearers of the narrative may find themselves drawn to commiserate and ally themselves with the exodus generation. The first person plural language invites their participation, and the alternation between participants past and present exemplifies the temporal solidarity of all Israel.

When Moses places the story "in the mouth" of Israel, even if they have not truly appropriated it, he fulfils the "obligation to tell" and the summons to enter into the story mandated by the primary exodus story. In SIA language, the rhetoric of the retelling offers an emotional portrayal of Israel's shared fate that is inclusive of past and present members. Moses, or the narrative, will have to find a way, however, to transfer the story to a new generation of Israel if it is to become her enduring identity story. This will become evident in the exodus stories of Deuteronomy.

Introduction to Retold Exodus Stories in Deuteronomy

The most extensive collection of retold exodus stories is found in the book of Deuteronomy. Nine passages meet the criteria of an exodus story as defined in the introduction. Deuteronomy portrays a new generation of Israel poised on the border of the Promised Land, preparing to enter and begin a new life. Although logically this group should have included the children of the exodus, the persuasive literary discourse of Numbers portrays them as new. For God declares in Numbers 14:22 that none of those who saw his glory and the signs done in Egypt would enter the land. Also, the census taken after the death of the old generation (Num 26) emphasizes only the discontinuity between generations and not continuity. Apart from any historical reality (hinted at only in 14:31–32), the narrative claim is that the generation that stood on the edge of the land was new and not a witness to God's glory and signs performed in Egypt. The experiences of wilderness and hardship, however, were certainly fresh in her mind. The presumed

---

22. Noth, *Numbers*, 149.
23. Ashley, *Book of Numbers*, 390; Noth, *Numbers*, 149.

narrator, Moses, calls this new generation to a new commitment to God and a fresh understanding of the nature of what it means to be the people of God.[24] The greatest danger to Israel's success is forgetfulness. The means to avert forgetting is the recital of the formative story of exodus, upon which her uniqueness and her defining relationship with God is grounded. Remembering her story will in turn motivate single-minded obedience and exclusive allegiance to the God of exodus.

Deuteronomy 4:20

On the surface, Deuteronomy 4:20 appears to be an incomplete exodus story, narrating only the final plot element—being brought out of Egypt. The term "iron-smelter," however, represents the prior state of oppression or enslavement.[25] Thus it expresses the first plot element. In addition, the phrase "to become a people of his very own possession, as you are now" connects this verse to the more complete story in Deuteronomy 4:34–38 that ends with "giving you their land for a possession, as it is still today." Whether designed as an independent reference or as a disconnected part of the Deuteronomy 4:34–38 story, Deuteronomy 4:20 meets the qualifications of a retold exodus story, albeit one of the shortest.

Identity constructing and reinforcing formulations are found in both the form and the content of the story.

Cognitive and Emotional Formulations

In this retold story, cognitive formulations are cast in emotive terms, thereby serving a dual function with respect to identity formation. Two group labels categorize Israel. Israel's previous identity as a people in an "iron-smelter" is contrasted with her present status as "a people of [God's] own possession." The iron-smelter metaphor (also found in 1 Kgs 8:51 and Jer 11:4) conjures images of immense heat, pain, toil and suffering, all of which were present in the Egyptian oppression. However, connotations of punishment[26] or testing[27] are untenable here due to the absence of any such overtones in the

---

24. Craigie, *Book of Deuteronomy*, 7.
25. Vieweger, "... und führte euch heraus aus dem Eisenschmelzofen," 272–76.
26. Singer, *Die Metalle Gold, Silber, Bronze, Kupfer und Eisen*, 130.
27. Driver, *Critical and Exegetical Commentary on Deuteronomy*, 71. See also Christensen, *Deuteronomy 1:1—21:9*, 89.

story or the surrounding literary context, though they are clearly present in the re-use of the term in the exilic context (Isaiah 48:10).[28]

The claim here is that Israel—implicitly valued by God—has been taken from an unstable, agonizing existence and reconstituted into the people of God. Her identity is defined in part by this prior state of being, a constituting experience that Israel is commanded not to forget. Braulik highlights the special dignity of Israel as God's possession, delivered from adversity: "Er Selbst hat es dem "Schmelzofen" Ägypten, einem qualvollen Verlust seiner Existenz als goj, entrissen, um es zu seinem 'am, seinem "Volk", genauer: Seiner Familie, zu machen. Mehr noch: Israel ist durch die Herausführung zum "Erbvolk" Jahwes geworden, also zu einem Besitz, den er letzlich nicht mehr veräußern kann."[29] God placed himself in a unique position when he snatched those who had become devoid of any sense of peoplehood out of the Egyptian iron-smelter. Not only did he fashion them into a people, but he made them his non-transferable possession.

The retold story paints an emotionally charged image of attachment and belonging that is present even in the assertion that Israel has become for God an עם נחלה. "His possession" does not have the impersonal connotations found in the current use of this expression. Tigay perceptively notes that the term נחלה "expresses not only God's sovereignty over the people of Israel but also His attachment to them 'since a person's personal property and his portion are dear to him.'"[30] This term demonstrates a Deuteronomic construction of Israel's exodus identity not evident in the primary exodus story. In Exodus 15:17, Israel is brought out of Egypt and planted on the mountain of God's inheritance (נחלה). However, here in Deuteronomy 4:20, as in 9:26; 9:29, and 1 Kings 8:51, Israel *becomes* his inheritance (עם נחלה). Removed from the exodus generation, Deuteronomy is able to reflect on and interpret the significance of exodus from its retrospective vantage point. This is the first of many interpretations of exodus as representing God's love for Israel that promote the emotional formulations of attachment and belonging.

Evaluative Formulation

In addition to using group labels that define Israel both in terms of adversity and deliverance, Deuteronomy 4:20 implicitly makes positive and negative evaluations of groups and their membership. The context of the retold

---

28. Vieweger, "... und führte euch heraus aus dem Eisenschmelzofen," 272–76.
29. Braulik, *Deuteronomium 1–16*, 17, 43.
30. Tigay, *Deuteronomy*, 51 quoting Saadia, *Book of Beliefs and Opinions*, 2:11.

story differentiates Israel from other nations and their non-gods (4:15–19).³¹ Describing the objects of other nation's worship (sun, moon, and stars) as "allotted to all the peoples everywhere under heaven" (4:19) is not intended to express tolerance for the practices of the "other."³² Rather it prepares the way for highlighting Israel's positive distinctiveness in verse 20.

Behavioral Formulation

As mentioned, the immediate literary context of Deuteronomy 4:20 portrays Israel's as the possession of God, distinct from the other nations who worship the creation rather than the Creator (4:19, 23–28). Idolatry in incongruous with her exodus identity.

Temporal Formulations

An important temporal image of Israel as coherent over time is also presented. A new generation of Israel is addressed as if they were the prototypical exodus generation itself, and God's inheritance of Israel is portrayed as one inheritance from the exodus to the present day (כיום הזה). The second-person address ("But the Lord has taken you ... ") and the singularity of the inheritance to "this day" welcome other hearers of the narrative into the collective identity. Vieweger infers that this passage may have had an identity constructing effect on exilic hearers who would have found identification with the exodus generation and the hope of a new leading out because of the similarity of their situations.³³ The SIA offers a more thorough explanation of their identification. The rhetoric of the narrative, with its second-person address and its emotional images, draft all subsequent hearers of the narrative into a shared life story which offers them a sense of both corporate identity and hope.

Deuteronomy 4:34–38

The second plot element characteristic of exodus stories—the supernatural intervention of God—that was missing in the retold stories of Numbers 20:14–16 and Deuteronomy 4:20, dominates Deuteronomy 4:34–38. Vocabulary tying this story to the primary narrative includes אתת ובמופתים

---

31. Christensen, *Deuteronomy 1:1—21:9*, 86.
32. Mayes, *Deuteronomy*, 154.
33. Vieweger, " ... und führte euch heraus aus dem Eisenschmelzofen," 276

and יד חזקה ובזרוע נטויה, as well as the recurrent, third plot element and anchoring phrase ויוצאך ממצרים. Deuteronomy employs this vocabulary differently than the primary narrative. The latter, for example, uses each of the phrases יד חזקה and זרע נטויה independently (Exod 13:9; 6:6). The same is true for the use of אותות (Exod 10:1–2) and מופתים (Exod 11:9–10), with the complete phrase אתת ובמופתים only appearing in Exodus 7:3 of the primary narrative. Deuteronomy, by contrast, uses יד חזקה ובזרע נטויה (Deut 4:34; 5:15; 7:19; 11:2; 26:8) and האתת והמפתים (Deut 4:34; 6:22; 7:19; 26:8; 34:11) as idiomatic wholes. Set within a literary context that repudiates the practice of idolatry, this vocabulary of God's supernatural intervention serves to emphasize the power of God displayed in exodus and his right to exclusive worship.

Another unique vocabulary usage noted here and in Deuteronomy 7:18–19[34] is the appropriation of the term מסה for the retelling of exodus. Elsewhere, this term evokes images of Israel testing God in the wilderness (Exod 17:7; Deut 6:16; 9:22; 33:8; Ps 95:8). However wilderness has no place in Israel's ideal social identity as established through the exodus story. Only one of the nine retold exodus stories in Deuteronomy includes a wilderness account (Deut 11:2–7). Here the anecdote of Dathan and Abiram is employed to portray a threat to Israel's identity.[35] Three of Deuteronomy's exodus stories portray Israel as transported directly from Egypt to the land (Deut 4:34–38; 6:20–23; 26:5–9). Deuteronomy 4:34 and 7:19 appropriate מסה and combine it with האתת והממתים and יד חזקה ובזרע נטויה to describe God's supernatural intervention in Egypt.

Cognitive and Evaluative Formulations

The social identification processes of defining and evaluating groups are interwoven in Deuteronomy 4:34–38 as they were in Numbers 20:14–16. Due to its retrospective literary vantage point, it is able to incorporate an interpretation of the exodus into its retelling. It portrays both Israel and her redemption from Egypt as unique.[36] As social memory, the selectiveness of Deuteronomy 4:34–38 is aimed at promoting a positive evaluation of the ingroup.[37] The rhetorical question of 4:34—"Has any god ever attempted to

---

34. This term is also used in the same way in the short reference to exodus in Deut 29:3.

35. מסה is used elsewhere in Deuteronomy to remind Israel of her wilderness experience, but not in exodus stories.

36. See also 2 Sam 7:23–24 // 1 Chr 17:21.

37. Bikmen, "History, Memory, and Identity," 21.

go and take a nation for himself . . . as the LORD your God did for you?"— is employed with that aim in mind. A more subtle devaluation of the outgroup through the use of idioms יד חזקה and an זרוע נטויה, however, is also surmised. These expressions describe God's redemptive action toward Israel, yet they are the same epithets found in Egyptian texts in regard to the power of the pharaohs.[38] If the Egyptian use of these terms was part of ancient Israel's common memory, then their use here would be polemical, underscoring Yahweh's superiority over Pharaoh and the gods of Egypt. As Hoffmeier says, "What better way for the exodus traditions to describe God's victory over Pharaoh, and as a result his superiority, than to use Hebrew derivations or counterparts to Egyptian expressions that symbolized Egyptian royal power."[39] While neither Currid nor Hoffmeier examines identity construction, their insights, nevertheless, illuminate the devaluation of the outgroup that is recognizable by the SIA as a characteristic element of identity formation. This same devaluation of the outgroup is implicit in the narrative claim that God took for himself גוי מקרב גוי (4:34).

Emotional Formulations

The images and language of hostile inter-group conflict used to devalue the outgroup also add emotional intensity to the story. Supernatural presence and strength on Israel's side of the conflict, as well as language of being loved, chosen, and brought out, would fortify her sense of attachment and belonging (v. 37). Deuteronomy is the first book of the Pentateuch to speak of God *loving* and *choosing Israel*,[40] thereby making the emotional dimension of God's relationship with Israel explicit. A similar effect is realized by the language of a shared fate: Israel was *taken out* of one nation, and other nations will be *driven out* before her until she is *brought into* her inheritance.

Behavioral Formulations

According to Deuteronomy 4:39–40, Israel's retold story and her identity as "the people whom God brought up out of Egypt" should give rise to certain behavioral norms, namely, the acknowledgement of Yahweh, the God of exodus, as the one true God and subsequent obedience to him.

---

38. Currid, *Study Commentary on Deuteronomy*, 114. A survey of the use of these terms in Egyptian texts is found in Hoffmeier, "Arm of God," 378–87.

39. Ibid., 386–87.

40. Tigay, *Deuteronomy*, 56.

Temporal Formulations

Numbers and Deuteronomy portray the adult exodus generation becoming extinct during the forty years of wandering in the desert.[41] Thereafter a new generation[42] is depicted. The narrative never breaks down the composition of this new adult generation by distinguishing between the children of the exodus and those born in the wilderness. In Deuteronomy 4:34-38 they are all addressed as one body as having witnessed God's displays of power before "your very eyes" עיניך (Deut 4:34). This recurring expression depicts all Israel as witnesses to God's acts and, therefore, as coherent over time. The same and similar phrases (עינינו and עיניכם) are found in successive exodus narratives (Deut 6:22; 7:19; 11:7; Josh 24:17) and in other short references to the exodus story (Deut 1:30; 10:21; 29:2-3) where they are used to create the same effect. In SIA terms, the rhetoric of the narrative creates collective identity by showing all Israel as participating in the experience of exodus. Persuading a new generation of Israel to remember an old generation's experience as if it occurred before her eyes is an invitation to actualize the group story, a temporal formulation of social identity made even more explicit in Deuteronomy 11:2-4, 7.

Not only does the phrase "your/our very eyes" contribute to a sense of Israel as coherent over time and invite her to enter into the group story, but the shift in pronouns from second to third and back to second—"loved *your* ancestors . . . chose *their* descendants . . . brought *you* out"—achieves the same effect. This is true not only for the purported community of the Deuteronomy narrative but for the hearer of the narrative as well.

Deuteronomy 5:15, 15:15, and 24:18

All three short retellings of exodus found in Deuteronomy 5:15, 15:15 and 24:18 begin with the phrase זכרת כי עבד היית followed by בארץ מחרים or במצרים. Deuteronomy 5:15 incorporates all three plot elements of the exodus story complete with common vocabulary linking it with the primary narrative (יד חזקה, יצא, and זרע נטויה). Deuteronomy 15:15 and 24:18 also begin with the same introductory phrase, making them easily recognizable, but then substitute פדה for יצא to express the final plot element. These

---

41. See Num 14:23, 30; Deut 1:35; 2:14-16; Josh 5:4.

42. This of course is with the exception of Joshua, Caleb, and Moses. However, as Greifenhagen notes, "Even Moses must expire outside the land in order for the break between Israel and Egypt to be final." Greifenhagen, *Egypt on the Pentateuch's Ideological Map*, 172.

very brief retold stories incorporate cognitive, emotional and behavioral formulations of identity.

Cognitive Formulations

These three retold stories go a bit beyond the referent of Exodus 13:3. Israel must not only remember the day of deliverance from בית עבדים but her former identity as a slave as well. An important group label for Israel is "a people who were slaves in Egypt." That is to say that Israel is cognitively defined by both her slavery and her emancipation (יצא in Deut 5:15; פדה in Deut 15:15; 24:18).

The use of עבד is significant for Israel's cognitive identity formation. In the book of Exodus, Israel is exhorted to refrain from mistreating or oppressing the גר (22:20-26; 23:1-9) since the people were once גרים (22:20; 23:9). Here, though, in addition to remembering being a גר, Israel is called on to remember being an עבד. Her prior condition links her not just to sojourners but to disenfranchised peoples in general (Deut 24:17-22). Therefore she is expected to "*revivre positivement une histoire d'humiliation et de souffrance.*"[43]

Emotional Formulation

The replacement of יצא, the most prevalent term of deliverance, with פדה in 15:15 and 24:18 evokes the particular exodus scene of the sparing and consecration of the firstborn (Exod 13:11-16).[44] These emotional images add to the perception of being loved and chosen that is distinctive to the Deuteronomic interpretation of exodus. Israel's cognitively and emotionally formulated identity—as a brought out/redeemed slave—in turn presents her with behavioral norms which both demonstrate and substantiate her identity.

Behavioral Formulations

These stories connect the remembrance of being a slave to keeping the Sabbath (5:15), to freeing fellow Hebrew slaves in the seventh year of servitude (15:15), and to practicing other humanitarian acts (24:18). As part of Deuteronomy, they are concerned with the possibility that Israel might

---

43. Pons, "La référence au séjour en Égypte," 171.

44. This is not an argument for developmental influence but rather speaks to how this story would be heard in conversation with the dominant exodus story.

fail to remember in general (4:9; 4:23; 8:11; 8:19; 9:7; 25:19) and with her forgetting the God of exodus in particular (6:12; 8:14). Childs argues, based on the syntactical structure of the narratives, that Israel is not commanded to keep the Sabbath day and Sabbath year and perform other humanitarian acts because of God's past redemption. Instead, she is to be obedient *in order* to remember the events of her redemption and thereby to participate again in the exodus event.[45] "The act of remembering serves to actualize the past for a generation removed in time from those former events in order that they themselves can have an intimate encounter with the great acts of redemption. Remembrance equals participation."[46]

Miller affirms Childs' interpretation in saying that while the Sabbath command in Exodus 20:8–11 follows the form of *remember in order to keep*, the Deuteronomic structure is reversed, namely, *keep in order to remember*. "So in the case of Exodus, the community is called to remember and to obey out of the memory; in the Deuteronomic form, the community obeys in order to keep alive the memory of redemption and to bring out the provision of rest from toil for all members of the community."[47]

The general pattern "remember ... therefore act"[48] is evident in much of the rhetoric of Deuteronomy and shows how the memory of exodus results in behavioral formulations of identity. But Childs and Miller add balance to the interpretation of these narratives by showing that traditions and social actions also remind Israel of her shared past. "Positively reliving a history of humiliation and suffering,"[49] "re-establishing a liberation perspective,"[50] "re-actualizing the exodus event,"[51] and even "keeping the memory of redemption alive"[52] draw those who remember into a collective identity, coherent over time and grounded in a shared story. The Israelite master, for example, is reminded that he once shared the same condition with the one who now serves him, and his identity as a freed slave is more valuable than the fruits of incessant labor or the profits gained through the subjection of others (Deut 15:15). Calendrical observances and humanitarian acts remind Israel of this common identity in the past and, therefore, of her solidarity in the present. The "keep in order to remember" structure

---

45. Childs, *Memory and Tradition*, 53.
46. Ibid., 56.
47. Miller, *Deuteronomy*, 80.
48. Nelson, *Deuteronomy*, 83.
49. Translated from Pons, "La référence au séjour en Égypte," 171.
50. Ibid., 173.
51. Childs, *Memory and Tradition*, 53.
52. Miller, *Deuteronomy*, 80.

becomes more apparent in Deuteronomy 26:5b–9's retold story, as will be demonstrated in the analysis of that narrative.

Since having been slaves is a boundary of Israel's identity, those sharing this identity are sympathetic to and, perhaps even, accommodating toward, others in comparable circumstances. Hearers of the narratives will observe the Sabbath and carry out other compassionate acts and, in so doing, will reactivate the memory of exodus and find coherence not only with one another, but with the exodus generation.

Deuteronomy 6:21–23

The retold story found in Deuteronomy 6:21–23 contains all three plot elements of the exodus story with the use of common shared vocabulary (עבדים, יצא, יד חזקה and אותת ומפתים). Like Exodus 15 the story takes Israel from the land of Egypt to the land of promise with no intervening narration of trials or testing. Full deliverance is symbolized by landedness, and the complete transformation of Israel's fate from Egypt to the land of promise is represented as the experience of one people rather than that of successive generations.

Cognitive Formulations

As in Exodus 12:26–27, this retold story is presented as the proper response to a child's question about the "meaning of the decrees and the statutes and the ordinances." Here though, the parent is to recite the exodus story beginning with the "named group" categorization of Israel as "Pharaoh's slaves," an echo of her prior identity. This specific reference to Israel's prior identity is uncommon in the Hebrew Bible,[53] overshadowed by the widely distributed group label identifying her as "the people whom God brought out of Egypt." The choice reflects, again, the particular concern of the producers of Deuteronomy that Israel not be allowed to forget who she used to be. Knowing who one was in the past is crucial to present identity.

---

53. There are more than seventy-five references to Israel being brought out of Egypt, but only fifteen of them describe Israel's prior enslavement, three of which are in the form of a metaphoric iron smelting furnace. Of the fifteen that describe enslavement, Deuteronomy contributes 9 (5:6; 5:15; 6:12; 6:21; 7:8; 8:14; 13:5; 13:10).

Emotional Formulations

Deuteronomy 6:21–23 represents social identity as relational. Not only are Israel's prior and present identities to be experienced corporately, but they are defined in terms of relationships. Israel's former identity was tied to Pharaoh and Egypt and her current identity to the "Lord, who brought you out of the land of Egypt, out of the house of slavery" (Deut 6:21). In the literary context of this retold story, פרעה—the prototype of the "other" who opposes יהוה—is reintroduced to make this contrast evident. Those who have been brought out of the house of *slavery* (עבדים) are instructed to *serve* (תעבד) God (Deut 6:13). As Craigie notes, "both words are derived from the same root and contrast vividly the old and the new masters of Israel."[54] While the categorization language defining Israel in the past and present is a cognitive formulation of social identity, the images of attachment and belonging, both to one another and to the God of exodus, potentially create an emotional identification. Israel is called on to remember not only her transformed state but also the vivid displays of God's power that brought about this new identity. This binds the people's hearts as well as their minds to one another and to their God.

Behavioral Formulations

In addition to the cognitive and emotional formulations of social identity noted above, behavioral formations found in 6:10–25 are similar to those that follow 4:34–38. Exodus identity is the motivation for exclusive allegiance to Yahweh and obedience to his law. Here, as in 26:5–9 and Joshua 24:2–7, there is no mention of the covenant at Sinai. This omission has nothing to do with the separateness of the Sinai tradition from the exodus-conquest tradition.[55] Instead, the form and content of these narratives suggest that the recounting of exodus elicits new acts of allegiance characteristic of covenant ratification, rather than the remembrance of prior obligations.

Temporal Formulations

The explicit admonition to parents to transmit the exodus story to future generations exemplifies a temporal formulation of social identity. While

---

54. Craigie, *Deuteronomy*, 173.
55. Rad, *Problem of the Hexateuch*, 1–78.

some see the retelling as necessary to retain a sense of history,[56] this writing argues that the obligation to tell the story is to maintain a sense of coherent identity over time. The child uses second-person pronouns, asking about that which "God has commanded *you*?" The parent, though, responds with inclusive pronouns: "*We* were Pharaoh's slaves . . . the Lord brought *us* out of Egypt". The child's question creates separation from the events, while the parent's response melds the generations. "The attempt by fathers to transform their uninvolved sons from '*dis*temporaries' to *con*temporaries, i.e., true-life sharers, is an issue of supreme and recurrent significance in the Bible."[57] That is to say, exodus must be actualized by generations not having eyewitness experience of it. As seen in the primary exodus story (Exod 10:2) the narrative seems to prioritize the retelling of the events over the actual experience of exodus. This contention will be further evaluated in the analysis of Deuteronomy 11:2–4, 7.

From the perspective of the SIA, Israel's coherency over time and space emerges from the telling of and participation in the story. The exodus story becomes her myth of common descent by which solidarity is traced to a cultural affinity with others. The retelling of exodus creates a memory for each new generation, regardless of where or when the child asks the question. The memory constructs and reinforces a unified identity, exemplified by a grateful response of allegiance and obedience.

Deuteronomy 7:18–19

Deuteronomy 7:18–19 contains two plot elements of an exodus story: the supernatural acts of God and the bringing out of Israel. No mention is made of her initial state of adversity or crying out to God. The focus is clearly on the supernatural act of God, laid out in emotive terms, namely, Israel being brought out of Egypt by means of great trials,[58] signs and wonders, and the mighty hand and outstretched arm. The emphasis on the second plot element in this retelling reflects the explicit purpose of the narrative, namely, to counter apprehension and inspire faith in God, so that Israel will act in accordance with God's plan. The memory of her earlier refusal to trust God, which led to her failure to possess the land (1:26–36), undoubtedly informs this story.

---

56. Merrill, *Deuteronomy*, 174.
57. Fishbane, *Text and Texture*, 81–82.
58. See the notes on the use of this term in Deut 4:34–38.

Evaluative Formulations

Evaluative formulations of differentiation between Israel and the nations are evident in the literary context leading up to this exodus story. Deuteronomy 7 "fervently asserts the distinctiveness of Israel that is to be affirmed and appreciated in the contexts of the other nations.... The anxiety of this chapter is that the next generation will fail to recognize and cherish Israel's distinctiveness."[59] This concern with Israel's positive evaluation is reflected in exhortations not to make treaties with the other nations, not to intermarry with them, to destroy them without pity, and to demolish their altars and idols. Although the nations are cast as mightier and more numerous than Israel (7:1), the promise is that God will give the nations over to Israel (7:2). If, in the face of this imminent war with the nations, however, Israel finds herself fearful and unsure, she is charged emphatically to remember (זכר תזכר) the exodus,[60] the unequivocal proof of her distinctiveness.

Emotional Formulations

In this short retelling of exodus, Israel's emotional attachment to the God of signs, wonders, and power is emphasized through the threefold repetition of יהוה אלהיך. The shared fate of Israel, set in contrast to that of the nations, further bolsters a perception of shared identity. The narrative portrays exodus as the prototypical way God will differentiate Israel from all other nations. As God dealt with the "other" in Egypt, he will deal with the "other" peoples. The paradigmatic exodus not only provides the rationale for war and the strict prohibition against assimilation, but it creates a perception of shared fate.

Temporal Formulations

The promise of supernatural deliverance for the new generation is like that of the prototypical exodus generation. Again, the "you" of Israel extends beyond a single generation. The temporal formulation of remembering exodus brings the past to bear on the present. Remembrance is essential to handling that which threatens Israel's distinctiveness. Whereas in the primary narrative, the exodus event asserts Israel's distinction with respect to a particular context and threat of assimilation, retellings of exodus maintain

---

59. Brueggemann, *Deuteronomy*, 93.
60. The emphatic infinitive absolute is used together with the verb.

and reinforce this distinctiveness for other narrative casts and subsequent hearers, unifying them over time and space.

Deuteronomy 11:2–4, 7

Set within a broader recollection of the great and awesome thing God had done for Israel (beginning in Deut 10:21), the retold exodus story in Deuteronomy 11:2–4, 7 takes on a distinctive quality. Not only does it emphasize the second plot element of God's supernatural intervention on behalf of Israel, but it begins the story there. There is no indication of Israel's initial state of adversity. The familiar expression ידו החזקה וזרעו הנטויה is followed by the unconventional phrasing ואת־אתתיו ואת־מעשיו. The narrative moves seamlessly to the third plot element, showcasing God's awesome deeds at the Red Sea with no use of the familiar verb יצא. The replacement of מופת, which in exodus retellings refers specifically to God's supernatural interventions in Egypt, with the more general term מעשה allows for the use of derivatives of עשה to connect all of God's interventions (11:3–7). Thus, the bringing up (יצא) from Egypt is replaced by what God did (עשה) at the sea. The unconventional construction and phrasing of this retold story places emphasis on the uniqueness of the God of exodus rather than on Israel's experience of it.

Although the emphasis of this story is on God's actions, the narrative nevertheless contains important evaluative, behavioral, and temporal formulations of collective identity.

Evaluative Formulations

Rather than defining Israel or her boundaries (cognitive formulation) this story defines God as the enemy of Egypt. The retold exodus story emphasizes God's punitive actions against Egypt, placing heavier emphasis on the devaluation of the "other" than in any of Deuteronomy's other exodus retellings. The devaluation is thorough; Pharaoh, his country, his army, his horses, and chariots are overwhelmingly enduringly shattered. The inclusion of the story of Dathan and Abiram (v. 6; cf. Num 16) is innovative and unique. This provides the first hint of the partial categorization of Israel as "other," which will be found repeatedly and more explicitly in retellings examined in chapter 5.

God stamps out all threats to Israel's identity, external (i.e., Egypt) and internal (i.e., the households of Dathan and Abiram). God's efforts to separate out a distinctive people are underlined by the rather hymnic, fivefold repetition of אשר עשה that joins these two stories (vv. 3–7).

Behavioral Formulations

Behavioral formulations of collective identity are found in the immediate context of this retold story: exhortations to fear, love, and obey God, with a promise of blessing for obedience and curses for disobedience (10:2–11:1; 11:8–32). Enveloping the exodus story within these formulations implicitly places the remembrance of exodus—with an emphasis on God's deeds—at the core of covenantal obedience. It is the impetus and rationale for acceptable group attitudes and behaviors, "the springboard of action for the present."[61]

Temporal Formulations

The emphatic contribution of this passage is the assertion that God's discipline (i.e., the lessons learned from these mighty acts of judgment) is the experience of *this* generation of Israel. The story is bracketed by that which "your children have not known or seen" (v. 2) and that which "you have seen" (v. 7). The contention—that God's miracles to set apart a people were not experienced by the children of the listeners but by the listeners themselves—should be heard in conversation with Deuteronomy 5:3, which argues that God's covenant was not with the listener's ancestors but with the listeners themselves. The exodus story is neither a second-hand memory nor a child's acquired inheritance. Instead, hearers must personally experience and participate in it. Otherwise, the statues and ordinances of God, subsequently presented in Deuteronomy 12–26, will be groundless and inexplicable.[62]

The design and content of this exodus retelling emphasizes Israel's positive evaluation and her need to actualize the exodus in personal experience. The latter is the core of covenant obedience. This passage clarifies the tentative interpretation drawn from Deuteronomy 6:21–23, namely, that the retelling of exodus takes priority over the experience of exodus. While the retelling may take priority over the historic event, this recollection of exodus is the primary entry point into the ongoing experience of exodus.

---

61. Clements, "Book of Deuteronomy," 2:369.
62. Mann, *Deuteronomy*, 103.

The living memory of exodus is more crucial to Israel's self-definition than a historically verifiable event.

Common to all the retellings in Deuteronomy, the exodus story blurs the line between the exodus generation and succeeding generations. A rhetorical bridge binds together Israel's many generations, creating a sense of unity and reasserting the claim of God on every generation of Israel.[63] There is no question; Israel's identity is represented as coherent over time.

Deuteronomy 26:5b–9

With the exceptions of the short retellings of Deuteronomy 15:15 and 24:18, all other retold exodus stories in Deuteronomy are found prior to the legal portion of chapter 12 through 26. The final story meeting the qualification of an exodus retelling is found near the end of this section. Deuteronomy 26:5b–9 contains all three major plot elements of the primary exodus story and the two minor ones—the descent in Egypt and entry into the land—as well. Images and vocabulary shared with the primary narrative consist of the portrayal of Israel as becoming עצום and רב in Egypt (Deut 26:5b; Exod 1:9; 5:5), language of affliction (עניענה, Deut 26:6–7; Exod 1:11–12; 3:7; 3:17; 4:31), hard labour (עבדה קשה; Deut 26:6; Exod 1:14; 6:9), oppression (לחץ; Deut 26:6; Exod 3:9), the supernatural intervention of God (יד חזקה ובזרע נטויה and האתת והמפתים), and of being brought out (יצא). As previously noted, Deuteronomy uses some of these phrases in ways that are distinct from the primary narrative.[64] It also shares with Numbers 20:14–16 the language of Egypt's mistreatment (רעע), of Israel crying out (צעק) and of God hearing Israel's voice (וישמע קלנו). Finally, Deuteronomy contains unique exodus vocabulary, מרא גדל (Deut 4:34; 26:8; 34:12) and עמל (Deut 26:7).

Both the shared and the innovative exodus vocabulary found in this retelling have significance with respect to collective identity formulation. Firstly, shared life stories with stable elements create a sense of coherence among hearers and storytellers across time and space. Secondly, innovative, dynamic elements alongside of the stable elements allow the story to be "translated"[65] so as to be taken up by successive social actors.

Deuteronomy 26:5b–9 weaves together cognitive, emotional, and temporal formulations all with the potential of creating social identity.

---

63. Clements, "Book of Deuteronomy," 369.
64. See the earlier discussion on Deut 4:34–38.
65. Condor, "Social Identity," 291.

Cognitive Formulations

Deuteronomy 26:5b–9 is an identity constructing narrative presented as a story. It captures key understandings about what it means to be a member of Israel, reducible to "we are a people who . . . ."[66] As Israel recites the exodus story, she divests herself of all personal concerns and aligns herself with the community[67] of all who have been brought out of Egypt. This act cognitively and collectively defines her; the exodus story encapsulates what it means to be a member of Israel. "Us" and "them" language also categorizes Israel as separate from Egypt.

Evaluative Formulation

Israel's story differentiates between the "us" and "them" categories by emphasizing the positive valuation of Israel as going from being "few in number" and "an alien" to "a great nation, mighty and populous" (26:5), favored by God, and gifted with "a land flowing with milk and honey" (26:9). Egypt on the other hand is devalued by God's "mighty hand and an outstretched arm, with a terrifying display of power, and with signs and wonders" (26:8).

Emotional Formulations

The words and images used to evaluatively differentiate Israel from Egypt integrate the hearers emotionally and bind them to the group. A "surprising, 'undeuteronomic' memory"[68] is unique to this exodus story: "A wandering Aramean was my ancestor" (v. 5b). The phrase fittingly refers to Jacob, who took his small family down to Egypt. He is "Aramean" due to his marriage to two Aramean women. While this retold exodus story traces Israel's old identity back a step further than slavery in Egypt, "wandering Aramean" does not primarily anchor Israel's identity in the patriarchs. The indirect mention of Jacob allows for the attachment of the adjective "wandering" to describe Israel's ancestor. When this phrase, set at the beginning of the exodus story, is placed in relation to the ending of this particular story—Israel's landedness (v. 9)—it becomes clear that its purpose is to trace all Israel back to a common condition, rather than to a common ancestor. The old identity defined by

---

66. Cornell, "Story of Our Life," 42.
67. Brueggemann, *Deuteronomy*, 246.
68. McConville, *Deuteronomy*, 384.

homelessness and misery is powerfully contrasted with Israel's new identity of being delivered by God and being given a lavish homeland.

Behavioral Formulations

Here, as in Numbers 20:14, the exodus story is placed in the new generation's mouth, as if telling this story were crucial to its identity. Israel is commanded to observe her first celebration of Firstfruits. The precise purpose of the celebration is to remember exodus. Landedness and fruitfulness are not viewed here as a fulfilment of ancestral promises but as the accomplishment of exodus. Israel's slavery and deliverance from Egypt is relevant to her present situation and gives meaning to her acts of worship. All Israel is to celebrate this first Firstfruits in order to remember her exodus identity. Whereas the multiple retellings prior to the legal portion of Deuteronomy place a somewhat stronger emphasis on exodus identity as motivating covenant-keeping behaviors,[69] this unique retelling in the legal core portrays covenantal behaviors as reminding Israel of her exodus identity.

Temporal Formulations

In the midst of this drama of wandering, affliction, and deliverance, the narrative switches from talking about the plight of the ancestors to a "we" and "us" memory of suffering. Because of the shifting pronouns (from third-person masculine singular pronouns and verbs in verse 5b to first-person plural direct object in verse 6 and first-person plural verbs and possessive pronouns in verse 7), exodus group members are seen as coherent over time, descriptive of all Israel. That is to say, the identification process begins with a third person telling of the story and ends with the storyteller participating in the story.[70] This process is repeatable by every generation. The SIA recognizes that such temporal formulations are essential to corporate identity. Identity stories such as this cannot endure over time or space without being taken up by successive social actors. As the story is taken up, translated over time, and dispersed over space, the perception of an ontological continuity encompassing successive generations is created.[71]

---

69. The explicit exception to this is Deut 6:21–23 in which a commemorative service inspires remembrance of exodus identity.

70. Brueggemann, *Deuteronomy*, 247.

71. Condor, "Social Identity," 305–6.

Significance of Identity Formation in Numbers and Deuteronomy

When the retold stories of Numbers and Deuteronomy are considered in conversation with one another and with the primary exodus story, several additional effects on the hearers come to light. Firstly, these retold stories make explicit for hearers that which was only implicit in the primary exodus story (Exod 15:1–21), namely, that all Israel (present and future) must not only tell the exodus story, but they must participate in it. Deuteronomy portrays a non-exodus-generation transmitting the story as if the obligation were their own. They identify themselves by telling the story. Further, they not only tell this shared life story, but they tell it as if they were, every one of them, eyewitnesses to it, having seen it with their "very eyes."

Being the "people whom God brought out of Egypt" is achieved rather than ascribed. Deuteronomy's exodus narratives claim that this identity is not just achieved by painting doorframes with blood or being present at a historical event. Deuteronomy makes explicit, even in a way that Numbers 20:14–16 cannot, that exodus identity is achieved by participation in the story. Remember, retelling, and participating in the exodus story becomes the definition of a prototypical group member.

The shifts from third to first-person plural subjects reflect the experiential participation of new generations in this share life story. The gap between generations of Israel is blurred and collapsed, resulting in a sense of coherence and unity across time. The boundaries are flexible enough to allow for additional participants to be added to the superordinate group of the "people whom Yahweh brought out of Egypt." Along with the patriarchs, the exodus generation of Israel, and the mixed multitude (assigned to this category by the primary narrative), a new generation is added as they tell the exodus story.

The exodus stories of Numbers and Deuteronomy are also significant in that they enlarge the concept of the "other" against which Israel may define herself. The outgroup category is expanded from a literal Egypt to include both Edom (e.g., Num 20:14–16) and the other nations (e.g., Deut 4:20; 7:18–19). This allows for the exodus story to maintain Israel's distinctiveness over time and space. The distinction that is created, however, is less ethnic and more cultural-ideological. Therefore, the exodus generation herself may be "other" because of her failure to participate in an internal separation from Egypt.

Finally, these retold stories represent an exodus identity that is cognizant not only of deliverance but of oppression and homelessness. The dominated and the landless of the hearer's generation might readily identity with these retold stories of a previous generation. The exodus story becomes relevant to the contemporary generation, and it offers them a cultural-ideological myth of common descent, unifying them with the exodus generation. The identity story endures because it is relevant to the present situation, and the social identity rhetoric of the narrative persuades hearers to take it up and enter into it.

5

Social Identity Formations in Retold Exodus Stories: Prophets and Writings

IN CHAPTER 4, THE retold exodus stories of the Pentateuch were examined for the various literary formulations of social identity presented in chapter 2. The content of these identity formulations was compared and contrasted with that of the primary exodus story, and then the possible effect of these formulations as identity resources for later hearers was considered.

The current chapter examines the remaining eight retold exodus stories for the same types of cognitive, evaluative, emotional, behavioral, and temporal formulations of social identity. The order of consideration of the retold stories will be based on their narrative perspectives. The first is from Israel's perspective following conquest and settlement in the land. Subsequent stories have narrative vantage points of transition from the rule of judges to kings, of impending exile, and of the post-exilic period. The retold stories from the Psalms, lacking explicit narrative perspectives, will be considered last.

The actual compositional order of the stories is not necessarily indicative of how these stories may have been used as identity resources in ancient Israel once they became available. Instead, similarities in language, ideology or theme, and the logical succession of narratives in the larger story of Israel may have affected how the stories were heard in relation to one another. The exodus story of Joshua, for example, would have been heard in relation to Deuteronomy, not because of editorial influence or development but because the story of Joshua, as a whole, continues the story of Deuteronomy. In addition, commonly recognized correlations between the language and ideology of Deuteronomy and that of Joshua,

1 Samuel, and Jeremiah would have caused any of the latter to be considered in conversation with the former.[1]

Literary constructions of identity will be exposed in these eight retold stories as they have been in the previous two chapters. The stories and their identity constructs will be considered in conversation with one another and with the primary exodus story to determine their mutual resonance, variance, or dissonance.

Joshua 24:2–7, 17

The recital of exodus in Joshua 24 may be divided into two retellings. The first in verses 2–7 is set within a broader recollection of God's gracious acts toward Israel. The second, verse 17, is a response to the first. Both are narratively portrayed as prefacing a covenant renewal ceremony initiated by Joshua following Israel's conquest and settlement.[2] In Deuteronomic style, "all Israel" is assembled for the retelling of exodus at this transitional time in her history. Her leader, Joshua, calls Israel to covenant faithfulness and asks her to choose between idolatry and serving Yahweh, the one who gave Israel the land. Two of the primary plot elements are present: the supernatural acts of God and the bringing out of Israel from Egypt.

In the primary exodus story and the retellings examined thus far, God is often represented as *responding* to Israel's cries for deliverance. Here, however, God is depicted as *initiating* exodus. The commissioning of Moses and Aaron and the afflicting of Egypt are unprovoked. There is no mention of oppression in the story, and the only instance of Israel crying out to God is at the edge of the sea as the Egyptian army overtakes her. Yet, even this hint of trouble is overshadowed by the narrations of Israel's already accomplished bringing out (24:5–6; cf. Exod 14:10). Narrated in the divine first-person, this retold exodus story contrasts God's direct actions (taking Abraham, leading him, etc.)[3] with the misdirected actions of both Israel and Egypt. The form and content highlight God's superiority over other gods

---

1. This is not intended as an argument for (or against) the construct of the Deuteronomistic History. This study focuses on the finished form of the text and on the rhetorical shape and effect of the whole. It acknowledges that the finished text contains evidence of various layers of memory and tradition and speaks with a multiplicity of voices, but it does not address the formative or developmental history that created it.

2. Howard, *Joshua*, 428. Other recitals of exodus related to covenant ceremonies have been identified by Boling and Wright, namely, Exod 19:3b–6; Deut 6:20–25; 26:5–9. Boling and Wright, *Joshua*, 534.

3. Cf. Deut 26:5–9 where the ancestors "went down," "lived," and "became."

and other human powers, thereby, preparing the hearer for the call to allegiance that follows.[4]

The dissonance between this retelling and the primary narrative and the other retellings grips the attention of the listener. Here, the listener is taken further back than the wandering Aramean of Deuteronomy 26:5 to Terah's purported worship of other gods beyond the rivers. God is portrayed as intent on freeing Israel from the worship of other gods, attributed to her distant, pre-patriarchal ancestors (24:2, 14–15) as well as her immediate ancestors in Egypt (24:14). This is the only instance where exodus is presented as God's response to Israel's worship of other gods. Here, Israel is not portrayed as unfortunate or oppressed but as culpable. This goes to the heart of the ancient Jewish debate of whether Israel's disgrace prior to the exodus was that she was a slave or that she was an idol-worshipper.[5]

The retelling continues with the uncharacteristic inclusion of Israel's wilderness experience, the significance of which will be examined below. This contrasts with the more common narration that takes Israel from Egypt directly to the land.[6] Verse 14 continues the story with Joshua expounding upon the ramifications of God's historical review. The narrative perspective shifts again when the people respond to the exodus memory with consternation (24:16) and then with their own, distinct retelling of exodus (24:17). Israel does not admit to worshipping other gods. Her retelling is more consonant with the primary exodus story and the retellings of Numbers and Deuteronomy than with God's retelling. The familiar vocabulary of being brought out (עלה) of Egypt and of having been eye-witnesses of God's miracles are the only connections between the two retellings in Joshua 24. The identity formulations in these two retellings will be examined together as the second story is portrayed as a response to the first.

Cognitive Formulations

The two exodus stories provide conflicting definitions of Israel. The first, in 24:2–7, identifies her as descendants of idolatrous patriarchs (and idolatrous forefathers in Egypt—24:14–15), the second as prior slaves or descendants of slaves (24:17). The boundaries of Israel, thus, are contested as either "those who were idolaters" or "those who were slaves." Both images are set in temporal terms connecting her to the exodus generation, creating myths of common descent and discordant, possible social identities.

---

4. Butler, *Joshua*, 267.
5. This debate is summarized in Kulp, "We Were Slaves," 59–75.
6. See for example Deut 4:34–38, 6:21–23, 26:5b–9; 1 Sam 12:8, Jer 32:20–22.

Therefore, the analysis of these images will be deferred to the section on temporal formulations.

Evaluative Formulations

Joshua 24:2–7, 17 displays all three representations of evaluative formulations of identity. Firstly, and common to most exodus stories, there is a clear differentiation between Israel and Egypt: God plagued Egypt but brought out Israel (24:5), put darkness between *you* (Israel) and the *Egyptians* (24:7), and made the sea cover *them* while *you* (Israel) saw what occurred (24:7). Secondly, verses 5–7 also highlight God's overt devaluation of the Egyptians. The bringing down of Egypt, both literally and in negative evaluation, is adequately described. All that remains is an example of the elevation of Israel. This is certainly implied in God's actions on her behalf. Nevertheless, this implicit positive evaluation is followed in the first story by a subtle, devaluation of Israel: ותשבו במדבר ימים רבים (7d). Terse and lacking specifics, the reference to her wilderness experience nevertheless contaminates Israel's identity story and is augmented by the final phrase "for a long time." This contamination is corrected by Israel's responsive retelling. The use of עלה rather than יצא emphasizes the bringing *up* and not just the bringing *out* of Israel. Israel's rebuttal also addresses the negative reference to her wilderness experience. It does this with the counterclaim that the desert experience is evidence of God's extended care for Israel: ישמרנו בכל־הדרך אשר הלכנו בה ובכל העמים אשר עברנו בקרבם

Emotional Formulations

Evaluative and emotional formulations are intertwined in this retelling of exodus. The negotiation between the two exodus retellings, just described, creates emotional formulations of collective identity, poignant images of God acting against Egypt and for Israel. All Israel—the new generation and their ancestors (אתנו ואת־אבותינו)—are bound together in the language of the shared fate of those brought up out of Egypt, out of בית עבדים. These emotional formulations of identity in turn motivate behavioral norms.

Behavioral Formulations

With the corrective from the second exodus retelling in Joshua 24, the supernatural acts of God are shown to result in the positive valuation of Israel and her corporate sense of belonging to God. As such, these acts serve as the foundation for Joshua's imperative identity norms (vv. 14–15) and the people's commitment to them (vv. 16–18). Remembrance of exodus and God's other exodus-like interventions on behalf of Israel (vv. 8–13, 17–18) are portrayed as the grounds for all acceptable group behaviors and attitudes.

Like the first Firstfruits celebration described in Deuteronomy 26:1–11, the covenant renewal narrated in Joshua 24 offers Israel the opportunity to remember exodus. It reminds the people that their identity and behavior are grounded in the telling of and participation in the story of exodus. As in Deuteronomy's retellings, the exodus story is the nucleus of covenant.

Temporal Formulations

The Joshua retellings are unique in that they differentiate between two possible social identities for Israel: a feckless, polytheistic one and a faithful one that worships the true God. Both God and Joshua paint Israel's present identity in terms of the former.[7] The patriarchs are mentioned only to illustrate the long history of idolatry leading up to the narrative present. In other words, Israel is presented as a coherent, idolatrous group over time. God's actions on behalf of Israel are portrayed as precursors to the creation of a new identity for Israel, one that is devoid of idolatry. The implication is that Israel had never truly rid herself of false worship, despite God's faithfulness, and he urges her to do so in the strongest terms possible.[8]

Israel is silent with respect to Joshua's/God's myth of common descent from idolatrous ancestors and the accusation that she is currently worshiping foreign gods. The people affirm that they will serve God and not forsake him to serve other gods (v. 16), but they never respond directly to Joshua's warning about serving other gods or to his exhortations to throw away foreign gods (vv. 14–15). The people respond with a proper retelling that highlights their prior condition as slaves, God's supernatural intervention and his bringing up of Israel (v. 17).

While the brief recollection of exodus in verse 17 may have served a liturgical purpose,[9] its placement following the God/Joshua speech and its content—reverting to a more conventional expression of the exodus story than verses 2–13—appear designed to contest the implied accusation that Israel's identity is polytheistic. That is to say, in the face of a dissonant exodus retelling with a discordant identity claim, Israel reclaims her traditional

---

7. See Josh 24:2, 14, 23.
8. Howard, *Joshua*, 435.
9. See Nelson, *Joshua*, 270; Boling and Wright, *Joshua*, 538.

expression of exodus identity. Her ideal possible social identity is grounded in the primary exodus story. Israel refuses to be drafted into a different identity, past or present, that portrays her as a worshiper of foreign gods. Hearers of the retellings, however, influenced by their own context of interpretation, may see in this identity negotiation not only a foreshadowing of the history of Israel, but a real choice of possible social identities.

The coherence of Israel over time is seen, once again, in the shifting pronouns used to describe exodus. In the first retelling, the divine narrator switches between second and third pronouns—"when *they* cried out ... he put darkness between *you* and the Egyptians"—as if there is no difference between the exodus generation and those now present. This is overtly stated near the end of the retelling, "and *your* eyes saw what I did in Egypt," the significance of which will be discussed below. The alternation between "you" and "they" unifies the contemporary generation with their ancestors in connection with exodus.[10] Further, the shifting pronouns "invite any reader to make personal identification with those whose story is recounted."[11] The result is a "transgenerational unity of the exodus experience."[12] That is to say, the story incorporates successive social actors as a clear example of Israel's coherence over time as the "people whom God brought out of Egypt." The retelling also emphasizes that the exodus story is a shared life story.

In the second retelling, the first-person is consistently used by the present Israel: "The LORD ... brought *us* and *our ancestors* up from the land of Egypt" (v. 17). The speakers actualize themselves as among those "brought up." The expressions "your eyes saw what I did to Egypt" (Josh 24:7) and "before our eyes" (Josh 24:17) are similar to the language of Deuteronomy, and hearers who had access to both narratives would easily make the connection. Israel's assembled masses are cast as coherent over time and as genuine witnesses to exodus.

When Joshua's retellings are heard in conversation with those of Deuteronomy, the dissonance arising from Joshua's first exodus story is further underscored. The second retelling affirms the new generation's *discontinuity* with Joshua's version of a possible social identity: idolatrous Israel. Thus, the retellings implicitly assert that exodus is the shared experience of both the exodus generation and the new generation only if the story is properly narrated. For later social actors, however, who could no longer deny the culpability of Israel, the initial, dissonant exodus retelling would offer a possible expansion of what it means to be included in the ingroup. That is to say,

---

10. Howard, *Joshua*, 431.
11. Boling and Wright, *Joshua*, 535.
12. Nelson, *Joshua*, 276.

exodus identity might expand further to include not only the innocent, oppressed, or homeless (as in Deut 26:5b–9), but guilty idol worshippers who also had seen exodus. As the exodus story is adjusted to fit Israel's changing identity, it might persuade successive, culpable generations to identify themselves as "the people whom God brought out of Egypt."

1 Samuel 12:6–8

The retold story found in 1 Samuel 12 is represented as being narrated just prior to the establishment of Israel's monarchy. It is part of a pattern of prominent characters retelling the exodus during times of significant transition: prior to entry into the land (Num and Deut); after the conquest (Josh 24); just before (Jer 32) and after exile (Neh 9).

The literary context is key to understanding the retold story in 1 Samuel, and it will be exposed here and throughout the treatment of identity formulations. Samuel and God are displeased that Israel has asked for a king. Once again, "all Israel" is gathered to hear a message. Samuel begins with a legal defense of his time as judge. His claim to covenant faithfulness is clearly meant to stand in contrast to his characterization of the self-serving "manner of the king" in 1 Samuel 8:11–17.[13] Samuel reminds Israel of the oppressive ways and practices of kings and how God had delivered her from Egypt and from the hand of all the kingdoms that were oppressing her (1 Sam 10:18).

The specific setting—at the time of the wheat harvest (i.e., Feast of Weeks), ties yet another commemorative celebration to the remembrance of exodus (as the primary exodus story did with Passover and Deuteronomy 26 with Firstfruits). Samuel exhorts the people to listen to all the evidence of God righteous acts performed for them and their fathers (v. 7). He ends his speech with a parallel entreaty to consider what great things God has done for them (v. 24).

1 Samuel 12:6–8 contains two of the three major plot elements that define an exodus story: Israel's prior condition of suffering (represented by her crying out in זעק not צעק) and the bringing out (יצא) of Israel. The two minor elements are also present: Jacob's descent into Egypt and settlement in the land. Samuel twice states that God sent Moses and Aaron and brought Israel's ancestors out of Egypt. Only this retold exodus story and those of Joshua 24:2–7 and Psalm 105 portray Moses and Aaron as characters in the exodus. This representation also ties these stories to the primary exodus story. Like most other retellings, the narration skips wilderness and conquest,

---

13. Klein, *I Samuel*, 115. Brueggemann agrees with this allusion in Brueggemann, *First and Second Samuel*, 90.

portraying a direct transport from Egypt to the land. The specific plot elements of exodus that are clearly stated (being in the land of the "other," crying out, being delivered) are subsequently revisited by Samuel as he inveighs against the ancestor's response to the repeated saving acts of God.

Cognitive Formulations

In the exodus story found in 1 Samuel 12:6–8, the ingroup that cries out from Egypt and is delivered remains nameless. The exodus generation is simply referred to as "they," or in relation to Samuel's listeners as "your forefathers." Israel is not mentioned by name in the subsequent conflicts with named groups either (12:9–12). Instead, she is represented stereotypically as forgetful of exodus from the time of her settlement in the land to the present time in which she has asked for a king. Israel's namelessness in the exodus story seems to be tied to her present crisis of identity. The literary context of the retold story implies that the God of exodus and his exodus-like paradigm of deliverance are all that Israel requires. While the narrative rhetoric is not univocally anti-monarchical, the institution of monarchy clearly does not define Israel. Samuel minimizes the theological significance of the king, his relevance to Israel's life and self-definition. When Israel is presented with the if/then blessings and curses evocative of Deuteronomy 28, even the king is included as one more member of the community subject to the covenant (12:20–25).

Evaluative Formulations

Samuel's ongoing speech following the retelling of exodus is a devaluation of the assembled Israel, the current ingroup. Even the note of positive reassurance—"the LORD will not cast away his people, for his great name's sake, because it has pleased the LORD to make you a people for himself" (v. 22)—is dampened by the final warning that persistence in evil will result in Israel being swept away (v. 25). Israel's uniqueness and positive valuation are sustained only in the retelling of the exodus with its two references to God's deliverance through Moses and Aaron (12:6, 8).

Emotional Formulations

Not only does the retelling of exodus promote Israel's sense of uniqueness and positive value in contrast to the remainder of Samuel's speech, but it rehearses God's relational commitment to Israel. His unfailing attachment to Israel would bolster her feelings of attachment and belonging. By tying present characters to exodus and later generations, Israel is represented as sharing one fate, whether of rejection (12:15) or of blessing (12:22).

Behavioral Formulations

The experience of exodus expressed God's relational commitment to Israel, and should have defined Israel's behavioral response. Yet, immediately following Samuel's retold exodus story is a historical review that shows otherwise, beginning with the opening words, "But they forgot the Lord their God" (12:9a). This phrase implies that the forefather's behavior was not in keeping with God's righteous acts. The experience of exodus should have engendered certain acceptable group behaviors and attitudes (i.e., identity norms). Instead, and in greater detail than his description of exodus, Samuel describes the period of judges as characterized by recurring cycles of forgetting God, resultant bondage, crying out to God, and deliverance by one of God's chosen judges. The narrative is clear that Israel brought bondage on herself. The cycle continues until the people ask for a king, and the story arrives at the narrative present.

Samuel exhorts Israel to התיצבו וראו. The connection to the primary exodus story is clear as this phrase is only used in 12:7, again in 12:16, and in Exodus 14:13. Furthering the conversation with the primary exodus story, the manifestation of God's power is framed on the other side by the people's response—"all the people greatly feared the Lord and Samuel" (1 Sam 12:18), which resembles Exodus 14:31—"the people feared the Lord and believed in the Lord and in his servant Moses." The manifestation of God's power in images of thunder and rain is analogous to the plague of Exodus 9:23–33. Direct and indirect references to exodus and the exodus paradigm are the primary focus of Samuel's theodicy.

1 Samuel 12 ends with a look forward to Israel's future. Samuel affirms God's faithfulness to "the people he was pleased to make his own" (v. 22). In Deuteronomic style, he exhorts and warns of future blessings or curses conditioned on Israel's willingness or unwillingness to remember and serve God. The remembrance and experience of exodus is represented as foundational to the people's obedience and crucial to their successful transition to a new era.

The retold story of exodus does not primarily call Israel, however, to look backward. Instead, Israel brings exodus forward into the present as motive for covenant keeping. Even the Philistine "other" who remembers the

God of exodus acts judiciously (according to 1 Sam 6:6ff). As in the theology of Deuteronomy, Israel's forgetting of exodus and of the God of exodus is a threat to her own identity, putting her at risk of being "othered."[14]

Remembrance of exodus and of the God of exodus will motivate Israel's espousal of behavioral norms unlike those of her forefathers, ones that are consistent with her exodus identity, which can be taught to her by Samuel (12:23). The commemoration of the wheat harvest becomes, therefore, an occasion to remember exodus as the basis of covenant (cf. Firstfruits in Deuteronomy 26:1–9).

Temporal Formulations

In this story, there are no radically shifting pronouns to unite the present generation with the exodus generation. However, the two generations are united by the theophany-like thunder and rain that come down at Samuel's request, reminiscent of the wind, darkness, and fire that came when Moses stretched out his hand over the sea (Exodus 14:13–31). Also, twice Samuel argues that Israel's fate is bound to her "fathers" (vv. 7, 15). In this context "fathers" refer to the exodus generation and their descendants.[15] The Israel who gathered to hear Samuel is only the most current iteration of the people, tracing her lineage in an unbroken line back to exodus. She was a witness to כל־צדקות יהוה אשר־עשה אתכם ואת־אבותיכם. The insinuation is clear: Israel will once again witness God's acts, but the hand of God will turn against her as it did to her fathers in the times of the judges. From Egypt to the present, Israel is represented as being coherent over time, because Yahweh was pleased to make her לו לעם (12:22). The cyclical return to oppression should not be the expression of her coherence over time. In order to successfully make the transition into the new era, Israel must remember and live in response to exodus.

Jeremiah 32:20–23a

Scholars have long noted the Deuteronomic phrasing and cadences of the Jeremiah tradition, including "rigorous covenantal conditionality" in which "blessings and curses are meted out in strict response to obedience or disobedience."[16] The bulk of Jeremiah, fittingly, speaks of Israel's impend-

---

14. Edelman, "YHWH's Othering of Israel," 41–69.
15. Römer, "Le cycle de Joseph," 3–15; and de Pury, "Le cycle de Jacob," 82.
16. Brueggemann, *Theology of Jeremiah*, 20–41.

ing exile, vindicating the dismantlement of the nation as the intention of Yahweh.[17] However, Jeremiah is also un-Deuteronomic at times with messages of hope, of return from exile, of the restoration of Israel, and of the making of new covenants between God and Israel (chapters 30–33).

In the prior literary context of the story to be considered, Jeremiah is called on to redeem the field of his cousin despite the impending Babylonian siege of Jerusalem. The legal minutiae of the transfer are noted, and this action takes on symbolic meaning. It "put Jeremiah on public record as claiming that there is indeed 'life after Babylon,'"[18] and it had "sacramental significance as a sign more widely relevant concerning God's future intentions for his people."[19]

The retold exodus story (32:20–23a) follows this transaction and is included in a prayer offered by Jeremiah (32:16–25). Prayers in written prophecy are rare, so its presence takes on particular ideological and theological significance. It is an attempt to make sense of the profound incongruity between the present experience of destruction and displacement and God's voiced purpose of rehabilitation and resettlement.[20]

Jeremiah's retelling of the exodus story contains two of the three major plot elements: the supernatural acts of God in Egypt and the bringing out of Israel. It focuses specifically on the displays of God's ability to accomplish his purposes. It is linked contextually to God's creational power. Connections to the primary exodus story are found in verses 20–21 in the phrase האתת והמפתים. Also, this retelling shares the general form, content, and vocabulary of Deuteronomy 26:8–9. Common to both are the idiomatic phrases יד חזקה ובזרע נטויה, האתת והמפתים and מרא גדל (Jer 32:21; Deut 26:8; cf. Deut 4:34; 5:15; 6:22; 7:19; 11:2; 26:8; 34:11–12). The retelling in Jeremiah also contains the common image of Israel going from Egypt directly to the land.[21]

Beyond shared vocabulary, this retelling and those in Deuteronomy both present an unreservedly positive recital abruptly broken off.[22] Like Samuel's speech, Jeremiah's prayer acknowledges that Israel has sinned, thus meriting devastation. The Deuteronomic deed-consequence sequence[23] is

---

17. Brueggemann, *Commentary on Jeremiah*, 264.
18. Ibid., 302.
19. Clements, *Jeremiah*, 194.
20. Brueggemann, "A 'Characteristic' Reflection," 19.
21. Deut 4:34–38; 6:21–23; 26:8–9; 1 Sam 12:8.
22. Brueggemann, "A 'Characteristic' Reflection," 20.
23. Ibid., 21.

visible in verses 18, 23, and 24, and disobedience results in punishment extending across generations (32:18; cf. Deut 5:9–10).

The acknowledgement of a drastic outcome for Israel would be the anticipated end to Jeremiah's prayer. Instead, not only does it depart from Deuteronomy's typical deed-consequence sequence,[24] but it exceeds even Deuteronomy's "more developed tradition"[25] which offers the possibility of a return to God's favor conditioned on repentance and a return to obedience. The proclamation of God's greatness and the thematic affirmation "nothing is too hard for you" (v. 17),[26] results in the prophet's seemingly illogical confession of faith: "Yet you, O Lord GOD, have said to me, 'Buy the field for money and get witnesses'—though the city has been given into the hands of the Chaldeans" (v. 25).

Cognitive and Evaluative Formulations

All of the methodological tool's identity formulations, with the exception of behavioral, are evident in this exodus retelling and its literary context. Because of the overlap, cognitive and evaluative formulations will be examined together, as will the emotional and temporal ones.

The exodus retelling in this passage both categorizes Israel and differentiates her from the "other." God brought a named group—"your people Israel"—out of Egypt; this is what it means to be Israel. No prehistory or prior existence is discussed. Israel's identity is attached directly to the God of exodus, and her distinctiveness is in contrast to Egypt. The narrative contends that this distinction was powerfully wrought, not only with the familiar signs and wonders, with a strong hand and outstretched arm" but also with "great terror" (v.21). Implicit in the decimation of Egypt is her devaluation as the outgroup. Israel's positive evaluation is also implied as the object of God's attention. It is muted, however, by the statement "they did not obey your voice or follow your law."

Emotional and Temporal Formulations

Jeremiah's retold story intimates emotional and temporal connections between Jeremiah's Israel (v. 20) and the people God brought out of Egypt (v.

---

24. Brueggemann demonstrates that these elements are characteristic of Deuteronomic theology. Brueggemann, *Theology of Jeremiah*, 143.

25. Ibid., 37.

26. The affirmation, "Nothing is too hard for you" in verse 17 is paralleled by God's rhetorical question, "Is anything too hard for me?" in verse 27.

21). Coherence between the two groups is sustained by a myth of common descent with the mention of Israel's ancestors. However, it is exodus that truly unifies Israel past and present. They are also united by a shared fate, both negative and positive in nature. The disaster threatening Jeremiah's Israel is linked to the previous generation's lax attitude toward obedience. Also, the wonders perceived "to this day" in Israel are described as a continuation of those performed in the primary exodus story.

Israel's coherence over time, however, is not demonstrated by shifting pronouns or phrases indicating that the present generation was also an eyewitness to exodus. Notably different from Deuteronomy 26, Jeremiah's retelling of exodus does not portray Yahweh's deliverance as a response to Israel's actions (descent into Egypt, oppression, and crying out). Instead, like creation, the supernatural acts of exodus are unprovoked, of God's own initiative.[27] Also different, God's current intervention does not follow the patterns and covenant obligations of Deuteronomy. Instead, "by the end of the poem, it is clear that the claims of creation are all mobilized toward Israel."[28] The prayer affirms that hope is based on God's character alone. It is unaffected by Israel's misdeeds or politics. The prayer, including the noble exodus story, utters "a newness that violates all trusted rhetoric."[29] These expressions and images of exodus, like that of Jeremiah's field, become the source of Israel's illogical future hope—exodus wonders that continue "to this day." God's identity is coherent over time and Israel's hope is in his exodus-like interventions throughout time and on her behalf.

Nehemiah 9:9–12, 36

The exodus retelling of Nehemiah 9—set within a larger prayer of praise, confession, and entreaty—is the only example from an explicitly post-exilic narrative perspective. It contains all three plot elements of the primary narrative.

Links with the primary exodus story include the setting. The people of Israel are led in prayer by the Levites, as in Exodus 15:1–21 when Israel is led in the Song by Moses, also a Levite. In addition, there is an extensive amount of shared vocabulary between Nehemiah 9 and Exodus 14—15:21. Present in both is the familiar vocabulary of suffering (עני), crying out (זעקה), and signs and wonders (אתת ומפתים). The drama at the sea is compacted into a single verse that includes the division of the sea (בקעת הים; cf.

---

27. Cf. Josh 24:2–7.
28. Brueggemann, *Theology of Jeremiah*, 47.
29. Brueggemann, "A 'Characteristic' Reflection," 24.

Exod 14:16, 21; cf. Ps 78:13), the passing through on dry ground (יבשה; cf. Exod 14:16, 22, 29; 15:19), the pursuit (רדף; cf. Exod 14:4, 8, 9, 23; 15:9), and the hurling of the adversary into the depth (מצולה; cf. Exod 15:5) like a stone (אבן; cf. Exod 15:5).

Following the rehearsal of exodus, the narrative recites how God saved Israel from other self-induced dangers, demonstrating goodness, patience, and mercy. Israel's response, however, was forgetfulness, disobedience, and rebellion. Perhaps the most devastating criticism is in verse 17 where the people of Israel are described as "determined to return to their slavery."[30] Israel's history after the exodus is characterized in terms of cycles of sin, bondage, crying out to God, and merciful deliverance, similar to 1 Samuel 12's retold exodus story. As in the narratives following the primary exodus story, the Nehemiah context traces Israel's forgetfulness back to the wilderness. This contrasts with Samuel's placement of culpability after settlement in the land and Joshua's attributing its beginnings to forefathers in Egypt or "beyond the River" (cf. Josh 24:14). In Nehemiah, wilderness failings are represented as stereotypical of Israel's ongoing behavior, just as exodus deliverance becomes paradigmatic of God's actions.

The Levites cry out, in typical wilderness fashion, for God to see Israel's "hardship" and "distress" (9:32, 37). This is not explicitly the hardship of Egypt but rather the self-inflicted תלאה that occurred after leaving Egypt (Exod 18:8).

Israel's situation in the narrative present is then described as slavery, brought on by her sin. The narrative is not explicit whether this slavery stems from the arrogance and disobedience of previous generations or from the present generation's own disobedience and defiance. The cycle has come full circle and once again Israel is in bondage. If the pattern holds true, the next action rests with God alone: the conferral of mercy and deliverance. However, the supplicants do not presume to solicit this directly. Instead the people enter into a binding agreement to keep the Law of God, determining to make a break with the cycle of sin, suffering, and bondage. Hope of deliverance is only implicit.

Cognitive, evaluative, emotional, and temporal formulations of identity are all found in the prayer of Nehemiah 9 with behavioral formulations in the subsequent narratives.

---

30. Some manuscripts, including the Septuagint, have added "in Egypt" possibly based on the resemblance of this text to Num 14:4.

Cognitive and Evaluative Formulations

The protagonist in this retold exodus story and surrounding context is referred to primarily as אבתינו. Foreign peoples and adversaries are both named (9:8–9, 22, 24) and unnamed (9:22, 27, 28, 30, 37). The unnamed are referred to as kingdoms and nations, foes, enemies, peoples of the land, and simply as "they" in contrast to "we" (vv. 22, 27, 28, 36–37).

Nehemiah 9 describes the prototypical member of Israel, however, as one who is arrogant and unmindful of God's marvelous exodus-like deeds (נפלאות; cf. Exod 3:20; 15:11). This theme is emphasized throughout the prayer, which moves quickly from brief reflections on creation and Abram to a more lengthy contemplation of exodus. Israel is portrayed stereotypically like Egypt. The hiphil perfect third-person plural form of זיד used to describe the insolent Egyptian outgroup in Nehemiah 9:10 is reused to describe Israel in Nehemiah 9:16 and 29. The devaluation of the Egyptian outgroup, represented in images of mocking and fall (9:10–11), not only resembles that of the primary exodus story, but serves by comparison as a subtle warning to Israel.

Emotional Formulations

Despite the negative cognitive and evaluative formulations of Israel's identity in this prayer, the narrative contains abundant language and imagery of attachment to Israel. God's tender mercies are repeatedly displayed toward Israel in the exodus, the giving of the law, and in various earthy expressions of his goodness: fertile land, clothes that did not wear out, feet that did not swell, and wells already dug. Israel is shown as a well-nourished people who should be reveling in God's goodness.[31]

Temporal Formulations

The prayer of the Levites is similar to the summary speeches of Moses, Joshua, Samuel, and indirectly Jeremiah. Looking backward and forward and recalling exodus, whether through speeches or through prayers, is essential to Israel's collective identification and to her successful transition from one context or period to the next.

Israel is portrayed throughout this narrative as an unbroken succession of fathers and sons from the time of their suffering in Egypt onward (9:9, 16,

---

31. Klein, "Ezra & Nehemiah," 813.

23, 24, 32, 34, 36). Initially, only the sins of the forefathers are recounted in the prayer. A shift occurs in verses 33–37, as the sins of the past and present are intermingled. The speakers are united with their ancestors in guilt, and the history of sinning becomes their personal history. They share the same fate of oppression and distress and can only hope for a future deliverance like that of their ancestors. In this portrayal of hardship (9:32) and slavery (9:36), Israel is coherent over time.

The purpose of the narrative, though, is not primarily to proclaim the present Israel's continuity with the ancestors in forgetfulness, culpability, and subsequent slavery nor to extend those lines of continuity into the future, as Throntveit claims.[32] Instead, the rhetoric of this narrative acts to highlight the inappropriateness of the ancestors' response to exodus from the wilderness period to the present.

Throughout Nehemiah's prayer, אבתינו refers to the exodus and subsequent generations, rather than to the patriarchs. While identity construction in the post-exilic period increasingly appealed to genealogical continuity with Abraham (cf. 1 and 2 Chronicles), Abram is introduced in the narrative prior to the retold exodus story for a different purpose. Abram is introduced in Nehemiah 9:7 as an example of one who, like Israel, was "brought out" by God.[33] As Klein notes, "the verb 'brought out' (יצא yāṣā'), used of God's guidance of Abraham from his southern Mesopotamian home in Ur of the Chaldees (cf. Gen 11:28, 31; 15:7), suggests a kind of deliverance, or exodus, also for him."[34] Rather than upholding Abraham as the father of Israel, the narrative endorses Abram's example as a possible social identity for those who have been "brought out." Abram's response of faithfulness is then contrasted with Israel's own response.

While no behavioral formulations of identity are explicitly endorsed in the prayer, the possible social identity represented by Abram—as a "brought-out one" who responds with faithfulness—offers a more desirable identity for Israel than her present one, and may be the motivation for her response in 9:38–10:39.

Narrative Perspectives of the Psalms

Four different Psalms (78, 105, 106, and 136) have language that meets the definition of a retold exodus story. They are considered below.

---

32. Throntveit, *Ezra-Nehemiah*, 92.

33. The similarities in Abram's exodus from Ur are less obvious than in the exodus of Abram narrated in Gen 12:10-20 (see chap. 4).

34. Klein, "Ezra & Nehemiah," 810.

Because their poetic form is not bounded by a prose narrative like the poems and poetic patterns of Exodus 15, Nehemiah 9, and Jeremiah 32, they do not fit into a precise place in Israel's larger story. They are characterized by indistinct narrative speakers and narrative audiences. References to specific events or contexts are most often blurred or non-existent. The advantage is that they are able to speak more easily across generations. Their ability to express in words profound emotions also accounts for their enduring use.[35] While the surveys of Israel's past in Psalms 78, 105, 106, and 136 may all initially resemble that of Nehemiah 9, a careful analysis will reveal that they each offer a creative retelling of Israel's story with a particular purpose in mind.[36] They are, in the words of Hossfelt, "history in poetic refraction."[37]

Some contextual analysis may be possible. For instance, examining the placement of adjacent psalms, the "Book" into which the psalm has been grouped or the "type" (e.g., historic psalms) may reveal clues about the compilers and their interpretative decisions. Organizational decisions, however, were made very late in the canonical process. Even as late as the Qumran community, the order and grouping of the Psalms in manuscripts were still fluid.[38] Because the canonical groupings may not offer additional insight into how the message and purpose of an individual psalm was understood by ancient Israel, they will first be considered as independent constructions. An introduction to the overall message of each psalm will be given before identity formulations are evaluated.

Psalm 78:11–14, 42–53

Psalm 78 exhorts hearers to heed the shared life story transmitted to them and to recognize their obligation to transmit it to the next generation. The retold exodus story is part of a larger recollection of Israel's failure to live up to her identity as the people of God. Like Nehemiah's version, Psalm 78 portrays the failure as beginning in the wilderness and continuing to the narrative present.

Only two of the plot elements that define an exodus story are explicitly present in the two-part retelling found in Psalm 78. Verses 11–14 narrate the dividing of the sea and the bringing out of Israel (third element). Verses 42–53 narrate God's supernatural intervention in Egypt (second

---

35. Curtis, *Psalms*, xxii.
36. McCann, "Book of Psalms," 989.
37. Hossfeld, "Psalm 78," 286.
38. Curtis, *Psalms*, xxiv.

element) and Israel's deliverance at the sea (third element). As will also be seen in Psalm 105, the plagues are central to this retelling, though the number and order seems to be of no interest to the psalmist.[39] Therefore, rather than investigating how the differences in plague lists may have arisen from independent traditions and sources[40] or out of particular theological-contextual concerns,[41] the possible literary effect of their use will be the focus this study. For example, the portrayed effect of the plagues in Psalm 78 is more severe than in Psalm 105, narrating the unleashing of God's anger against Israel's enemies.

The exodus story is told in a context of forgetfulness of exodus, resulting in ingratitude and rebellion. The psalmist's stated purpose is to offer a conundrum (חידה) for the people to consider (78:2), namely, that in spite God's ample care of Israel, her forefathers were insubordinate and presumptuous toward him.

Cognitive Formulations

The Psalm begins in the first-person singular, with the speaker authoritatively calling "my people"—subsequently identified as Israel/Jacob—to listen (vv. 1–2). A shift to first-person plural occurs in verse 3, as the speaker joins himself to the "we" group and speaks of "our ancestors." The SIA recognizes both the named group—Israel/Jacob—and the plural pronoun as categorization language and a potential resource for the formation of collective identity. Israel's unbroken chain and ideal boundary of "ones who remember exodus"—past, present, and future—is also established.

After the introductory exhortations the exodus story is retold as part of an extended, historical survey. As in the primary exodus story, Israel as a people begins in exodus. Thus, the "ancestors" begin with the exodus generation—not the patriarchs (78:12–13)—and extend through the wilderness generation. The ancestors—prototypes of Israel—comprise both the faithful fathers who have transmitted the stories of God's praiseworthy deeds and the stubborn and the rebellious fathers who forgot them (vv. 1–11). The ingroup is characterized by identity confusion.

---

39. Bullock, *Encountering the Psalms*, 105.

40. Allen, *Psalms 101–50*, 54–55; and Choi, *Traditions as Odds*, 124–27.

41. Hossfeld, "Psalm 78"; Lee, "Context and Function of Plagues Tradition," 83–89; Tucker, "Revisiting the Plagues," 401–11.

Evaluative Formulations

Both parts of the retold exodus story (11–14 and 42–53) hint at the positive evaluation of Israel by a God who orchestrates her deliverance and works wonders on her behalf. Prototypical Israelites put their trust in God and do not forget his deeds. This in turn leads to keeping his commands (v. 7). In verses 9–12 and 17–43, however, the psalmist—employing a third-person designation commonly used as a label for the outgroup—exhorts hearers to differentiate themselves from a "they" who is negatively and stereotypically defined by lawlessness, rebellion, unfaithfulness, and disloyalty. This "other" is formerly and genealogically part of the self. Twice the negative behaviors of this outgroup are linked to its forgetfulness of exodus and God's other נפלאות. Israel's covenant relationship was grounded in God's mighty acts, which "they" have forgotten.

Two "theys" are positioned side by side in the second part of the retold exodus story (42–53). The first is the one just described—the "other" who is part of Israel's ancestry (42a). Then, following a subtle transition in 42b–43, verse 44 distinguishes the prototypical "other"—the Egyptian "they"—who is afflicted by plagues. Because there is no clear, intervening antecedent[42] to explicitly distinguish the Egyptian "other" introduced in verse 44, the line is blurred between these two groups of "other." That is to say, the culpable forefathers are barely distinguishable from Israel's primary outgroup and both are the object of devaluation. This contrasts with a more obvious distinction between the Egyptian other and the non-culpable forefathers ("his people" vv. 51–53).

The Psalm ends by rejecting two tribes and choosing the tribe of Judah. But Ephraim had been "made culpable from the beginning"[43] as verses 9–11 reveal. The narrative expressly binds Ephraim's failure to live in a covenant relationship (v. 10) to their forgetfulness of exodus (v. 11). While boundaries normally allow for both the inclusion of the ingroup and the differentiation of the outgroup, Israel's ideal boundary of "ones who remember exodus" now also excludes those who were once part of the self.

---

42. Because צר is singular (78:42b) and מצרים is used as a geographic indicator, there is not a clear antecedent for the masculine plural pronouns and subject that begin in v. 44.

43. Hossfeld, "Psalm 78," 287.

Emotional Formulations

The listeners in the narrative, and later unresisting hearers of it, are persuaded to identify with the faithful who retell the awe-inspiring wonders of God and to reject the forgetful and insubordinate forefathers. Belonging to the ingroup is inseparably linked to remembrance of God and his wonders. The story, with its focus always on God, is the basis of their relationship with God and subsequent trust and obedience. As in the retellings of Deuteronomy and Joshua, remembrance of God's mighty deeds—with an emphasis on the exodus—is at the core of the covenantal relationship.

Behavioral Formulations

While the narratives of Joshua, 1 Samuel, Jeremiah, and Nehemiah also trace the people's rebellion from the exodus generation to the contemporary one, Psalm 78 does not accuse the contemporary generation of unfaithfulness. Rather, the implication is that such faithlessness may be avoided by hearing and telling the stories of God's great deeds. Hearers and tellers alike are exhorted to trust in God rather than turning from him by forgetting, being stubborn, or rebelling like their forefathers.

Notably, the unfaithful ancestors are said to be from the northern tribes (cf. Ps 78:9, 67).[44] Although not explicit, the exile of the northern kingdom may be represented in 78:59–67. If so, the exhortations to remember and retell God's glorious deeds would then represent a call to covenant renewal so the southern kingdom might avoid an imminent national catastrophe.[45] Regardless of historical intent, however, Greenstein argues that the psalmist "practices memory, not to recount the past, but to prompt the kind of remembrance that leads to change."[46] The purpose of receiving and transmitting the story of God's great deeds is to guard participants against the stubbornness, rebelliousness, disloyalty, and unfaithfulness that characterized previous generations (78:6–8) and, thus, "to avoid becoming negative characters in such a sad story."[47] Remembering and telling the story is the behavioral norm that motivates covenant keeping and creates and maintains ingroup identity. But the order of the narrative in Psalm 78:10–11 and 32–42—with the covenant breaking preceding the forgetting

---

44. These two particularities are discussed by Niccacci, "Exodus Tradition in Psalms, Isaiah and Ezekiel," 13.
45. Terrien, *The Psalms*, 565.
46. Greenstein, "Mixing Memory and Design," 197.
47. House, "Examining the Narratives of Old Testament Narrative," 240.

of exodus—may also suggest that forgetfulness of exodus is an example of covenant breaking or even the result of it. The latter is consonant with the retold stories of Deuteronomy and Joshua that portray specific acts of covenant keeping provoking the remembrance of the exodus. Remembering exodus and keeping covenant exist in mutual relationship according to the retold exodus stories.

Temporal Formulations

Psalm 78 portrays Israel's collective identity as coherent across generations in several distinct ways. As in Exodus 15, there is a violation in the temporal sequencing of the story line. In verses 9–11, the omniscient narrator portrays narrative actors as looking backward in time with forgetfulness. Then time moves forward from Egypt to Canaan as Israel's story is remembered. In verses 43–72 time is turned back once again to remember that which has been forgotten. Hearers are called on to remember twice that which only "happened" once, and to take up this "collective memory" of the group without having had personal experience of the events remembered.[48]

This narrative portrayal strips the exodus of its particular historical context and invites all Israel to participate in it. The remembrance of exodus is constantly relevant to the present, and ingroup identity is achieved by receiving, transmitting, and participating in the story of God's great deeds (vv. 1–8). Ingroup members (the collective "we") are not defined primary by genealogy but by this cultural/ideological myth of common descent. That is to say, the unbroken line to the past is marked by remembering and telling. This sets up the conflict between those faithful ancestors and "*their* ancestors—a stubborn and rebellious generation" (v. 8) Forgetting exodus results in loss of identity, while rehearsing exodus reorients life to the relationship that gives identity and hope.[49]

The representation of the ingroup as coherent over time—as transmitters and participants in the story—serves as an identity resource for later hearers of the narrative. In other words, the inclusiveness of the narrative allows Israel's stories to take on a formative nature. Later hearers will also become a chapter in the story, represented either as those who remember or as those who were forgetful, stubborn, and rebellious. This undoubtedly places Israel's shared life story at risk of being transformed so much that it

---

48. This according to Halbwachs is the task of a social group. Halbwachs, *On Collective Memory*, 52–53.

49. Brueggemann and Bellinger, *Psalms*, 343.

no longer sustains identity and continuity. At the same time, it allows each new generation to appropriate and participate in the story.

Psalm 78 also further enlarges the category of the "other" against which Israel may define herself. To the classical understanding of Egypt as "other" were added Edom (Num 20:14–16) and other nations (Deut 4:20; 7:18–19). Psalm 78 adds to this category those who were formerly part of self. This "other" explicitly includes the northern tribes but potentially includes the psalmist's audience if they fail to transmit the story. As with the retellings of Numbers and Deuteronomy, therefore, this is less an ethnic distinction than a redrawing of ingroup boundaries based on one's participation in the exodus story. The assertion of these exodus stories is that the "people whom God brought out of Egypt" is defined by remembering exodus, whether one is entering the land or returning to it, on the verge of a new kingdom or faced with impending siege. Even those who are ethnically Israel can be excluded from this superordinate identity by a stubborn forgetfulness of exodus. Prototypical members of Israel, however, are those who know and remember God's wonders and transmit them to the next generation.

Psalm 78's exodus retelling shares vocabulary and images with other exodus stories, which adds to Israel's perceived coherence over time. The compositional influence of the Pentateuch, in particular Deuteronomy, has been widely debated.[50] However, even if there were no compositional influences, similarities in language or themes would place Psalm 78 in conversation with the other retellings of exodus for those hearers who had access to them. It shares an extensive amount of vocabulary with the primary exodus story (e.g., 78:12 עשה פלא; Exod 15:11; 78:13 בקע ים; Exod 14:16; ויצב־ 78:13 מים כמו־נד; Exod 15:8).[51] Even though the psalmist's version of the plagues "diverges notoriously from both the sequence and the wording of the Torah"[52]—the series ends with an intractable link to the primary exodus story 78:51) ויך כל־בכור במצרים; cf. Exod 12:29).

More important than lexical connections, however, are the identity claims shared between Psalm 78 and the other retellings. Like the primary exodus story and Deuteronomy 6, Psalm 78 emphasizes Israel's perpetual obligation to remember and retell the exodus story (Exod 10:2; 12:26–27; Deut 6:20–23). Forgetting the God of exodus and the wonders he performed (Ps 78:7, 11; cf. Deut 4:9; 6:12; 8:14; 1 Sam 12:9) stands as a constant threat to Israel's identity.

50. A bibliography of the various positions is given in Leonard, "Identifying Inner-Biblical Allusions," nn14–16.

51. A comprehensive comparison is found in Greenstein, "Mixing Memory and Design," 205–8.

52. Ibid., 207.

Psalm 105:23–39

Like Psalm 78, Psalm 105 begins with a call to remember God's "wonderful works" (v. 2). However, this retelling is to be told "among the peoples" (בעמים), not to the next generation of Israel, and its focus is on God's promise, purpose, and his praiseworthy deeds, not on Israel's actions and reactions. The retold story stretches from God's promise of land (vv. 9–11) to Israel's entry into it (v.44). Like Joshua 24:17, the wilderness experience is remembered, but the narrative focuses on God's provision and avoids discussing Israel's failures.

The greatest amount of mnemonic space in Psalm 105 is occupied by Israel's exodus story—from descent into Egypt to her joyous deliverance (vv. 23–28), with anticipatory (vv. 2 and 5) and summary remarks (v. 43). While all the major and minor plot elements of a retold exodus story are present, Israel's experience of oppression is minimized. None of the language of the primary narrative or other retold stories is used here to describe Israel's distress. Only general images are offered of Israel's prior condition, first as foreigners and later as a hated people (vv. 23–25). True to the stated purpose in verse 2, the plagues are examples of God's power, evoking praise. The Psalm selectively recasts Israel's deliverance, eliminating Pharaoh's pursuit of Israel and her distress at the sea, instead asserting simply, "Egypt was glad when they departed" (v. 38).

The retelling of exodus in Psalm 105 serves not only to display reasons for praise but to model a possible social identity characterized by a faithful and grateful response to God's wonders. The psalmist calls the people to make known, sing, tell, and remember (vv. 1–5) and then exemplifies these actions for them.

All five types of identity formulations are present in this retelling and its literary context.

Cognitive Formulations

In the first five verses of Psalm 105, the audience is addressed anonymously by ten masculine plural imperatives. Other categorizing labels include משיחי (v. 15), עמו (vv. 25, 43), and עבדיו (v. 25). Collectively, they define Israel in relation to יהוה אלהינו (v. 7). The psalm also names the people "Israel" as they enter Egypt (v. 23) and a second time as they are brought out (v. 37). This highlights again that the sojourn in and departure from Egypt was commonly perceived as the formative point of the people known as Israel. Finally, the group label בחיריו occurs in both verse 6 and 43, thereby enclosing the exodus story. Similar to Deuteronomy, Psalm 105 interprets the significance of exodus for Israel in terms of being chosen.

Evaluative Formulations

Evaluative formulations of collective identity are numerous in Psalm 105. In verses 12–15, proto-Israel is differentiated from others as the recipient of divine favor and protection. This differentiation unambiguously raises the evaluation of the ingroup. This continues in Egypt where Israel's positive distinctiveness is acclaimed in verse 24: "And the Lord made his people very fruitful, and made them stronger than their foes." The outgroup, Egypt, is the target of devaluation as she is struck by decimating plagues emanating from Moses, Aaron, and God (vv. 26–36).[53]

Instead of devaluing Egypt by expounding on her demise (cf. Exodus 15), Psalm 105 exalts God's chosen by spatially differentiating Israel from Egypt twice (vv. 37, 43). The twofold "brought out" declarations violate the temporal sequence of the story line. This would allow both the narrative audience and the hearers of it to interpret the atemporal deliverance as inclusive of them as well as the exodus generation.

Emotional Formulations

The shared fate of "a thousand generations" (v. 8) unifies the entire psalm. Both the common usage of "thousand" in the Hebrew Bible[54] to signify "innumerable"[55] and the context describing the promise of land as an "everlasting covenant" (v. 10) indicate that Israel's shared inheritance extends over time and generations.[56] In the language of the SIA, this shared claim creates a sense of attachment for all Israel. Exodus is pivotal to the fulfilment of this promise and is, therefore, fundamental to Israel's identity. This is asserted rhetorically by the placement of the exodus story in the center of the narrative structure of the psalm.

---

53. Not part of the exodus story, a devaluation of other nations and people is similarly recounted in v. 44 as Israel is given the land and wealth of other nations and peoples.

54. Cf. Exod 34:6–7; and Deut 5:10.

55. Scott, "109a אלף (ʾelep) thousand," 48.

56. The covenant referred to here is the promise of land to Abraham. The leitmotif of land will be discussed in the section on temporal formulations.

Behavioral Formulation

A behavioral norm appears in the concluding verse of Psalm 105. Everything God has done for Israel is designed so that she might "keep his statutes and observe his laws" (v. 45). Although the content of this formulation is sparse, its placement at the end of the psalm enhances its impact and the significance for the hearer. Like the retellings of Deuteronomy and Joshua, Psalm 105 implicitly asserts that exodus must be remembered in order to keep Torah.

Temporal Formulations

Like Psalm 78, the dominant identity formulations here are temporal. Firstly, Israel is emphatically portrayed as a coherent group over time but not based on a strong genealogical myth of common descent as, for example, Mays claims.[57] Abraham, Isaac, Jacob, and Joseph are not mere illustrations of the ancientness of Israel's bloodline. The leitmotif of this psalm—land—with nine references, makes this apparent. Landless Abraham is promised a land (v. 11). His few descendants were not a people but strangers and wanderers (v. 12). While the Joseph story anticipates Israel's future identity formation, the homelessness of verse 12 is emphatically repeated in verse 23. So then, the patriarchs of Psalm 105 are like the stereotypical "wandering Aramean" of Deuteronomy 26:5b-9 who anchors Israel's prior identity not in her bloodline but in a common condition, a cultural-ideological myth of common descent, which is a stronger constructor of collective identity than genealogy.

Secondly, much of the language and images found in Psalm 105 would resonate with anyone familiar with the primary exodus story and its prologue. This includes Psalm 105's prologue to the exodus story that exhorts Israel to "tell of all his wonderful works" (v. 2), references to the Abraham-Isaac-Jacob triad (vv. 9–10), Joseph's story (vv. 16–22), and the plagues (vv. 26–36). The images of Israel being brought out with rejoicing (v. 43) and being exhorted to sing (v. 2) would link hearers with Moses's Song of Exodus 15. The shared language and images thereby join the psalmist's audience collectively with the exodus generation. Participation in remembering is essential to what it means to be Israel. Singing and telling the story of God's mighty deeds reminds Israel who she is and how she is to live.

---

57. Mays, *Psalms*, 338.

Psalm 106:7–12, 21–23

Psalm 106 begins and ends with praises to God, but its focus is squarely on Israel's failures. Her vocation to praise God is compromised by her sin and its consequences.[58] The psalm is mnemonically dense with wilderness images, eventually characterizing even her existence in the land. The dominate tone is mournful. Moses, Phinehas, and Yahweh himself have stood in the breach to prevent the destruction of Israel (vv. 8, 23, 30, 44–45). Unlike 1 Samuel 12 and Nehemiah 9, there are no cycles of returning to God, just a continual history of sin similar to Psalm 78. Verses 4 and 47 frame the psalm, indicating that the present Israel is once again in trouble, scattered among the nations, and in need of God's deliverance.

The only positive highlight of this selective "historical" review is the first part of the exodus retelling (vv. 8–12). The exodus story is prefaced with a dissonant narration, like Joshua 24, of the prior wickedness and failings of Israel in Egypt which continued even to the drama at the sea (v. 7). The story contains no hints of the first plot element (Israel's oppression or distress), moving instead directly to the third element, the "bringing out of Egypt." God is portrayed as the one who initiated the deliverance in order to make his name and power known and to prevent Israel's imminent demise. This is the only instance in the psalm when the people of Israel respond positively: יאמינו בדבריו ישירו תהלתו (v. 12).

Unfortunately, Israel's belief is short lived as she quickly forgets God's acts (v. 13). The verb אמן is used a second time after the next reference to the exodus story where Israel continues her sinful forgetting (v. 21–22). The second plot element—God's supernatural deeds, signs and wonders, and so forth—is half forgotten in the retelling just as the Israel of the narrative is characterized as having forgotten God "who had done great things in Egypt" (v. 21) Despite Moses's intervention, Israel לא־האמינו לדברו (v. 24). The correlation is once again clear: appreciating exodus resulted in belief/trust (אמן) in God, forgetting it culminates in incredulity.

The psalm ends with Israel finally raising an exodus-like cry for help (v. 47), followed by an exclamation of praise ending with the confirmation אמן. This hints at the hope of exodus expressed in the verb אמן, and together these two terms structure the psalm.

The exodus retelling and its narrative context in Psalm 106 is similar to that of Nehemiah 9, which recites God's goodness, patience, and mercy as well as Israel's failure. As with Joshua's first retelling, Israel's forefathers are accused of sinning even while in Egypt; but unlike Joshua's portrayal

---

58. Mays, *Psalms*, 341.

of the sinful forefathers as beginning "beyond the rivers" (Josh 24:2, 14), the forefathers in Psalm 106 are only those of the exodus generation. Also, in contrast to Joshua's precise portrayal of idolatry as the principal sin in Egypt, in Psalm 106 sin is characterized vaguely as the failure to remember God's חסד.

The purpose of Psalm 106 and its exodus retelling is found in verse 47: Israel needs deliverance. The exodus story confronts Israel with her current predicament and offers her hope. Deliverance in turn will result in the exultation of God's name (vv. 8, 47; cf. Exod 15; Psalm 105).

All the rhetorical formulations of identity, with the exception of explicit behavioral ones, are found in this retelling and its narrative context.

Cognitive and Evaluative Formulations

In verses 4 and 5 of the psalm, the present generation of Israel is identified by the categorical formulations "your people," "your chosen ones," "your nation," and "your heritage." The plural pronouns "we" and "us" are used in verses 6 and 47. Previous generations are referred to both as "our fathers" and "his people," designations highlighting continuity with the narrative present, and as "they" and "them," rhetoric of differentiation. In this way, Israel is portrayed as united with her forefathers in guilt (v. 6) and the need for deliverance (v. 47), and yet she is potentially made distinct by her projected response of praise and gratitude (vv. 47-48).

Emotional Formulations

In verses 9-11, inter-group conflict is evident as God overcomes unnamed adversaries and natural forces (ים־סוף) that resist his plans for Israel. These emotional formulations assert God's attachment to the exodus generation and her belonging to him. A sense of solidarity with the exodus generation is engendered by the present generation's analogous cries of distress (vv. 44, 47) and by God's response of love (v. 45).

Temporal Formulations

Once again temporal formulations of identity are evident as potential identity resources. Each generation over the centuries has contributed to a "backlog of sins" including the contemporary one.[59] Because of this, an

---

59. Allen, *Psalms 101-50*, 70.

exodus story narrating the deliverance of the innocent and oppressed (e.g., Exodus 14–15) would not do. Instead, Psalm 106 crafts the exodus retelling to fit the contemporary need for a Jeremiah-like, illogical hope based solely on the coherence of the exodus God over time. God is portrayed as one who defends his own name and reputation while simultaneously delivering a sinning people. In fact, the line between exodus and wilderness are blurred. While "in Egypt," Israel rebelled (מרה; v. 7; cf. Num 20:10, 24; 27:14), and her sea crossing on dry ground is creatively described as "as through a wilderness" (כמדבר v. 9).

Hope is possible for any generation, knowing that God has delivered the guilty in the past on the basis of his own commitment to covenant rather than theirs (vv. 43–45). The psalm itself ultimately offers all hearers an example of the confession and crying out for salvation that can change their own life story. A possible future identity that is discontinuous with the fathers is implicit. While the fathers responded to deliverance with rebelliousness and iniquity (v. 43), Israel vows to give thanks and glory in response to God's salvation (v. 47).

Psalm 136:10–15, 23–24

Psalm 135 was excluded from consideration as an exodus retelling since it contained only the second plot element, the supernatural intervention of God. Psalm 136, however, ties that plot element to the third, the "bringing-out" of Israel at the sea. Some argue that the first plot element is also present in the oblique references to "our low estate" (v. 23),[60] but there are no linguistic links with other exodus stories to support such an interpretation.

The psalm begins with a threefold imperative, "O give thanks," and it ends with a final repetition of the imperative. In between, the psalmist selectively recalls events from Israel's past. Some are specific (creation, exodus, wilderness, conquest, and settlement) while others are imprecise (being remembered while in a low estate and being freed from enemies). Each phrase is followed by the response כי לע ולם חסדו. The divine name יהוה is only employed once, in the opening verse, with אלהים in verse 2, אדון in verse 3, and the shortened אל in verse 26. Throughout, however, God is described as "the one who . . .", reinforcing his identity as being constituted by his wonderful deeds and benevolence. While he gives general care to all

---

60. This is suggested in Brueggemann and Bellinger, *Psalms*, 571; and Allen, *Psalms 101–50*, 299. The latter argues that "from our foes" (מצרינו) functions as wordplay for Egypt. Allen offers an extensive summary of other interpretations.

(v. 25), his partiality to Israel is evident. The exodus story is central both literally and theologically to the psalm.

Cognitive, Evaluative, Emotional, and Behavioral Formulations

Identity formulations are intertwined in Psalm 136 and will be examined together with the exception of temporal formulations, which will be considered separately due to their importance as a potential resource for identity formation.

The collective Israel is identified and differentiated from both Egypt (v. 10) and Pharaoh (v. 14). She is more personally designated עמו and עבדו in verse 16 and 22, respectively, in contrast to other named and unnamed enemies (vv. 17–24). Like the primary exodus story, Psalm 136 portrays Israel as born when God brought her out of Egypt (v. 11). Unlike that narrative, however, there is no prologue, no mention of promises, ancestors or the descent into Egypt. The narrative jumps directly from the creation of the universe to the precipitous creation of Israel. This not only differentiates between her and the "other", it positively evaluates Israel by portraying her as the second major creative movement of God.

God's actions in history are clear indications of his steadfast love in general, but the distinguishing feature of Israel is God's particular commitment to her as expressions of his חסד, another example of her positive evaluation as the ingroup. In verses 10–24, God's partiality toward Israel is evident in the unbalanced inter-group conflict and the devaluation and defeat of Egypt and Israel's other enemies. The enemies are not worthy foes of God as he delivers Israel. He passes Israel through the midst of Egypt and the sea (10–15). He tosses Pharaoh's armies (v. 15, cf. Exod 1:27). He not only strikes (נכה) Egypt through their firstborn (v. 10, cf. Exod 12) but he strikes (נכה) other kings as well. The category of "other" is broadened to include any who would pretend to stand in the way of God delivering Israel into the land. She alone and no "other" is able to interpret God's deeds with the refrain "his steadfast love endures forever."

This lyrical phrase, "his steadfast love endures forever," is repeated 26 times. The emotional element is evident, as the refrain adds dimension to what it means to understand God's power. His "great wonders" are dramatized through time and over space, converging on Israel. She is portrayed as a unique creation, evaluatively distinct, and particularly loved and favored by her God. The portrayal of exodus as an expression of God's love places this psalm in conversation with Deuteronomy's retold exodus stories of divine love and election (cf. 4:37; 7:8). What was only declared briefly in Deuteronomy's exodus stories is repeated six times in this retelling (vv. 10–15). While Deuteronomy conditions God's love on obedience, Psalm 136 simply declares that it "endures forever." The only behavioral requirement is to "give thanks."

Temporal Formulations

The community expressing thanks is unnamed in Psalm 136. Israel is named three times and referred to only in the third-person as the one whom God saved in exodus and resettled in the land. The repetition of the bringing out of Israel in verses 11–12 and then again in 13–14 interrupts the story's chronology (cf. Exodus 15). It portrays exodus deliverance as an atemporal or recurring experience.

In verses 23 and 24, the community is finally represented by means of first-person plural pronouns, as God is identified as the one "who remembered *us* in our low estate . . . and rescued *us* from our foes." This shift of pronouns constructs a sense of continuous identity, bridging the temporal distance between past ("them") and present ("us") generations. A clear understanding of the historical setting of the Psalm is not necessary to understand the meaning and significance of verses 23 and 24. Though there are no contextual references to contemporary events, these verses appear to be a summary of the preceding history with the contemporary generation "us" assuming the identity of the foundational generation in similar circumstances.[61]

Conclusion

The retellings of exodus in the psalms reveal distinctive identity resources. Their evaluative formulations, for example, expand the conception of the outgroup to a more symbolic interpretation of Egypt and allow for the inclusion of former members of the self in this designation (e.g., Ps 78). Mostly absent are the explicit behavioral formulations that are so prevalent in Deuteronomy. Instead of covenantal obligations, Israel is to live cognizant of exodus: remembering it, retelling it, and giving thanks to the God of it.

According to these psalms, Israel's past failure is not simply due to the fathers' "misconduct"[62] in general but because of their failure to remember

---

61. This is Nasuti's argument in Nasuti, "Historical Narrative and Identity," 138.
62. Gerstenberger, *Psalms, Part 2, and Lamentations*, 95.

and live by the exodus story specifically. Remembering exodus, therefore, is a solution—a way back—from failure. As in Psalms 78 and 106, Israel's failure is now an indisputable part of the story (cf. Joshua 24:2-7, 17). But the story has taken on a new, open-ended quality, and Israel is being drafted into the story. This story has even taken on some slightly modified forms at times, as in Psalm 106:7, so that Israel could find her place in it.

6

The Significance of Exodus Identity for Ancient Israel

PRIOR RESEARCH ON THE social identity approach (SIA) has shown that collective identity is manifest in certain cognitive, evaluative, emotional, behavioral, and temporal expressions. It has also shown that the texts of ancient collectives may express collective identity in analogous rhetorical formulations. With this in mind, a methodological tool for identifying narrative formulations of social identity was developed (chapter 2). This heuristic tool was applied to all exodus stories found in the Hebrew Bible (chapters 3, 4, and 5) in order to illuminate the social identification processes at work in them. The current chapter will consider the general and methodological findings of those chapters and their significance.

General Characteristics of Exodus Stories and Their Significance

Exodus 1:1—15:21, dubbed the primary exodus story, narrates the story of Israel's sojourn in and departure from Egypt. It presents itself as an objective narration of "real events." Its seemingly omniscient, although anonymous, narrator exhaustively reports not only "historical" details but overheard conversations, motives, and the internal musings of characters as well.

Two particular aspects of the primary exodus story's content shed light on its purpose. Firstly, the placement of instructions to commemorate (12:14–20), remember, and tell (10:2; 12:25–27) interrupt the story's sequential narration. Secondly, the story concludes with a poetic, paradigmatic song that invites ongoing participation in exodus (15:1–21). This content indicates that the chief purpose of the narrative is not to present a sober historiographic account but rather to emphasize the importance of the persistent, ongoing participation of Israel in this exodus. As Alexander maintains, "The exodus was not merely a past event but an ongoing activity. Even those who have never been in Egypt were meant to see themselves as having been liberated from there."[1]

Eighteen retold exodus stories were identified using the definition set out in the introduction. All eighteen appear as retrospective accounts of the exodus. The nine Deuteronomic retellings present themselves as the first existential appropriations of this story by a non-exodus generation in their transition from the wilderness to the conquest of Canaan. As mentioned in chapter 4, this is the literary—not historical—claim of the narratives. The retold exodus stories in Joshua 24:2–7, 17 are set in the transition from conquest to settlement, 1 Samuel 12:6–8 in the transition from the period of judges to the monarchical era, Jeremiah 32:20–23 in the transition from this kingdom period to exile, and Nehemiah 9:9–12, 36 in Israel's transition back to the land after exile. Like Exodus 15:1–21, the retold exodus stories in the Psalms are presented as timeless, poetic rehearsals of exodus.

The retold exodus stories portray Israel's rehearsal of and ongoing participation in the exodus, as was anticipated by the primary exodus story. In their final form, they have narrative settings at every major socio-cultural transition in Israel's history up to her post-exilic restoration in the land. This suggests the potential identity-forming purpose of retold exodus stories even prior to an analysis of identity formulations. Cornell posits that during significant socio-cultural changes ("periods of rupture") people retell collective life stories in order to re-narrate group identities that have lost their taken-for-granted quality.[2]

The density of exodus stories set at the transition between the wilderness period and the conquest of the land, following the death of the exodus generation, are particularly significant. They illustrate the fundamental importance of the first transitional event when the story changes hands and is appropriated by those not present at the story's events. Taking on another's experience as relevant to one's own is crucial to continuing the life of the story.[3]

---

1. Alexander, *From Eden to the New Jerusalem*, 86.
2. Cornell, "Story of Our Life," 45–46.
3. Linde, *Working the Past*, 73–74.

Differences in Meaning, Vocabulary, and Content and Their Significance

The retold exodus stories unabashedly re-present the exodus imaginatively and interpretively. Differences between the retold stories and the primary narrative are meaningful and apparent. They include differences in the interpretative meaning of exodus, differences in vocabulary use, and the inclusion or exclusion of various plot elements.

Interpretive additions to Deuteronomy's and Jeremiah's retellings are made possible by the retrospective vantage point that characterizes retold exodus stories. Deuteronomy's retellings interpret exodus in ways that could not ostensibly be expressed by the primary narrative's "objective" account of events. They interpret exodus as representing God's love for and choosing of Israel. Deuteronomy 4:20 asserts that though exodus Israel became God's עם נחלה. Deuteronomy 4:34–38 explicitly states that God brought Israel out of Egypt because he loved and chose her. Deuteronomy's repeated inclusion of behavioral norms *in* (5:15; 15:15; 24:18) or *immediately after* retold exodus stories (4:39–40; 6:24–25; 11:8–9), however, sustains its overall theology: that God's ongoing favor displayed in exodus rests on Israel's obedience.

In contrast to Deuteronomy's interpretation of exodus as an expression of God's conditional love, Jeremiah's retold exodus story (32:20–23a) proposes a future, illogical hope and unconditional valuation of Israel. The implicit promise of deliverance does not depend on Deuteronomy's deed-consequence sequence. It is neither a reward for proper behavior nor clemency for repentance. Instead, exodus is its own premise of hope, reflecting the extraordinary and unsolicited intervention characteristic of God. Psalm 106 appears to share this interpretation of the hope of a new exodus in the life of Israel.

Differences in vocabulary usage in retold stories compared to the primary exodus story also have particular significance. Deuteronomy 5:15, 15:15, and 24:18 all begin with an image of Israel—consistent with the primary exodus story—as having been an עבד in Egypt. The replacement of יצא, the most prevalent term of deliverance, with פדה in 15:15 and 24:18, however, evokes the particular exodus scene of the sparing and consecration of the firstborn (Exod 13:11–16). This vocabulary change supports Deuteronomy's interpretation of exodus as representing God's election of and love for Israel.

The second exodus retelling in Joshua (24:17) substitutes יצא with עלה to emphasize the bringing *up* and not just the bringing *out* of Israel. This was a necessary response to the first retelling in 24:2–7, which had both explicitly and subtly devaluated (i.e., "brought down") Israel by accusations of idolatry and unwelcome references to her wilderness experience.

Another difference in vocabulary is the re-appropriation of wilderness language by exodus retellings. Unlike the linking of the primary exodus story to the subsequent wilderness stories, which narrate Israel's many failures prior to entry into the Promised Land, the retold exodus stories commonly portray Israel as going up out of Egypt and directly into the land (Deut 4:34–38, Deut 6:20–23, Deut 26:5–9, 1 Sam 12:6–8, and Jer 32:20–23a). When exodus stories narrate wilderness experiences, they use them for the "othering" of Israel, as in Joshua 24:2–7 (cf. Deut 11, Neh 9, Pss 78, and 106). In addition to the absent or different use of wilderness narratives with respect to the retold exodus stories, the exodus retellings of Deuteronomy 4:34–38 and 7:19 re-purpose the term מסה.[4] Instead of evoking images of Israel's testing of God in the wilderness (cf. Exod 17:7; Deut 6:16; 9:22; 33:8; Ps 95:8), Deuteronomy 4:34 and 7:19 appropriate and incorporate this term into the description of God's supernatural interventions in Egypt. That is to say, מסת is added to יד חזקה ובזרע נטויה דנא האתת והמפתים as a means used to deliver Israel from Egypt. The treatments of wilderness themes in Joshua 24:2–7, Deuteronomy 4:34–38, and Deuteronomy 7:19 show the incompatibility of "wilderness" with Israel's ideal social identity. By contrast, entry into the land is part of Israel's ideal identity, namely, as the completion of exodus.

In addition to the differences in the interpretative meaning of exodus and differences in vocabulary used in exodus stories, the varying use of exodus plot elements has particular significance. Retold exodus stories, as defined here, include two or more of the major plot elements of the primary exodus story linked to one another in causal, sequential, or associational ways. These provide the stable essence that makes them recognizable across generations. The stories vary, however, as to which major elements they employ.

All retold stories include the final plot element, the bringing out of Israel. In 11 of 18 stories, however, only one other plot element is present, either the prior oppression of Israel (five stories) or the supernatural deliverance of God (six stories). In some narratives, the presence and design of the additional plot element highlights the function of the exodus retelling. This is seen in Deuteronomy 7:18–19's exclusion of any mention of Israel's descent into Egypt, her former condition of oppression, and her crying out to God. This retold story places, instead, an increased focus on

---

4. This term is also used in the same way in the short reference to exodus in Deut 29:3.

the supernatural acts of God that brought Israel out of Egypt. The stated purposes of the retelling are to relieve the narrative audience's apprehension concerning "all the peoples you now fear" and to inspire faith in God. In a similar way, Deuteronomy 4:34–38, Deuteronomy 11:2–4, 7, Jeremiah 32:20–23a, Psalm 106, and Psalm 136 exclude any mention of Israel's negative prior fate. Excising this extraneous plot element supports their purpose of emphasizing God's power at work in Israel. By contrast, the exodus story retold in Numbers 20:14–16 makes no mention of supernatural acts. Its purpose is not to counter apprehension or inspire faith in God. Instead, the focus is on Israel's endurance of the long-foretold hardship that would entitle her to possess the land (cf. Gen 15:13, 16). In 1 Samuel 12:6–8, the absence of this plot element in the narrative parallels Israel's own failure to remember God's supernatural acts in the exodus. In each of these cases, including elements of supernatural deliverance would only serve to weaken the narrative's function. Deuteronomy 4:20, 15:15, and 24:18, however, appear to exclude the second plot element simply for brevity's sake.

Other differences in exodus narratives are visible in the specific use of diverse literary formulations of identity. The sections that follow will examine the overall significance of these.

Significance of Cognitive Formulations

According to the primary exodus story and retold exodus stories, Israel initially came to regard herself as a collective entity because of her shared experience of oppression, divine intervention, and deliverance. Although narrative rhetoric may not reflect the actual socio-historical reality, this is the identity claim of the stories on their hearers.

Israel's Boundaries

Being "the people whom God brought out of Egypt" was the feature of the group that was regarded as significant and defining—the *boundary* of the group. Several of the identity formations observed in chapters 3–5 support this finding.

Emergence of "Israel" in the Primary Exodus Story

In the Genesis prologue to the exodus story, categorical designations of Israel as a community are virtually absent. The designation "Israel" and other such instances of a named group (e.g., Hebrews, my people) to represent a broad populace first appear in the primary exodus story. That is to say, the sojourn in and deliverance out of Egypt defines Israel's existence.

Dramatic Representation of Israel's Emergence in Psalm 136

Psalm 136 dramatically represents the implicit contention of the primary exodus story. With no mention of promises, ancestors or the descent into Egypt, the narrative jumps without interruption from the creation of the universe to the precipitous creation of Israel, in her emphatic "bringing out" (vv. 11, 14) from Egypt.

Use of "the Fathers" to Trace Ancestry Back to Egypt

With the exception of Deuteronomy 26:5, Jeremiah 32:22, and Joshua 24:2–7, references to Israel's ancestors in the retellings (Num 20:15; Deut 4:37; Josh 24:17; 1 Sam 12:6–8; Ps 78:12;[5] 106:6–7) refer consistently to the exodus and later generations, not the patriarchs,[6] reinforcing the impression that Israel as a people may be traced back only as far as Egypt. Deuteronomy 26:5 and Jeremiah 32:22 refer to an earlier father simply to illustrate Israel's prior condition of landlessness and the promise of land but not to represent an older collective identity. Joshua 24:2–7 tries to present a negative collective identity traced back to the patriarchs and their ancestors "beyond the River." Joshua 24:17, however, rejects this interpretation and again traces "fathers" back only as far as Egypt. Nehemiah 9:7–8 offers Abraham as an example of a "brought out one" who responded with faithfulness rather than as a "father" of Israel.

Significance of Abraham, Isaac, and Jacob in Defining Israel

The primary exodus story contains seven reminders to Moses or Israel of their genealogical ties to Abraham, Isaac, and Jacob (Exod 2:4; 3:6, 15, 16; 4:5; 6:3, 8). After the last of these, the narrative notes: "Moses told this to

---

5. Non-specific "fathers" are also mentioned in Ps 78:3, 5, and 8.

6 See the analyses on these narratives in chapter 5, Römer, "Le cycle de Joseph," 3–15; and de Pury, "Le cycle de Jacob," 82. While, "fathers" in these stories does not refer to the patriarchs, it has been noted in both chapter 3 and in the analysis of Nehemiah 9 that various narrative attempts were made to incorporate the patriarchs in the exodus story.

the Israelites; but they would not listen to Moses, because of their broken spirit and their cruel slavery" (6:9). This narrative does not deny common ancestry but it portrays it as a feature of the group that its members do not regard as significantly defining of their identity as a people. Instead, the narrative depicts them as seeing themselves unified by oppression and, later, by deliverance. It is important to note, therefore, that the later expressions of Israel's identity in Judaism and Christianity defined in terms of a common ancestry may not have been definitive for all of ancient Israel or for the producers of exodus narratives.

Prior Identity as Slaves

Israel's representation of her emergence as a collective body is found in exodus stories that trace the origin of the prototypical Israelite back as far as slavery in Egypt. Israel's first sense of solidarity or "us-ness" is portrayed in the primary exodus story with images of collective suffering and crying out (Exod 2:23, cf. 6:8–9). That is to say, slavery is prototypical of Israel prior to deliverance. Her condition is described as "oppressed" (ענה) in Exodus 1:11–12 and Deuteronomy 26:6, "oppressed" (רעע) in Numbers 20:15 and Deuteronomy 26:6, "in slavery" or "the house of slavery" (עבדה, עבדים or בית עבדים) in Exodus 2:23, 6:5, 6:6, 6:9, 13:3, 13:14, Deuteronomy 5:15, 6:21, 15:15, 24:18, and Joshua 24:17, and "in an iron-smelter" (כורהברזל) in Deuteronomy 4:20.

Since the primary exodus story's concluding, paradigmatic song (Exod 15) only rehearses Israel's deliverance, it might be conjectured that Israel would, thereafter in her story, be defined only by deliverance. This is not the case. Deuteronomy 4:20 says that Israel was brought out of the iron-smelter, out of Egypt, to become a people of God's very own possession. It is this poignant transformation of selfhood and transfiguration of Israel's fate that continues to define her as a people. Her present status cannot be understood except in comparison to her former existence marked by debilitating heat, pain, and suffering. Remembrance of this prior condition is essential to keeping Sabbath (5:15), to freeing Hebrew slaves in the seventh year of servitude (15:15), and to other humanitarian acts (Deut 24:18). Thus, Israel's prior condition as a slave is essential to defining her present identity. This is made clear by the retellings of Numbers 20, Deuteronomy 5:15, 15:15, 24:18, and Nehemiah 9. Despite their retrospective and interpretative perspective, they all portray exodus identity as an ongoing identification with suffering and slavery, as well as deliverance. The latter enhances but does not replace the former in defining Israel's collective exodus identity. Israel is expected to "*revivre positivement une histoire d'humiliation et de souffrance*."[7]

The importance of a rightly portrayed prior identity—as a slave—to Israel's self-definition is illustrated by the exodus stories of Joshua 24. In the face of a dissonant exodus retelling presenting an undesirable idolatrous prototype (Josh 24:2–7), Israel maintains her desired expression of exodus identity by means of a conventional retelling (24:17). She is represented as refusing to be drafted into a faith story that changes her prior identity from slave to idolater. Whereas social memory studies recognize that memory is malleable and constantly reinterpreted, this narrative demonstrates its claim that collective memory also has a stable essence.[8]

Delineation of a Prototypical Israelite

The primary exodus story portrays Moses and Aaron, explicitly and implicitly, doing everything that God commands (Exod 7:10, 20; 8:6, 17; 9:10, 23; 10:3, 13, 22). They represent the ideal Israelite. As Israel emerges as a distinct people her initial characterization is identical to that of Moses and Aaron: she "did just as the Lord had commanded" (12:28).

In retold exodus stories and their literary contexts, an all-embracing obedience is not a definitive characteristic of Israel. Nevertheless, obeying God's commands inserted into the primary exodus story—to retell and to participate in exodus (10:2; 12:25–27; 12:14–20, 15:1–21)—is continually portrayed as central to Israel's inclusion in "the people whom God brought out of Egypt." The prototypical member of every new generation is the one who does this. Thus, the retold exodus story in Psalm 78 exhorts hearers to heed the shared life story transmitted to them and to recognize their obligation to transmit it to the next generation (vv. 1–8). This is how membership is achieved. Ingroup members are defined by an unbroken line to the past marked by remembering and telling. Because the exodus story defines Israel's existence and distinctiveness, it is viewed as a shared belief whose historical factuality is never internally questioned.

While the obligation to tell a shared life story has been designated in our tool as a temporal formulation of identity, Israel's exodus stories have

7. Pons, "La référence au séjour en Égypte," 171.

8. Schwartz rejects the constructionist conviction that social memory can undergo such modification to serve present needs that it is rendered unrecognizable. While acknowledging that memory is malleable and constantly reinterpreted, he argues that it, nevertheless, retains a stable essence that makes it recognizable across generations; Schwartz, "Where There's Smoke," 7–37. See also Schwartz, "Social Change and Collective Memory," 221–36; and Schwartz, "Christian Origins," 43–56.

also shown that retelling exodus was categorically definitive of Israel. Both the exodus story and the telling of the exodus story define Israel. Numbers 20:14–16 exemplifies the former and Psalm 78 the latter. In Number 20:14 the introductory identifier "your brother Israel" is followed by the carefully positioned exodus story, which alludes to its epithetical nature. Psalm 78 advances Israel's obligation to tell the story and ties forgetfulness of this story to covenant breaking. Deuteronomy 6:20–23 and 26:5b–9 provide Israel with explicit models of how to properly tell the story.

Significance of Evaluative Formulations

Israel is not portrayed as a collective prior to the primary exodus story, and in the story she is initially represented as an indistinct collective, ambiguously linked to Egypt.[9] Moses's personal identity crisis ensuing from his mixed identity is prototypical of the identity crisis of this Israel, newly conceived by Egypt's oppression, yet lacking distinction. Evaluative formulations, however, begin to distinguish Israel from Egypt as a separate, well-defined collective entity. These include purported Egyptian distinctions (Exod 1:9–22; 2:6), the poignant and unremitting divine demand, "let my people go" (Exod 5:1; 7:16; 8:1, 20; 9:1, 13, 10:3), and the devaluation of the "other" (Exod 1:12, 19; 7:14–15:12; cf. Deut 4:34–38).

Differentiating Israel from an "Other"

The principal outgroup of the primary exodus story is Egypt, represented by Pharaoh. Egypt, often portrayed in a rather positive light (Exod 2:5–10; 7:24 cf. 7:23; 8:19; 9:20; 11:3; 12:33) makes a poor candidate for the "other." Pharaoh, by contrast, is unambiguously depicted as arrogant, obdurate, recalcitrant, and opposed to God. Pharaoh, then, emerges as the primary, prototypical depiction of "other." While the story narrates two Pharaohs, it names neither, adding to the stereotyping effect of "the other" as an enemy and oppressor of God's people who is set in contrast to them. Conflict between the two peoples underscores their distinction.

The rhetoric of exodus narratives asserts that being "a people whom God brought out of Egypt" is the significantly defining boundary of Israel. These narratives make the claim that group membership in Israel is not simply genealogically ascribed. It is defined with respect to an "other."

---

9. Ambiguous language and images of both integration and separation from Egypt were described in detail in chap. 3.

Expanding the Other Category

The primary exodus story represents the dominant voice of the exodus story. Retold exodus stories contribute a pluriformity of voices. This is illustrated, for example, by their expansion of the "other" category. The first example of this is found in Numbers 20:14–16. Edom fails to take up or acknowledge Israel's story, which is required for ingroup membership, and thus becomes part of the outgroup. Also, because a prior condition as a slave is definitive of the ingroup, Edom is further disqualified by her lack of participation in the trials of Egypt. Israel's endurance of the hardship of Egypt differentiates her from Edom. This exodus retelling distinguishes Israel not only from the radically other (Egypt/Pharaoh) but from the "proximate other" (Edom).

Deuteronomy 7:18–19, in turn, expands the outgroup category further to include other nations. The nations who occupy Israel's Promised Land are not only viewed as "other" but they will be brought down in the same way as Egypt: with great trials, signs and wonders, and "a mighty hand and an outstretched arm." The lack of precision of the "other" (two nameless Pharaohs) in the dominant narrative invites the expansion of this category. Such reinterpretations of the exodus story allow for it to address new situations, incorporate new members, and create a sense of commonality between the past and the present.

The "Othering" of Israel

Identity stories cannot be adjusted to include those who do not exhibit the features that are group defining. The "people whom God brought out of Egypt" are defined by their telling of and participation in the story of exodus. An identity crisis is indicated when the prototypical Israelite is depicted as one who forgets the story.

In Psalm 106, the previous generations going back as far as Egypt are referred to as "our fathers" (v. 6) and "his people" (v. 40), designations highlighting continuity with the narrative present. These same prior generations, however, are also referred to throughout the psalm as "they" and "them," drawing on a non-inclusive rhetoric of differentiation. The internal audience hearing the narrative is portrayed as united with her forefathers in guilt and the need for deliverance. At the same time, however, the narrative of Psalm 106 is incomplete. Neither the deliverance nor the response to deliverance has been narrated. The narrative portrays the hearers as potentially distinct in their anticipated response of praise and gratitude ("that we may give thanks to your holy name and glory in your praise," Ps 106:47).

Membership in "the people whom God brought out of Egypt" is anticipated, although two possible identities are conceivable.

Retold exodus stories portray the "other" as anyone who threatens Israel's distinctiveness, even those who might previously or otherwise be classified as Israel. An undesirable, but possible, identity for Israel in the present and future is one in which Israel is characterized by forgetfulness of the exodus, of the story of the exodus, and of the God of exodus. This results in the "othering" of those who were formerly believed to be part of the Self (i.e., Israel). Psalm 78 depicts an unbroken line of those who tell the story of God's wonders—including exodus—from the fathers of the past to the present hearers to the children yet to be born (vv. 1–6). Ingroup members are defined and positively evaluated by this unbroken line of remembering and retelling. Within the ingroup, though, there are those who are negatively and stereotypically differentiated because "they" did not remember God's displays of power (vv. 17–42a). This group of "they" is practically indistinguishable from the Egyptian "they" whom God devalues and utterly decimates (v. 42b–50).

In Nehemiah 9, Abram is represented as a prototype of one who is brought out and responds faithfully to his deliverance (vv. 7–8). Those who experienced exodus from Egypt, by contrast, "acted presumptuously and stiffened their necks and did not obey your commandments" (v. 16), and "failed to remember the miracles you performed among them" (9:17 NIV). Throughout this retold exodus narrative, Israel is referred to as "they." The boundaries that should separate "us" (Israel) from "them" are blurred. Israel is equated with the Egyptian outgroup based on her arrogant dealings with God (vv. 16, 29).

The othering of Israel allows a means of discriminating between authentic members of the ingroup and those who bear a strong resemblance to the outgroup. The "other" is not defined ethnically but by boundaries drawn on the basis of their participation in and appropriation of the exodus story. Only by participating effectively in the exodus story does Israel avoid devaluation as "other" and achieve positive distinctiveness as the ingroup. These representations of social identity serve as resources for hearers. They should persuade hearers of the greater desirability of an identity that provides a positive evaluation.

Significance of Emotional Formulations

With the exception to the exodus stories of Joshua 24:2–7 and Psalm 106:7–12, unresisting hearers are drawn to sympathize with Israel in her prior identity, either of oppression and bondage or of wandering and landlessness. One of the most stable elements of the exodus stories are their poignant images of God acting powerfully on Israel's behalf, whether in response to her cries for help (explicit in the primary narrative, Num 20:14-16, Deut 26:5b-9, and Neh 9:9-12) or out of his own initiative and purposes (Josh 24:2-7 and Psalm 106:7-12). Such actions on behalf of his people are extended against all whom Israel fears (Deut 7:18-19) and "to this day" (Jer 32:20-23a).

Deeper ties of attachment and belonging between God and Israel are created in Deuteronomy's retold exodus stories by the language of being valued, loved, and chosen by God. The replacement of יצא, the most prevalent term of deliverance, with פדה in Deuteronomy 15:15 and 24:18 evokes the particular exodus scene of the sparing and consecration of the firstborn (Exod 13:11-16). Although Deuteronomy ties Israel's ongoing belonging to covenant-keeping behavior, Jeremiah's exodus story offers a future "illogical hope" of God's deliverance based on God's character alone. God's attachment to Israel is portrayed as unaffected by her misdeeds or politics.

Significance of Behavioral Formulations

There are only a few behavioral formulations of identity evident in the primary exodus story: the anachronistic injunctions to commemorate and retell the exodus at a future time (Exod 10:2, 12:14-20, and 12:26-27) and an implicit summons to all Israel—not just to the generation at the sea—to enter into the exodus story by taking up the Song of Deliverance (Exod 15:1, 21). As "the people whom God brought out of Egypt" is expanded temporally, the behavioral norms that distinguish them are illuminated. Thus, in contrast to the primary exodus story, the retold stories contain numerous behavioral formulations of identity. They assert that the ongoing experience of exodus is at the core of covenant allegiance and renewal.

Deuteronomy 11 illustrates how the exodus story is at the core of Deuteronomy's commitment to covenant obedience. Behavioral formulations of collective identity are found immediately prior and subsequent to the exodus retelling in 11:2-4, 7—exhortations to fear, love, and obey God—with promises of blessings for obedience and curses for disobedience (10:2-11:1; 11:8-32). The implicit claim of this form is that exodus is central to (or at the core of) covenant obedience.

In other retold stories, covenant obedience (Deut 6:21-23; 26:5-9) and covenant renewal (Josh 24) seem to point toward and inspire the remembrance of exodus. Commemorative celebrations and traditions (e.g., Firstfruits in Deut 26 and the wheat harvest/feast of Weeks in 1 Sam 12) similarly remind Israel of her shared story. Israel is to be obedient *in order* to remember the events of her redemption and thereby to participate again in the exodus event.

Deuteronomy is concerned, in general, that Israel "not forget" (e.g., 4:9, 4:23, 8:11, 8:19, 9:7, and 25:19). In particular, she is not to forget the God of exodus (6:12 and 8:14). The immediate narrative contexts of other retold exodus stories illustrate the effect Israel's failure to remember exodus has on her behavior (1 Sam 12:9–15, Neh 9:16–35, Ps 78:17–42, and Ps 106:13–43). The remembrance of exodus inspires certain behavioral norms and these same norms inspire the remembrance of exodus. The retold exodus story of Jeremiah 32 uniquely notes that, while collective identity grounded in exodus has behavioral implications for Israel (vv. 18, 23), her exodus identity is also the premise of a future illogical, exodus-like hope, independent of behavioral qualifications.

Identity norms in retold exodus stories significantly redefine covenant keeping. Of the 18 retellings of exodus only two include the giving of the covenant at Sinai (Neh 9:13 and Ps 106:19). Retold exodus stories do not view covenant allegiance as primarily based on a remembrance of or adherence to the Sinai Covenant, but on a present-day encounter and oath of allegiance of each generation when confronted with the remembrance of exodus (e.g., Deut 11:1–32, Joshua 24:2–27, and Psalm 105). Covenant sustains and is an expression of exodus identity. Covenant keeping reminds Israel of exodus, but remembrance of exodus is primary and definitive for Israel.

Significance of Temporal Formulations

Temporal formulations are the most dense and most prominent formulations found in the primary exodus narrative and retold exodus stories.

Temporal Expansion of "The People Whom God Brought Out of Egypt"

Both the primary exodus story and the retold stories assert that "the people whom God brought out of Egypt" consists of more than just Israel's exodus generation. If group membership is achieved, rather than simply ascribed, the stories must answer the question of how new members are added to this group across time. They accomplish this by representing new members crossing the boundary into this identity through the appropriation and transmission of a shared life story—the exodus story. This is demonstrated in various ways in the primary exodus story and retold exodus stories.

Proleptic Inclusion of the Patriarchs

The creative narration of patriarch stories represents Abraham and Jacob going down and up from Egypt (Gen 12:10–20; 46:1–7; 50:5–13) in an exodus-like pattern. These narratives do not, however, succeed perfectly in revealing the patriarchs as proleptic participants in the exodus story. This impedes the patriarchs from crossing the boundary fully into the group membership defined by participation in exodus. Retold exodus stories, however, further accommodate the patriarch's membership in the "people whom God brought out of Egypt." Because a prior condition as a "slave" is not particularly apt for describing Abraham and Jacob, the story is adapted to include shared initial fates of wandering and landlessness leading up to the exodus (Deut 26:5b; Ps 105:8–13).

A significant contribution of the application of the SIA to exodus stories is the illumination of an origin tradition that traces Israel's origin back to Egypt and the exodus. This tradition either coexists or completes with the more familiar origin tradition that genealogically traces Israel's origins back to the patriarchs. Exodus stories compellingly promote a cultural-ideological myth that links generations by means of their experience of slavery and deliverance.

Inclusion of Present and Future Others into the Primary Exodus Story

While the Genesis prologue to the primary exodus story creatively, but imperfectly, incorporates the patriarchs into "the people whom God brought out of Egypt," various rhetorical devices within the primary exodus story expand this category. Exodus 12:38 delineates the group as inclusive of a "mixed multitude" (JPS) and not just ethnic Israelites. The hyperbolic count of 600,000 plus people purportedly participating in exodus (12:37) may represent the anachronistic incorporation of subsequent generations into the exodus.[10] Passover and Firstborn commemorations inserted into the primary exodus story prior to the narration of the exodus event itself, symbolically incorporate later generations into the initial deliverance (Exod 12:14–20 and 13:5–16). Taken together, these examples may represent creative, editorial attempts to integrate all Israel into the initial redemptive

---

10. See chap. 3.

event. Even if the identity formulations of these narratives were spontaneous and unintentional, they would have fostered perceptions of incorporation and inclusion in hearers of the narratives.

Inclusion of Later Generations through Shifting Pronouns in Retold Stories

The less-than-perfect incorporation of the patriarchs and the theoretical inclusion of later generations by means of commemorative instructions illustrate the expansiveness of the category of "the people whom God brought out of Egypt." New generations of social actors are also integrated by the use of shifting pronouns in retold exodus stories. An implied pronoun shift, in the form of a temporally inclusive second person narrative, occurs in Deuteronomy 4:20. Here the narrative audience is addressed as if they were the prototypical exodus generation itself: "But as for you, the Lord took you and brought you . . . out of Egypt" (NIV). This same second person narrative occurs in Deuteronomy 5:15, 15:15, and 24:18. A new generation of Israel is portrayed as those who experienced the exodus. A similar implied pronoun shift occurs in the form of a temporally inclusive first person narrative in Deuteronomy 6:21: "We were Pharaoh's slaves in Egypt, but the LORD brought us out of Egypt with a mighty hand." The introduction to this assertion indicates the future generations should repeat this first person narrative to their children.

In contrast, 1 Samuel 12:6–8, Nehemiah 9:9–11, Psalm 78: 11–14, 42–53, and Psalm 106:7–12, 21–23 simply tell the story as it occurred to their ancestors, and Joshua 24:17 claims that God "brought *us and our ancestors* up from the land of Egypt." Psalm 105:23–39 and Jeremiah 32:21 use the indefinite language of "Israel" or "your people."

Shifting pronouns that narrate the exodus story partially as happening to "them" and partially to "us" occur in Deuteronomy 26:5–9, Joshua 24:2–7, and Psalm 136:10–15, 23–24. Joshua 24:6–7 offers a key example:

> When I brought *your ancestors* out of Egypt, *you* came to the sea; and the Egyptians pursued *your ancestors* with chariots and horsemen to the Red Sea. When *they* cried out to the LORD, he put darkness between *you* and the Egyptians, and made the sea come upon them and cover them; and *your eyes* saw what I did to Egypt. Afterwards *you lived* in the wilderness a long time.

All of these pronouns shifts contribute to dissolving the gap between past and present members of Israel. Israel is, thus, an atemporal expression of collective identity. The use of the second person plural and first person plural have the potential to draft hearers of any epoch into the shared life story and thus to enter into "the people whom God brought out of Egypt." This identity is inclusive and may be definitive of any generation of Israel who participates in the story.

Inclusion of Later Generations by Eyewitness Language

The narratives of Numbers amplify the discontinuity (and minimized the continuity) between the new generation and the old so that—from a literary point of view—the new generation is depicted as not having actually witnessed the exodus events (Num 14:21-23). Thus, the claims of Deuteronomy 4:34, 6:22, 7:19, 11:7, and Joshua 24:17 that the events of exodus occurred before "your/our very eyes" accomplish the same effect as that of the shifting pronouns described above: they portray the inclusion of later generations in "the people whom God brought out of Egypt."

Adjusting the Shared Life Story

Israel's identity is anchored in her collective perception of self as "slaves" (or wanderers or homeless ones) whom God brought out of Egypt. Nehemiah's and Psalm 106's exodus stories, however, are dissonant in this respect. Beginning with a conventional recollection of Israel's suffering, crying out to God, and deliverance from Egypt, Nehemiah 9:36 then describes the present people of Israel as still slaves in distress. Similarly, Psalm 106 portrays Israel as having returned to her prior condition of homelessness ("gather us from among the nations," v. 47). In these dissonant retellings, both continuity and discontinuity are represented as existing between the Israel depicted in the narratives and the exodus generation. Continuity is seen in the analogous cries of distress. Discontinuity is represented in the depiction of the supplicants as unequivocally guilty rather than presumably innocent. Deliverance is an implicit hope rather than a foregone, future reality and exodus is a paradigm of God's repeated deliverance (1 Sam 12, Neh 9, and Ps 106). These dissonant stories demonstrate that, at times, only a re-narration of the exodus story can fit the experience of "all Israel" and provide a coherent exodus identity.

Possible Social Identities for Hearers of Exodus Stories

While exodus narratives represent the "concretization" of collective memory, they are neither uniform nor inflexible, reflecting instead the adjusting of stories to fit identities. They offer Israel distinct possible social identities.

Slaves or Heedless and Idolatrous People
"Whom God Brought Out of Egypt"

Psalm 106 equates Israel's present identity with a pre-exodus generation's identity characterized by rebelliousness, failure to remember God's kindnesses, and heedlessness of God's miracles (Psalm 106:7). Exilic hearers of this particular exodus story may find hope for a similar deliverance.

While the retelling in Joshua 24:2–7—of an Israel characterized by idolatry—meets with resistance and re-narration in Joshua 24:17, it certainly foreshadows such a situation. Thus, Joshua 24:2–7 may ring true with exilic and post-exilic hearers of the retelling who are familiar with Israel's history of idolatry. The hearer of the narrative may view the undesirable identity of an "idolater set free" as a real choice of possible social identities for the narrative characters and for him or herself.

It is significant that retold exodus stories provide a pluriformity of voices. Modifications of the exodus story are possible while still maintaining a stable essence. They provide the possibility of diverse, even undesirable, social identities. These make the stories potentially transferrable to a variety of hearers. This is crucial since the key to a social group's endurance is found in it having "successive social actors."[11] Exodus identity may not always signify transformation from oppression to deliverance, but may include a shift from wandering to landedness (Deut 26 and Psalm 105). There is no indication that such a redefinition distresses Israel's identity. Instead, it allows the tellers to emphasize aspects of Israel's desired exodus identity that may have been of particular relevance to the producer's generation.

Exodus stories construct a prototypical identity for Israel that is not anchored in bloodlines. They embrace a prior identity of slavery and oppression but are agreeable to a previously shared fate of wandering and homelessness. They portray a prior identity as an idolatrous people as conceivable though undesirable.

---

11 Condor, "Social Identity," 291.

Faithful Remembering Response or Forgetfulness

Identity formation generated by the proper telling of and incorporation into the exodus story creates both an exclusive and inclusive boundary within Israel. It excludes those who forget the story, even though previously considered part of the Self, and it includes those who remember and narrate it.

Some retold stories prompt Israel to *embrace* continuity with her ancestors (e.g., Deut 4:37–40; 6:22–25; Josh 24:16–18) while others call her to *reject* them (e.g., Ps 106:7). At least one retelling calls for both (Josh 24:14, 16–18). When expressed positively, exodus narratives promote Israel's continuity with the past as a means of extending the lines of continuity into the future. In cases where Israel's past is cast in negative terms, as exemplified in the retold stories of 1 Samuel 12 and Nehemiah 9, the future possibility of a faithful response to exodus is portrayed as discontinuous with the past and the present. In Psalm 78, the present Israel, who is not accused of unfaithfulness, is presented with a choice of identities. She may embrace continuity with a chain of the faithful by telling the exodus story, as the psalmist prompts her to do, or she may join herself to the unfaithful ancestors who forgot God's deeds, particularly his wonders performed in Egypt.

Hearers of the story, both the characters in the narrative and those who hear the narrative, are constrained not only to relay the story forward to the next generation but to choose between various possible social identities as they become social actors in the story. To avoid becoming a tragic "other" in a sad story, Israel is presented with a desirable social identity represented by a faithful and grateful response to God's deliverance. An example of this is the anachronistic response in Nehemiah 9. Abram is incorporated into the exodus story as prototypical of one who not only is "brought out" but also responds faithfully to exodus.

Actualization of the Shared Story

Telling the exodus story is cognitively definitive of Israel. But remembering and retelling the story also serves as the entry point into a corporate identity. Those who know the story are obliged to *transmit it*, and those who subsequently hear the story are *reconstituted by it*. Even a return to Egypt, literally or symbolically as narrated in Nehemiah 9, does not threaten Israel's collective identity as much as forgetting the story or failing to participate in it.

The significance of this, based on the claims of the exodus stories, is that Israel's identity across time cannot be validly traced simply through bloodlines. Similarly, new generations of Israel are not just descendants of "the people whom God brought up out of Egypt." They are the people who tell the story of being brought up out of Egypt. The primary narrative hints, and the retold stories more explicitly state, that Israel is distinguished by a proper retelling of and incorporation into the exodus story. The extent to which this exodus story became a permanent feature of Jewish imagination is proof of its success in identity construction. Thus, modern Israel reminds herself in the Passover Haggadah: "Therefore, even if we were all sages, all men of understanding, all advanced in years, and all expert in the Torah, it would yet be our duty to tell of the departure from Egypt, and the more a man tells about the departure from Egypt, the more praiseworthy he is."[12]

This analysis of exodus stories has revealed reinterpreted understandings of the prototypical exodus generation and the exodus story that are capable of addressing new situations and of creating a sense of commonality between the past and the present. The narrative assumption that the exodus story has relevance to and bearing on "current" events, while needing "translation"[13] for successive social actors apparently legitimizes such reinterpretations of the exodus story. Having elaborated in detail on the methodological findings and their significance, the final chapter will examine the significance of this new method of exposing identity formulations in narrative with respect to previous scholarship. It will also explore opportunities for further, related study.

---

12 Zakovitch, "*You Shall Tell Your Son . . .*" 9.
13 Condor, "Social Identity," 291.

7

Conclusion

THIS BOOK HAS ATTEMPTED to elucidate how a long-lasting collective identity may have been created and maintained through persuasive narrative rhetoric. It built upon previous research from diverse fields of study to approach this question. Prior social memory studies had established that group memory is selective and that memories deemed worthy of representing the group are the ones brought forward in fixed form. Therefore, the social memory occupying the most mnemonic space in the Hebrew Bible—Israel's sojourn in and departure from Egypt—was chosen to be examined for its identity-creating potential. Previous literary studies had revealed the centrality of the narrative genre in identity construction. As a result, the research sample was limited to exodus *stories*. The principles of the social identity approach (SIA) had been shown to be applicable not only to face-to-face relationships but also to ancient cultures and their narratives. Hence, the SIA was called on to offer insight into how these exodus stories may have contributed to ancient Israel's identity. Using a methodological tool introduced in chapter 2, this analysis exposed various rhetorical identity formulations in the primary exodus story and in multiple retold stories of exodus. By doing this, it demonstrated that exodus narratives reflect identity rhetoric capable of creating or reinforcing collective identity in their hearers.

Significance of This Analysis

This study has significant implications for the field of biblical studies. Firstly, it shows the advantages of appreciating biblical texts as narratives before they are used as historical sources. When stories are examined first for what they "say," clues can be found that more accurately reveal the function they served. For example, exodus narratives claim that all Israel was conceived in oppression and born in deliverance. While a historical-critical approach would promptly dismiss the claim as invalid, a narrative approach cannot do so. The latter recognizes the rhetorical devices that are employed throughout the exodus narratives to reinforce the claim and to incorporate past and future generations ("all Israel") into the exodus experience. The narrative approach helps to appreciate the purpose of the claim. In this case, the assertion was not intended as a historical contention but rather as an affirmation of solidarity and collective identification.

Not only does this study show that narrative analysis can illuminate the function of biblical texts, but it demonstrates how a heuristic tool from the human sciences, namely the Social Identity Approach, can offer additional insights into the narrative analysis of ancient texts. The use of this tool helps in answering the "why" question posed of the narrative. In the case of the exodus story, it shows that the retold stories were preserved, revised, and transmitted not simply to safeguard the past but to persuade Israel of a still relevant, present and future collective identity. Although narrative analysis does not provide unambiguous clues as to how a text *should* be read,[1] characteristics of narratives show how they tend be read and the effect they are apt to have on their interpretative audiences. Analysis of recurring exodus stories has demonstrated that whether the producers of the narratives were consciously instigating an identity project to fend off assimilation and create an identity, or unconsciously reflecting a contemporary ideological struggle, the artistry and design of the narratives, particularly their rhetorical formulations of identity, highlight their potential as identity resources. Thus, in addition to promoting the narrative study of the Hebrew Bible and elucidating the purpose of biblical narratives, this study narrows the gap between social identity theories and biblical narrative by demonstrating once again that narratives are important culture tools by which collective identity can be created, maintained, or even transformed with continued usage.

Because possible social identities are limited by resources and socialization into those resources, the significance of the recurring exodus story in mediating identity to those who used the text cannot be ignored when studying the Hebrew Bible's exodus narratives. Rather than assenting to or contradicting those who have tried to answer the question of when the exodus tradition may have contributed to Israel's corporate identity, this study adds to their research by showing how characteristics of the tradition in its final literary form may have constructed or maintained such identity. Instead of demonstrating how a narrative may have historically served Israel's changing identity needs at a particular point in time, this

---

1. Berquist, "Identities and Empire," 12.

study surmises that the persistence of these narratives may have had an enduring effect on ancient Israel's identity.

Significance of the Heuristic Tool

This study adds depth and objectivity to the examination of social identity in ancient texts made by others.[2] Rather than examining a single biblical text[3] or book of the Bible,[4] this study presents an innovative example of applying the SIA to a narrative motif. The result is a broader application of the approach than previously has been undertaken.

Prior to this examination, five scholars specifically claimed an application of the SIA to the Hebrew Bible.[5] Their efforts were reviewed in chapter 2. Baker's work lacked a specific examination of the rhetoric of the narrative. He focused instead on the nature of the text as a fresh source of common identity at a time when evidence of the original identity-sustaining covenant had been lost.[6] Bosman, Jonkers, Finitsis, and Lau, in contrast, did attempt to uncover the underlying dynamic of how social identity was constructed through narratives. Their treatment of the rhetoric of their respective narratives was broad, but lacked systemization and the appropriation of specific social identity language. Bosman alludes to many of the social identity formulations specified in our methodological tool, while Jonkers, Finitsis, and Lau focus on a more limited set.[7]

Compared to the systematic examination of identity rhetoric in exodus narratives in this study, Bosman's approach interspersed narrative observations of social identity rhetoric with historical and theoretical interpretations. For example, Bosman notes the identity chaos created in Nahum 1:9-14 by the shifting second person pronouns. The term "you" first represents the outgroup, then the ingroup, and then the outgroup again. Rather than allowing other rhetorical formulations of identity to inform the significance of this, Bosman jumps to an interpretative question of whether this observation supports Jeremias's theory that Nahum was not a cultic

---

2. See the previous works applying social identity to ancient texts in chap. 2 and Appendix 1.

3. See for example Baker, "New Covenant, New Identity," 5.1–5.11.

4. See Bosman, *Social Identity in Nahum*; Jonker, "Reforming History," 21–44; Jonker, "Textual Identities in Chronicles," 197–217; Lau, *Identity and Ethics in Ruth*; and Finitsis, "The Other in Haggai and Zechariah1-8," 116–31.

5. See nn3 and 4 above.

6. Baker, "New Covenant, New Identity," 5.6–5.9.

7. Bosman, *Social Identity in Nahum*; Jonkers, "Reforming History"; Jonker, "Textual Identities in Chronicles"; and Lau, *Identity and Ethics in Ruth*.

prophet and Dietrich's contention that the ingroup *you* represented King Manasseh.[8] Using a more systematic approach and focusing on the identity rhetoric of the narrative would have revealed how the ingroup "you" is not only overpowered in the narrative by the outgroup "you," but that there is a change of shared fate being narrated for both the ingroup and outgroup. Judah—who has been bound and afflicted by God—will be afflicted no more, and Nineveh—who has been "at full strength and many"—will "be cut off and pass away" (Nahum 1:12). Exposing these additional emotional formulations of identity helps to understand the significance of the shifting "you" as God, acting in the narrative, redefines the ingroup and outgroups. Thus, although our methodological approach—using the newly formed heuristic tool—is not determinative or predictive of biblical phenomena, it prompts the search for patterns, correlations, and coherency within narratives, and it permits comparison between them.

In Jonker's examination of the reign of Hezekiah in 2 Chronicles, the use of this heuristic tool would have offered specific examples to support his claim that the "reforming history" in Chronicles stood in the service of identity formation in the Persian province Yehud.[9] It would have illuminated Hezekiah's offer to Israel of a possible social identity in 2 Chronicles 29–31—one that is temporally continuous with ancestors descending from Abraham, Isaac, and Jacob, and yet discontinuous with their stubbornness and unfaithfulness. The tool would also expose how Hezekiah and his ancestor David, in contrast with the other kings of Israel and Judah, are shown as prototypes of this new identity.

Finitsis's work primarily examines what the methodological tool designates as cognitive and evaluative formulations of identity in Haggai and Zechariah, and Lau's book mainly explores behavioral expressions in Ruth. The application of our methodological tool offers them a more systematic approach which focuses on what is remembered and how it is told, and brings social identity formations in biblical narratives into direct conversation with the SIA. The use of this tool would ensure a thorough examination of the narrative construction of identity.

The application of the SIA methodology to exodus narratives has shown how a rhetorical and systematic approach reveals a plethora of insights into the possible narrative constructions of social identity. It represents the broadest and most systematic application of the SIA to the Hebrew Bible. While historical and interpretative questions are important, they are not the first that should be considered when examining the possible effect

---

8. Bosman, *Social Identity in Nahum*, 130.
9. Jonker, "Reforming History," 37.

of a narrative on its hearers. What hearers know and understand is dependent on how events are remembered, shaped, and narrated. For many generations of ancient Israel, the exodus was a collective memory rather than a lived experience. What Israel knew and believed was dependent on the cultural tools available to her—oral and written memory and cultic recital. This was the pertinent evidence that informed her worldview and motivated her actions. Therefore, primary consideration must always be given to the content, arrangement, and presentation of her memory (i.e., the "accessible narrative resource").

The application of my methodological tool to exodus narratives showed that the categories and verbal/imaginal representations chosen were valid. The only representation not found in exodus narratives was that of interdependence. Explicit verbal representations of cooperation and reliance were not noted within the narrative rhetoric. This is due to the nature of the story, which focused on God's intervention for Israel, rather than on a task to be accomplished by the ingroup. Cooperation and reliance are only implicit in Israel's original situation of adversity—making mortar and bricks, and building supply cities for Pharaoh. Interdependence would have been explicitly evident, however, in task-centered stories such as the building and rebuilding of the Temple. Therefore, this representation of an emotional formulation is considered appropriate to the tool despite the lack of examples in exodus narratives.

Not only is our methodological tool useful and presumably comprehensive, but it incorporates a new aspect into the temporal dimension of the SIA. Genealogical and cultural-ideological myths of common descent have been explored in studies of ethnic identity but have not previously been assimilated into the SIA. Not only is ethnic identity a subset of the more inclusive category of social or collective identity, but our analysis of exodus narratives has shown that myths of common descent are temporal formulations of identity, contributing to a group's sense of coherence over time.

Several limitations of this tool should be noted. Although the tool is useful for showing narrative constructions of identity, it cannot show that these constructions were intentional or that they resulted in subjectively perceived identity on the part of hearers.

Establishing intentionality is difficult in the best of circumstances, and when one is working with ancient texts written in a dissimilar culture and context, it is almost certainly impossible. The rhetorical formulations that were identified, however, are similar to those implicated in the creation and maintenance of a coherent collective identity in other contexts of study. Even though we cannot show that the producers of exodus narratives were consciously committed to an "identity project," we have shown that rhetorical devices similar to those found in face-to-face relationships are present in exodus narrative and, therefore, have the potential to produce identity in hearers.

Just as this study cannot presume knowledge of the motivations of the producers of the exodus narratives, it cannot demonstrate that exodus identity was subjectively perceived or keenly felt by ancient Israel. That is to say, an investigation of narrative rhetoric cannot demonstrate that Israel as a people actually consumed and assumed the collective identity constructed by the narratives. We can conclude, however, that the narrative rhetoric was of such a nature that it would have persuaded the unresisting hearer and socialized him or her into this identity.

Opportunities for Further Study

Several opportunities for further study have emerged as a direct result of this analysis.

Applying the Methodology to Short References to Exodus

Short references to exodus were excluded from consideration in this study. These either contain only a single plot element of the primary exodus story (e.g., Deut 1:30 and 34:10–12) or elements that are not linked together in the form of a story (e.g., Exod 32:11). Limiting the present study to only exodus stories was justified by prior research in literary studies, which had specifically established the involvement of the narrative genre in social identity construction. Now that *exodus* stories have been shown in this analysis to rhetorically construct identity, however, other articulations of *exodus* may also be evaluated for evidence of identity formulations. Also, since all retold exodus stories contained the third plot element—the bringing out of Israel—short references containing this element in particular should be carefully analyzed. Again, to avoid charges of determinism, the methodological tool must be used carefully as a heuristic device, examining and comparing the short references in a search for patterns, correlations, and coherency.

An application of the methodological tool to the short reference to exodus identified in the third section of Appendix 2 may either confirm the comprehensiveness of identity formulations established in the methodological tool or bring to light other formulations that previously have been overlooked. Such a study will undoubtedly identify other settings and periods of social change in which the memory of exodus purportedly constructed identity. This, for example, might give support to studies by Hoffman, van der Toorn, and Albertz who view the establishment of the Northern Kingdom as a setting in which the exodus myth was vital in constructing Israel's collective identity.[10]

Inscribed memories of Joshua's and Josiah's initiatives to commemorate the Passover (Josh 5:10–12; 2 Kgs 23:21–30) are another possible area in which to examine identity formulations. Examining these commemorations of exodus may provide additional imaginal formulations of identity that were not evident in the more verbal remembrances of exodus.

Exploring Conflicting Myths of Israel's Origin

Another area of further research arises from the claim of these narratives that being "the people whom God brought out of Egypt" was the feature of Israel that was boundary forming (i.e., significant and defining for the group). This contrasts with another myth of common descent evident in the Hebrew Bible, later Judaism, and Christianity that traces Israel's identity by means of genealogical descent from the patriarchs. This analysis showed how exodus stories compellingly promote the myth of cultural-ideological kinship. Nevertheless, it leaves questions about the origin of the genealogical myth. Understanding when, where, and why genealogical expressions took on significance for Israel's identity formulation are important to this conversation and require further research.

Examining Historical Contexts of Plurivocal Exodus Stories

Exodus narratives likely constructed and maintained ancient Israel's group identity at various periods of transition and social upheaval throughout her history. Although exodus stories were set at key places within Israel's overall story, the narratives, in reality, may not have informed Israel's collective identity in those particular socio-historical contexts. Their placement there may simply express an ideological stance of the producers of the narratives who were attempting to emphasize the importance of these particular transitions in Israel's history.

Having accomplished the aim of this analysis, namely the recognition of rhetorical formulations capable of constructing and maintaining group identity, and having noted a plurivocity of exodus stories and formulations, the subsequent challenge would be to see if the ideologies,

---

10. Hoffman, "North Israelite Typological Myth; Van der Toorn, "Exodus as Charter Myth"; and Albertz, "Exodus."

reinterpretations, and adaptions made to the various exodus stories offer insight into the context in which each story was composed or the audience for which it was intended.

Some narrative clues may initially seem quite obvious. Jeremiah's and Nehemiah's stories suggest exilic and post-exilic redactions respectively. The portrayal of pre-exodus Israel as idolatrous in Joshua's retelling and as heedless and un-remembering in Psalm 106's exodus story suggests at least an exilic redaction, when such culpability in Israel was undeniable. The stories of Deuteronomy and Psalm 136, with their added interpretations of exodus as evidence of God's love and election, may also have been redacted with a demoralized and marginalized exilic Israel in mind.

Compositional history is more complex, however, than these seemingly obvious narrative clues. Several of the retold exodus stories examined, for example, represent Israel going directly from Egypt to the land (Deut 4:34–38, Deut 6:20–23, Deut 26:5–9, 1 Sam 12:6–8, and Jer 32:20–23a). Following a tradition-historical approach that views themes (such as wilderness) as having been gradually added to the earlier exodus theme, one would have to conclude that these retold stories were composed earlier than the primary exodus story, which shows Israel moving from the exodus, to the wilderness and finally into the land. This is clearly not the case. Hakola cautions against assuming a direct correlation between narrative rhetoric and existing socio-historical context. It is possible that narrative rhetoric is simply a product of the effort to construct a clearly defined social identity rather than a direct reflection of the real world.[11] In the exodus stories mentioned above, group identification processes are seen as constructing an ideal identity for Israel that excludes the narration of wilderness failings. The absence of wilderness themes, therefore, is not a good indication of a particular time of composition, but rather of an ideological stance.

Identification of the historical context of exodus narratives will allow for a mnemohistorical discourse analysis[12] that traces the chronology of memory and seeks out the threads of connectivity working behind the narratives, such as intertextuality, evolution of ideas, recourse to forgotten evidence, shifts of focus, and so forth. Developmental ordering of exodus narratives may also permit an application of Baker's narrative identity model,[13] showing how identity-shaping processes evident in one exodus narrative may interact with hearers' pre-existing identities to either reinforce or transform them.

---

11. Hakola, "Burden of Ambiguity," 453.
12. See Assmann, *Moses the Egyptian* and Delumeau, *History of Paradise*.
13. Baker, *Identity, Memory, and Narrative in early Christianity*, 28–30.

Further efforts to identify the historical context of exodus narratives will require a complex examination of social context, linguistic clues, storylines, webs of intertextuality, and diachronic continuities and discontinuities.

Examining Exodus Narratives in Conversation with Other Identity Narratives

It is also important to note that the plurivocity of these exodus stories came together in conversation at some point in Israel's history, likely in the post-exilic period. While ancient Israel existed as a collective from the Iron Age I though the Roman Period, self-definition was particularly critical to the survival of ancient Israel during the exilic and post-exilic periods. Due to her central concerns of identity, continuity, and self-definition, the rhetoric of exodus narratives and other available narrative resources would have had a significant effect on her identity construction and maintenance. While ancient Israel may not have been homogeneous even during the final periods of narrative editing and reception, scholars have noted some of her characteristic features. The loss of national autonomy and the dissolution of Israel as a geographic entity occasioned by the exile generated shame and self-blame. Israel found herself a conquered, scattered, endangered, and marginalized people.[14] Brueggemann maintains that

> For ancient Israel, [the exile] was the end of privilege, certitude, domination, viable public institutions and a sustaining social fabric. It was the end of life with God, which Israel had taken for granted. In that wrenching time, ancient Israel faced the temptation of denial—the pretense that there had been no loss—and it faced the temptation of despair—the inability to see any way out.[15]

Cornell notes that following "periods of rupture," when people experience such large-scale changes, the normally taken-for-granted collective identities are questioned by those who carry them, contested by others and severely tested by events.[16] Certainly, the post-exile period was one such time when the ruinous cultural effects of Israel's demoralizing crisis posed a significant challenge to her self-understanding.

---

14. Scalise, "The End of the Old Testament," 172.
15. Brueggemann, "Conversations among Exiles," 630.
16. Cornell, "Story of Our Life," 45. Cornell is speaking here in generalities and not specifically about the post-exilic period.

Japhet supports the assertion that this period is best defined by the central concerns occupying Israel: questions of identity, continuity, and self-definition.[17] The significant political and social reorientation of the restoration period required Israel to redefine herself in the context of a world empire.[18] Israel tackled the question, "What is it that really constitutes Israel?" with various identity resources in hand that had the potential to play a role in her negotiation of collective identity.

Cornell and Hartmann also argue that "identity construction is most apparent during periods of social change, such as migration or social upheaval."[19] This claim is endorsed by others[20] and bolstered by case studies on identity construction among immigrants.[21]

The narratives of the Hebrew Bible undoubtedly served as identity resources within contexts of social upheaval characterized by migration, conflicts with other nations, displacement, and domination.[22] The resources described in the works of Bosman, Jonkers, Finitsis, and Lau, namely, the texts of Nahum, Chronicles, Haggai, Zechariah, Ruth and, comparatively, Ezra–Nehemiah must be placed in conversation with exodus narratives. This will offer insight into the ongoing effect of exodus narrative on Israel's collective identity in both dissonance and consonance with other identity resources.

With additional study, the shared exodus story may be shown to be an attempt at a cohesive identity in Yehud, to achieve the "rebirth" of the nation as Finitsis posits.[23] When exodus narratives are placed in conversation with Finitsis's study of identity construction in Haggai,[24] however, at least one of his conclusions is challenged. The possibility of the "othering" of Israel does indeed exist in Israel's ancient narratives, particularly in the exodus stories of Psalm 78 and Nehemiah 9.

17. Japhet, From the Rivers of Babylon, 432.

18. This premise has been repeatedly reinforced in the compiled works of Lipschits, Knoppers, Oeming, *Judah and the Judeans in the Achaemenid Period*; and Lipschits and Oeming, *Judah and the Judeans in the Persian Period*.

19. Cornell and Hartmann, *Ethnicity and Race*, 211.

20. Assmann, *Das kulturelle Gedächtnis*, 32–33; Spaulding, *Commemorative Identities*; and Halbwachs, *Les cadres sociaux de la mémoire*, 185–86.

21. De Fina, *Identity in Narrative*; Peterson, *Popular Narratives and Ethnic Identity*; Arnone, "Journeys to Exile," 325–40; Ballinger, *History in Exile*.

22. Isbell argues that the final edition of the exodus story was framed in the crisis of the early exilic period. Such an argument is not germane to this analysis because the social, cultural, and theological crisis of exile extended far into the Restoration Period. Isbell, *Function of Exodus Motifs*, 6–11.

23. Finitsis, "The Other in Haggai and Zechariah 1–8," 120.

24. Ibid., 121.

CONCLUSION

Exodus narratives take collective identity back farther in time to a unified place in history and a foundational identity story. It moves away from a simply genealogical boundary for shared identity, as Lau notes in his study of identity construction in Ruth,[25] and makes possible the inclusion of outsiders. The conversation between myths of cultural-ideological and genealogical descent must be examined developmentally and ideologically to determine when, where, and why the genealogical myth was taken up as an expression of Israel's identity.

Exodus narratives portray coherent group identity as achieved and not acquired. Sometimes they call for a superior ethical behavior, as Finitsis notes in Zechariah[26] (Deut 4:34–39; 6:13–25; Ps 106:43–45), but more often this identity is portrayed as achieved by remembering, retelling, and living in light of the exodus. Some voices of the exodus, namely Jeremiah 32 and Psalm 106, even assert the possibility of a continuing and coherent identity in Israel despite her failure to live by exodus. This is based on the illogical paradigm of exodus deliverance and God's own exodus identity characterized by חסד (Ps 106:7; cf. Exod 15:13).

Exodus stories also seem to offer a response to the polarized identity of Ezra–Nehemiah: One does not have to be a "returnee" from Persia to have an "exodus" story and be a legitimate member of Israel. This is where future study on the development of the narratives is crucial to determining if one identity claim is a response to the other or if they existed as competing identity claims.

The mutual conversation of exodus identity and other identity narratives prominent in the post-exilic period must be considered. The goal would not be to harmonize these stories disingenuously but rather to recognize from the start that the question, "What is it that really constitutes Israel?" was negotiated with various resources from Israel's sacred scriptures in hand.

Various identity negotiations may attempt either to create cohesiveness or to promote exclusion. Further comparative research is needed to understand fully how exodus narratives participated in this identity conversation following the exile and throughout the remainder of Israel's history. Because possible social identities are limited by resources and socialization into those resources, the significance of the recurring exodus story in mediating identity should not be ignored.

* * *

---

25. Lau, *Identity and Ethics in Ruth*.
26. Finitsis, "The Other in Haggai and Zechariah 1–8," 130.

This study has shown that narrative resources in particular had the potential to influence the process and practice of collective identification in ancient Israel, mediating realities to the present experience of those who used them. Analysis of recurring exodus stories has demonstrated that whether the producers of the narratives were consciously instigating an identity project to fend off assimilation and create an identity, or unconsciously reflecting a contemporary ideological struggle, the artistry and design of the narratives, particularly their rhetorical formulations of identity, highlight their potential as identity resources.

Appendix 1

Prior Research on Identity and Memory in Text

1. General Studies on Collective Identity in Text

a. In Literature

De Fina, Anna. *Identity in Narrative: A Study of Immigrant Discourse.* Amsterdam: Benjamin's, 2003.
Linde, Charlotte. *Working the Past: Narrative and Institutional Memory.* New York: Oxford University Press, 2009.
Somers, Margaret R., and Gloria D. Gibson. "Reclaiming the Epistemological 'Other': Narrative and the Social Constitution of Identity." In *Social Theory and the Politics of Identity*, edited by Craig Calhoun, 37–99. Oxford: Blackwell, 1994.
Vila, Pablo. "Narrative Identities: The Employment of the Mexican on the U.S.-Mexican Border." *Sociological Quarterly* 38 (1997) 147–83.
Wertsch, James V. *Voices of Collective Remembering.* Cambridge: Cambridge University Press, 2002.
Whitmarsh, Tim. *Greek Literature and the Roman Empire: The Politics of Imitation.* Oxford: Oxford University Press, 2001.

b. In Biblical Texts

Esler, Philip F. "Ezra-Nehemiah as a Narrative of (Re-invented) Israelite Identity." *Biblical Interpretation* 11 (2003) 413–26.
George, Mark. "Constructing Identity in 1 Samuel 17." *Biblical Interpretation: A Journal of Contemporary Approaches* 7, no. 4 (1999) 389–412.
Greifenhagen, F. V. *Egypt on the Pentateuch's Ideological Map: Constructing Biblical Israel's Identity.* London: Sheffield Academic, 2002.
Jonker, Louis. "Reforming History: The Hermeneutical Significance of the Books of Chronicles." *Vetus Testamentum* 57 (2007) 21–44.
Knoppers, Gary N., and Kenneth A. Ristau, editors. *Community Identity in Judean Historiography: Biblical and Comparative Perspectives.* Winona Lake, IN: Eisenbrauns, 2009.

Linville, James R. *Israel in the Book of Kings: The Past as a Project of Social Identity.* JSOTS 272. Sheffield: Sheffield Academic, 1998.

Lipschits, Oded, Gary Knoppers, Manfred Oeming, eds. *Judah and the Judeans in the Achaemenid Period: Negotiating Identity in an International Context.* Winona Lake, IN: Eisenbrauns, 2011.

Lipschits, Oded, and Manfred Oeming, eds. *Judah and the Judeans in the Persian Period.* Winona Lake, IN: Eisenbrauns, 2006.

Liss, Hanna, and Manfred Oeming, eds. *Literary Construction of Identity in the Ancient World: Proceedings of a Conference, Literary Fiction and the Construction of Identity in Ancient Literatures: Options and Limits of Modern Literary Approaches in the Exegesis of Ancient Texts, Heidelberg, July 10-13, 2006.* Winona Lake, IN: Eisenbrauns, 2010.

Mullen, E. Theodore. *Ethnic Myths and Pentateuchal Foundations: A New Approach to the Formation of the Pentateuch.* Society of Biblical Literature Semeia Studies. Atlanta: Scholars, 1997.

Sparks, Kenton L. *Ethnicity and Identity in Ancient Israel: Prolegomena to the Study of Ethnic Sentiments and their Expression in the Hebrew Bible.* Winona Lake, IN: Eisenbrauns, 1998.

van Henten, Jan Willem, and Anton Houtepen, eds. *Religious Identity and the Invention of Tradition: Papers Read at a NOSTER Conference in Soesterberg January 4-6, 1999.* Studies in Theology and Religion 3. Assen, Netherlands: Van Gorcum, 2001.

2. Collective Memory in the Hebrew Bible

Greenstein, Edward L. "Mixing Memory and Design: Reading Psalm 78." *Prooftexts* 10 no. 2 (1990) 197–219.

Hendel, Ronald. *Remembering Abraham: Culture, Memory, and History in the Hebrew Bible.* New York: Oxford University Press, 2005.

Smith, Mark S. "Remembering God: Collective Memory in Israelite Religion." *Catholic Biblical Quarterly* 64, no. 4 (2002) 631–51.

Smith, Mark S. *The Memoires of God: History, Memory, and the Experience of the Divine in Ancient Israel.* Minneapolis: Fortress, 2004.

Yadin, Azzan. "Goliath's Armor and Israelite Collective memory." *Vetus Testamentum* 54, no. 3 (2004) 373–95.

Yerushalmi, Yosef Hayim. *Zakhor: Jewish History and Jewish Memory.* Seattle: University of Washington Press, 1982.

3. Exodus as Israel's Collective Memory

Blenkinsopp, Joseph. "Memory, Tradition, and the Construction of the Past in Ancient Israel." *Biblical Theology Bulletin* 27 (1997) 76–82.

Brettler, Marc Zvi. "Memory in Ancient Israel." In *Memory and History in Christianity and Judaism*, edited by M. Signer, 1–17. Notre Dame: University of Notre Dame Press, 2001.

Hendel, Ronald. "The Exodus in Biblical Memory." *Journal of Biblical Literature* 120, no. 4 (2001) 601–22.

Stargel, Linda M. "Social Memory and the Exodus Tradition." ThM thesis, Duke University, 2007.

Appendix 2

Direct References to Exodus in the Hebrew Bible

1. Primary exodus story—Exodus 1:1–15:21
2. Retold exodus stories

Num 20:14–16	Deut 6:21–23	Josh 24:2–7, 17	Ps 105:23–39
Deut 4:20	Deut 7:18–19	1 Sam 12:6–8	Ps 106:7–12, 21–23
Deut 4:34–38	Deut 11:2–4, 7	Jer 32:20–23a	Ps 136:10–15, 23–24
Deut 5:15, 15:15, 24:18	Deut 26:5–9	Ps 78:11–14, 42–53	Neh 9:9–12, (36)

3. Short references to exodus

   a. Recalling exodus as motivation for law keeping and for the fair treatment of others

Exod 19:4	Lev 11:45	Deut 10:19	Deut 29:1–2
Exod 20:2; Deut 5:6	Lev 19:34, 36	Deut 23:4–8	1 Sam 15:2, 6
Exod 22:20	Lev 25:38	Deut 24:9	2 Kgs 17:36; Hos 13:4
Exod 23:9	Lev 25:42	Deut 24:22	Jer 7:22
Lev 11:45	Lev 25:55	Deut 25:17	

   b. Recalling exodus in the observance of calendrical celebrations

Exod 34:8	Lev 23:43	Deut 16:1–3	Deut 16:12

   c. Recalling exodus as justification for other institutions such as the Levitical priesthood, inheritance of the land, the prophetic office.

Num 3:13	Num 8:17	Num 26:4	Deut 34:10–12

d. Recalling exodus as a historical watershed and means of measuring the passage of time.

Exod 16:1	Num 1:1	Num 33:38	Judg 19:30	2 Kgs 21:15
Exod 16:32	Num 9:1	Deut 4:45–46	1 Sam 8:8	Jer 7:25
Exod 19:1	Num 14:19	Deut 9:7	2 Sam 7:6	Jer 11:7
Exod 23:15	Num 33:1–5	Josh 5:4–6	1 Kgs 6:1	Hag 2:5

e. Recalling exodus to define Israel's God and to motivate confidence in times of stress.

| Exod 32:11 | Deut 20:1 | Is 43:16–17 | Is 63:11–14 | Ps 135:8–9 |
| Deut 1:30 | Judg 6:13 | Is 51:10 | Ps 77:13–20 | |

f. Recalling exodus as a means of defining Israel's unique covenant relationship to God.

Exod 16:6	Num 15:41	Deut 13:10	1 Kgs 9:9
Exod 29:46	Deut 1:27	Deut 29:25	2 Kgs 17:7
Exod 32:1, 4, 7, 8, 11, 23; 33:1 (1 Kgs 12:28)	Deut 4:20	Judg 2:1, 12	Jer 2:6
Lev 11:45	Deut 6:12	Judg 6:8–10	Jer 11:4
Lev 22:33	Deut 7:7–8	1 Sam 10:18	Hosea 11:1–5
Lev 25:38	Deut 8:14	2 Sam 7:23–24 (1 Chr 17:21)	Amos 2:10, 3:1, 9:7
Lev 25:55	Deut 9:26	1 Kgs 8:21	Micah 6:4
Lev 26:13, 45	Deut 13:5	1 Kgs 8:51, 53	Psalm 114:1–3

g. Recalling exodus to distinguish present situation from the past

Exod 16:3	Num 20:5	Isa 10:24–26	Ezek 20:5–10, 34–38
Exod 17:3	Num 21:5	Isa 11:16	Hos 2:15
Num 11:5, 18, 20	Num 32:11	Jer 16:14; 23:7	
Num 14:2–4	Deut 11:10	Jer 31:32	

h. Recognition of Israel's exodus identity by outsiders

| Exod. 18:1, 9–11 | Josh 2:10 | 1 Kgs 9:9 (2 Chr 7:22) |
| Num 22:5, 11; 23:22, 24:8 | Judg 11:13 | Jer 16:14, 23:7 |

Appendix 3

Three Translation Models for Exodus 15:13–18

Carol Meyers (NCBC)	Sarna (JPSTC)	Dozeman (ECC)
¹³In your steadfast love you **led** the people who you **redeemed**; you **guided** them by your strength to your holy abode.	¹³In Your love You **lead** the people You **redeemed**; In Your strength You **guide** them to Your holy abode.	¹³You **led** in your steadfast love the people whom you **redeemed**;
¹⁴The peoples **heard**, they **trembled**;	¹⁴The peoples **hear**, they **tremble**; Agony **grips** the dwellers in Philistia.	¹⁴People **heard,** they **trembled**. Pangs **seized** the inhabitants of Philistia.
¹⁵Then the chiefs of Edom **were dismayed**;	¹⁵Now **are** the clans of Edom **dismayed**; The tribes of Moab—trembling **grips** them; All the dwellers in Canaan **are** aghast.	¹⁵Then the chiefs of Edom **were terrified**. The leaders of Moab, trembling **seized** them. All the inhabitants of Canaan **melted**.
¹⁶Terror and dread **fell** upon them; by the might of your arm, they **became** still as stone until your people, O LORD, **passed by**, until the people whom you acquired passed by.	¹⁶Terror and dread **descend** upon them; Through the might of Your arm they **are** still as stone—Till Your people **cross over**, O LORD, Till Your people **cross** whom You **have ransomed**.	¹⁶Terror and dread **fell** upon them; at your great arm they **became** silent like a stone. Until your people **cross over**, Yahweh,
¹⁷You **brought** them in and **planted** them on the mountain of your own possession, the place, O LORD, that you **made** your abode, the sanctuary, O LORD, that your hands **have** established.	¹⁷You **will bring** them and plant them in Your own mountain, The place You **made** to dwell in, O LORD, The sanctuary, O LORD, which Your hands **established**.	¹⁷You **will bring** them in and **plant** them on the mountain of your inheritance, the place for your dwelling that you **made**, Yahweh,
¹⁸The LORD **will reign** forever and ever.	¹⁸The LORD **reigns** for ever and ever!	¹⁸Yahweh **will reign** forever and ever

Appendix 4
Methodology Worksheets

Genesis 12:1–50:26 (Prologue to the Primary Exodus Narrative)

Verbal or Imaginal Representations	Definition or Example
Cognitive Formulations	
Categorization	
Named Group (group name or label)	Hittites, Canaanites, and Perizzites (23:7; 34:30)—names of collective peoples. "Israelites" x 1 as a collective people—used anachronistically in 32:33. Otherwise, "Sons of Israel" is used literarily to refer to a fix set of sons and not to a people group. "Hebrews" is used twice as an ethnic designation of proto-Israelites (40:15, 43:32)
Plural Pronouns	
Boundaries	There are ill-defined boundaries between Israel and Egypt because of the conflicting images of Israel's integration with and separation from Egypt. Goshen—either as an actual location or an ideological construct—serves as a means of establishing a distinct identity for Israel.
Shared Beliefs	
Prototypes	
Stereotypes	

Verbal or Imaginal Representations	Definition or Example
Evaluative Formulations	
Differentiation	Conflicting images of Israel's integration with and separation from Egypt
Positive Evaluation of the Ingroup	
Devaluation of the "Other"	
Emotional Formulations	
Inter-Group Conflict	
Attachment and Belonging	
Interdependence	
Shared Fate	All members of Proto-Israel went down into Egypt
Behavioral Formulations	
Identity Norms	
Temporal Formulations	
Coherency Over Time	
Possible Social Identities	
Myths of Common Descent	
Genealogical	
Cultural-Ideological	
Shared Life Stories	
Obligation to Tell	Pre-tellings of exodus in 15:13–16 and 50:24
Actualization	Proto-exodus of Abram (12:10–20) and of Jacob (46:1–47:12; 50:-14)

Exodus 1:1–15:21 (Primary Exodus Story)

Verbal or Imaginal Representations	*Definition or Example*
Cognitive Formulations	
Categorization	
Named Group (group name or label)	"Hebrews" is used 13 times to designate a collective people, and "Israelites" is used 51 times. Israel is also referred to collectively as "the people" and "my people." "Israel" and "Egypt" take on increased significance as separate and distinct peoples.
Plural Pronouns	
Boundaries	Boundary of "Goshen" continues to set Israel apart from Egypt either literally or ideologically. Israel is also defined as a people capable of worship Yahweh, compared to Egyptians who find such practices detestable (8:25–26)
	Beginning of a new ingroup defined as "the people whom God brought out of Egypt." This group is exceedingly large (12:37), either literally or symbolically, and ethnically diverse (12:38). According to the second Passover narrative in 12:43–49, "the people whom God brought out of Egypt" has a boundary that may be crossed into by outsiders.
Shared Beliefs	
Prototypes	Moses and Aaron are the most visible members of the ingroup, notable for their obedience. As Israel emerges, their characterization is like that of Moses and Aaron, they "did just as the Lord had commanded" (12:28).
	Pharaoh—who is arrogant, obdurate, and recalcitrant—become the prototype for the outgroup, while the portrayal of Egypt itself remains more ambiguous.
Stereotypes	

Verbal or Imaginal Representations	Definition or Example
Evaluative Formulations	
Differentiation	Conflicting images of integration and separation give way to a clear and physical differentiation between Israel and Egypt in the stories of the plagues and the Israel's eventually coming up out of Egypt.
Positive Evaluation of the Ingroup	God acts supernaturally in favor of Israel
Devaluation of the "Other"	Mockery of Egyptian power (7:8–13)
	Mockery of Pharaoh's authority (10:28, 12:31–32)
	Mockery of Pharaoh's judgment (13:15, 14:3, 5, 23–25)
	Fall of the Outgroup (15:5, 10, 12)
Emotional Formulations	
Inter-Group Conflict	
Attachment and Belonging	Initial solidarity with one another in suffering (1:9–22). Eventual attachment to one another and Yahweh as "my people."
Interdependence	
Shared Fate	Shared fate first of suffering, oppression, and collective crying out. Later a shared fate of deliverance.
Behavioral Formulations	
Identity Norms	All Israel will commemorate exodus (12:14–20), will retell the story (10:2) and will participate in an atemporal Song of Deliverance (15:1–21)
Temporal Formulations	
Coherency Over Time	A family of individual actors ("sons of Israel") gives way to a collective ("sons of Israel"). Promises to the one becomes fulfillment to the other. The God of the patriarchs is the God of Israel. There is also a discontinuity as this new collective Israel is born out of the suffering in and deliverance from Egypt.

Verbal or Imaginal Representations	Definition or Example
Possible Social Identities	
Myths of Common Descent	
Genealogical	Israel's descent from the patriarchs
Cultural-Ideological	Israel's solidarity with those who suffered in and were delivered from Egypt
Shared Life Stories	
Obligation to Tell	Children and grandchildren are to be told of God's supernatural deeds on behalf of Israel and their meaning (10:2). Children who ask about the meaning of Passover during its annual re-performances are to be told of the original Passover and its meaning (12:25–27). Israel is to remember the exodus in the Feast of Unleavened Bread (13:3), telling children why it is celebrated (13:8). They are to tell about God's delivering of Israel from slavery when children ask why the first born in consecrated. They are to set up remembrances as a means of telling.
Actualization	Exodus is re-actualized in the experience of each generation that hears and commemorates it in the annual celebrations. New members are incorporated into the shared story. This is illustrated in the participatory nature of Exod 15:1–2

Numbers 20:14–16 (17–21)

Verbal or Imaginal Representations	Definition or Example
Cognitive Formulations	
Categorization	
Named Group (group name or label)	The named groups include "your brother Israel" (14), "our ancestors" x 2 (15). Also "us and our ancestors" comprise a single entity that can cry out and be heard. "Egypt" is portrayed collectively (15–16) as are Israel and Edom (17–20)

APPENDIX 4: METHODOLOGY WORKSHEETS

Verbal or Imaginal Representations	*Definition or Example*
Plural Pronouns	The collective pronouns "we"/"us" are used (x 6, 14–16). There is an absence of "them" when referring to the ancestors.
Boundaries	"Your brother Israel" is defined by the story of adversity, crying out, being heard, and being brought out of Egypt.
	Edom is portrayed as a brother to Israel.
Shared Beliefs	There is an implicit belief in the reality of the exodus
Prototypes	Messengers are portrayed as speaking on behalf of all Israel (past and present). They tell the exodus story.
	The King of Edom represents collective Edom (question addressed to King [17] is answered by the group [18–21]). As a collective, Edom knows of Israel's past adversity.
Stereotypes	Egyptians oppress.
	Edom (as a whole) refuses Israel and comes out against her
	Both Egypt and Edom are portrayed as antagonistic "others"
Evaluative Formulations	
Differentiation	A distinction is made between Israel and Egypt (oppressed and oppressor) and between Israel and Edom (*One brother suffered, the other apparently did not, One brother requests, the other refuses*)
Positive Evaluation of the Ingroup	The narrative makes the unresisting hearer sympathetic to Israel.
Devaluation of the "Other"	There is an implicit devaluation of Edom as the "other": Edom's knowledge of Israel's story and Edom's sibling status are meaningless

Verbal or Imaginal Representations	Definition or Example
Emotional Formulations	
Inter-Group Conflict	Israel experiences adversity at the hands of both Egypt (14–16) and Edom (18–21)
Attachment and Belonging	The story alternates between "our ancestors" and "us"
Interdependence	
Shared Fate	The shared fate of adversity extends across generations (14–16)
Behavioral Formulations	
Identity Norms	
Temporal Formulations	
Coherency Over Time	The past and present generation are portrayed as one across time; they share the story of adversity and deliverance
Possible Social Identities	
Myths of Common Descent	
Genealogical	Israel is linked genealogically by terminology only: "ancestors"
Cultural-Ideological	Ancestors are united with the present generation in their experience of oppression and deliverance
Shared Life Stories	
Obligation to Tell	Number 20:14–16 complies with the primary narrative's imperative to tell the exodus story. The story is portrayed as being retold within a different historical context.
Actualization	

Deuteronomy 4:20

Verbal or Imaginal Representations	Definition or Example
Cognitive Formulations	
Categorization	
Named Group (group name or label)	Egypt is depicted as an "iron smelter," Israel as "a people of his very own possession."
Plural Pronouns	You (pl.) x 2
Boundaries	
Shared Beliefs	
Prototypes	
Stereotypes	
Evaluative Formulations	
Differentiation	
Positive Evaluation of the Ingroup	The ingroup has implicit value: she was taken from an agonizing existence and reconstituted as the people of God
Devaluation of the "Other"	The context differentiates Israel from other nations and their non-gods (4:15–19)
Emotional Formulations	
Inter-Group Conflict	
Attachment and Belonging	Belonging is evident in the claim that Israel is "a people of his very own possession"
Interdependence	
Shared Fate	Prior identity as a people in an "iron smelter" is contrasted with present identity as "a people of [God's] very own possession"

Verbal or Imaginal Representations	Definition or Example
Behavioral Formulations	
Identity Norms	The exodus story is enveloped by exhortations to shun the idolatrous practices of other nations
Temporal Formulations	
Coherency Over Time	The new generation is addressed as the exodus generation. God's inheritance is portrayed as one from the exodus to the present
Possible Social Identities	
Myths of Common Descent	
Genealogical	
Cultural-Ideological	
Shared Life Stories	
Obligation to Tell	
Actualization	

Deuteronomy 4:34–38

Verbal or Imaginal Representations	Definition or Example
Cognitive Formulations	
Categorization	
Named Group (group name or label)	Israel is a "nation" from the midst of a "nation" (34)
Plural Pronouns	
Boundaries	
Shared Beliefs	
Prototypes	
Stereotypes	

APPENDIX 4: METHODOLOGY WORKSHEETS

Verbal or Imaginal Representations	*Definition or Example*
Evaluative Formulations	
Differentiation	Rhetorical question "Has any god . . .?" portrays the exodus as a unique intervention from God (34)
Positive Evaluation of the Ingroup	
Devaluation of the "Other"	"Strong hand," "mighty arm"—these epithets used about pharaohs were taken to describe Israel's God. The concept that God "took for himself" emphasizes his power over the other (34).
Emotional Formulations	
Inter-Group Conflict	There are images and language of hostile intergroup conflict (34, 38)
Attachment and Belonging	God took for himself a nation. He loved, chose, brought out (37).
Interdependence	
Shared Fate	Israel was taken from one nation by God's supernatural intervention. Other nations will be driven out until she is brought into her inheritance. Wilderness language (masa) is even hijacked as deliverance language (34).
Behavioral Formulations	
Identity Norms	
Temporal Formulations	
Coherency Over Time	Loved *fathers*, chose *seed*, led *you* out . . . (shifting recipients)
Possible Social Identities	
Myths of Common Descent	
Genealogical	
Cultural-Ideological	

Verbal or Imaginal Representations	Definition or Example
Shared Life Stories	Inclusive story (see above)
Obligation to Tell	
Actualization	New generation is persuaded to remember exodus generation's experience as if it occurred before their eyes.

Deuteronomy 5:15, 15:15, 24:18

Verbal or Imaginal Representations	Definition or Example
Cognitive Formulations	
Categorization	
Named Group (group name or label)	Previous corporate identity: a slave (sing)
Plural Pronouns	*You (sing) is used to address all Israel
Boundaries	Israel is being defined as a brought-out slave (5:15) or a redeemed slave (15:15; 24:18)
Shared Beliefs	
Prototypes	
Stereotypes	
Evaluative Formulations	
Differentiation	
Positive Evaluation of the Ingroup	
Devaluation of the "Other"	
Emotional Formulations	
Inter-Group Conflict	God brought out Israel with "a mighty hand and an outstretched arm" (5:15)
Attachment and Belonging	Israel is reminded that "the Lord your God" acted on her behalf
Interdependence	

Verbal or Imaginal Representations	Definition or Example
Shared Fate	Israel is portrayed as having a shared fate, first as a slave then as a brought-out/redeemed one
Behavioral Formulations	
Identity Norms	Remember exodus, and Israel's own transformation of fate, should result in keeping the Sabbath (5:15), freeing (with liberal provision) fellow Hebrew slaves in the seventh year of servitude (15:12–15), and treating equitably the poor, orphans, widows, and other disadvantaged people (24:18–22).
Temporal Formulations	
Coherency Over Time	
Possible Social Identities	
Myths of Common Descent	
Genealogical	
Cultural-Ideological	
Shared Life Stories	
Obligation to Tell	Israel has an obligation to remember in a transformative way
Actualization	

Deuteronomy 6:21–23

Verbal or Imaginal Representations	Definition or Example
Cognitive Formulations	
Categorization	
Named Group (group name or label)	Israel's past identity: Pharaoh's slaves (plural) in Egypt (21)
Plural Pronouns	
Boundaries	
Shared Beliefs	

Verbal or Imaginal Representations	Definition or Example
Prototypes	
Stereotypes	
Evaluative Formulations	
Differentiation	God acted for Israel and against Egypt, against Pharaoh and his entire household (22)
Positive Evaluation of the Ingroup	
Devaluation of the "Other"	
Emotional Formulations	
Inter-Group Conflict	Conflict is depicted in images of Israel being brought out of Egypt by a mighty hand, signs, and wonders
Attachment and Belonging	As slaves, Israel belonged to Pharaoh, as "brought out ones" she implicitly belongs to God and must serve him (24–25)
Interdependence	
Shared Fate	
Behavioral Formulations	
Identity Norms	Exodus is the motivation for exclusive allegiance to Yahweh and obedience to the law (24–25)
Temporal Formulations	
Coherency Over Time	This story narrates the exodus as happening "before our eyes" (22). The children are included in this eyewitness experience.
Possible Social Identities	
Myths of Common Descent	
Genealogical	
Cultural-Ideological	The solidarity of generations is portrayed in an inclusive exodus story
Shared Life Stories	

Verbal or Imaginal Representations	Definition or Example
Obligation to Tell	In the future when children ask the meaning of Israel's decrees, statutes, and ordinances (20), the parent is obliged to tell the child of exodus, including him/her in the story (changing the child's non-inclusive pronouns to inclusive ones)
Actualization	Exodus is re-actualized in the retelling to the young generation

Deuteronomy 7:18–19

Verbal or Imaginal Representations	Definition or Example
Cognitive Formulations	
Categorization	
Named Group (group name or label)	
Plural Pronouns	The second person singular is used throughout. The context, especially Deut 7:6, makes it clear that this singular "you" refers to a collective people rather than to an individual.
Boundaries	
Shared Beliefs	
Prototypes	
Stereotypes	
Evaluative Formulations	
Differentiation	The prior literary context differentiates between Israel and the nations. This is reflected in exhortations to not intermarry, to destroy them without pity, and to demolish their altars and idols (7:1–5, 16)

Verbal or Imaginal Representations	Definition or Example
Positive Evaluation of the Ingroup	Israel is holy, chosen, treasured, loved, and redeemed (7:6–8). Exodus is the proof of her distinctiveness and positive value
Devaluation of the "Other"	Exodus is portrayed as prototypical of the way God will differentiate Israel from all other nations (19)
Emotional Formulations	
Inter-Group Conflict	Trials, signs and wonders, mighty hand, and outstretched arm. The images of exodus are paradigmatic for war and prohibitive of assimilation
Attachment and Belonging	"The Lord your God" is repeated x 3
Interdependence	
Shared Fate	Exodus images become paradigmatic for those experiencing conquest, creating a perception of shared fate
Behavioral Formulations	
Identity Norms	Here it is not the remembrance of exodus that evokes certain behaviors but rather that Israel's acts of love and obedience toward God (7:9–18) allows her to remember exodus as a prototype for the present and future
Temporal Formulations	
Coherency Over Time	Supernatural deliverance of the new generation is likened to that of the prototypical exodus generation.
Possible Social Identities	Choosing an identity of loyalty and obedience toward God allows Israel to re-actualize exodus in the present and future
Myths of Common Descent	
Genealogical	
Cultural-Ideological	

Verbal or Imaginal Representations	Definition or Example
Shared Life Stories	
Obligation to Tell	Retelling exodus maintains and reinforces Israel's distinctiveness in the face of a new context and threat of assimilation, unifying generations over time and space, and bringing the past to bear on the present
Actualization	(See possible social identities above)

Deuteronomy 11:2–4,7

Verbal or Imaginal Representations	Definition or Example
Cognitive Formulations	
Categorization	
Named Group (group name or label)	
Plural Pronouns	
Boundaries	
Shared Beliefs	
Prototypes	
Stereotypes	
Evaluative Formulations	
Differentiation	The fivefold repetition "that he did" (2–7) emphasizes God's efforts to separate out a distinct people from external and internal threats
Positive Evaluation of the Ingroup	
Devaluation of the "Other"	This retelling emphasizes God's comprehensive, punitive actions against Egypt. The internal "other" in the midst of Israel (6) is similarly brought down

Verbal or Imaginal Representations	Definition or Example
Emotional Formulations	
Inter-Group Conflict	
Attachment and Belonging	
Interdependence	
Shared Fate	
Behavioral Formulations	
Identity Norms	Exhortations to fear love and obey God (10:2–11:1; 11:8–32) envelop the exodus story placing the remembrance of exodus at the core of covenantal obedience
Temporal Formulations	
Coherency Over Time	The story blurs the line between the exodus generation and succeeding generations creating continuity over time. Discontinuity, however, is also created by the "other" within.
Possible Social Identities	
Myths of Common Descent	
Genealogical	
Cultural-Ideological	
Shared Life Stories	
Obligation to Tell	
Actualization	God's discipline (the lessons learned from his mighty acts of judgement) is the experience of *this* generation of Israel (2, 7). The exodus story must be heard and experienced personally

Deuteronomy 26:5b-9

Verbal or Imaginal Representations	Definition or Example
Cognitive Formulations	
Categorization	
Named Group (group name or label)	"Great nation" vs Egypt
Plural Pronouns	We/us vs Egyptians
Boundaries	"We are a people who . . ."—Israel defines herself by a story and aligns herself with those who went down into and came up out of Egypt
Shared Beliefs	
Prototypes	
Stereotypes	
Evaluative Formulations	
Differentiation	
Positive Evaluation of the Ingroup	Israel is positively depicted as going from being few in number and alien to being a great nation, mighty and populous, favored by God, and gifted with land
Devaluation of the "Other"	Egypt is portrayed as being brought down by God's mighty hand, outstretched arm, terrifying power, and signs and wonders
Emotional Formulations	
Inter-Group Conflict	There are images of harsh treatment, suffering and crying out on account of Egypt
Attachment and Belonging	The God of our ancestors heard, saw, and brought us out
Interdependence	

Verbal or Imaginal Representations	Definition or Example
Shared Fate	Israel's fate of homelessness and wandering is exchanged for one of being given a lavish homeland
Behavioral Formulations	
Identity Norms	Israel celebrates Firstfruits in order to remember her exodus identity
Temporal Formulations	
Coherency Over Time	Coherency created by shifting pronouns from 5 to 6–7 (third person to first person plural)
Possible Social Identities	
Myths of Common Descent	
Genealogical	"Our ancestors"—a genealogical relationship is present
Cultural-Ideological	The corporate participation in exodus binds the generations together
Shared Life Stories	
Obligation to Tell	There is an obligation to take up this identity story at the time of the first Firstfruits
Actualization	Tellers of the story are incorporated into it. They tell it as eyewitnesses

Joshua 24:2–7,17

Verbal or Imaginal Representations	Definition or Example
Cognitive Formulations	
Categorization	
Named Group (group name or label)	
Plural Pronouns	

Verbal or Imaginal Representations	Definition or Example
Boundaries	There are conflicting definitions of who Israel was before exodus: descendants of idolatrous patriarchs (v. 2) or slaves (v. 17)
Shared Beliefs	
Prototypes	
Stereotypes	
Evaluative Formulations	
Differentiation	God's differentiated treatment of Israel and Egypt: he plagued Egypt but brought Israel out (v. 5), put darkness between *you* (Israel) and the *Egyptians* (v. 7), and made the sea cover *them* while *you* (Israel) saw what occurred (v. 7)
Positive Evaluation of the Ingroup	
Devaluation of the "Other"	Egypt is brought down metaphorically and literally. But rather than portraying the comparative elevation of Israel in this first retelling (2–7), Israel is also devalued subtlely: "Afterwards you lived in the wilderness a long time" (7b). Israel's counterclaim in 17 was that God brought her *up* (not just *out*) and that the desert experience was evidence of God's extended care for Israel
Emotional Formulations	
Inter-Group Conflict	There are poignant images of God acting against Egypt and for Israel
Attachment and Belonging	God initiated Israel's deliverance (2–7)
Interdependence	
Shared Fate	Israel shares the fate of being brought up out of Egypt

Verbal or Imaginal Representations	Definition or Example
Behavioral Formulations	
Identity Norms	Remembrance of exodus and of God's other interventions on behalf of Israel (8–13) serve as the foundation for Joshua's imperative identity norms (14–15) and the people's commitment to them (16–18). Conversely, covenant renewal offers an opportunity to remember exodus. The exodus story is the nucleus of covenant
Temporal Formulations	
Coherency Over Time	First retelling: Shifting pronoun are used—"when *they* cried out . . . he put darkness between *you* and the Egyptians (7). The minimization of the distance between the exodus generation and the new one is evident in the assertion "your eyes saw what I did in Egypt"
	Second retelling: Coherency over time is evident in the claims, "the Lord brought *us* and *our ancestors* up from the land of Egypt" and "before our eyes" (17)
Possible Social Identities	The two stories offer a choice of social identities: a polytheistic one and a faithful one
Myths of Common Descent	
Genealogical	There is a dissonant genealogical myth: Israel's descent from idolatrous patriarchs
Cultural-Ideological	
Shared Life Stories	
Obligation to Tell	Covenant renewal reminds Israel that her identity and behavior are grounded in the telling of and participation in the story of exodus. Implicit to second retelling: Exodus is the shared story of all Israel only when it is properly narrated.

Verbal or Imaginal Representations	Definition or Example
Actualization	Hearers included in the story by pronoun shifts from them to us

1 Samuel 12:6–8

Verbal or Imaginal Representations	Definition or Example
Cognitive Formulations	
Categorization	
Named Group (group name or label)	There is no named ingroup, they remain nameless
Plural Pronouns	They (your ancestors)
Boundaries	
Shared Beliefs	There is a shared belief in the reality of exodus
Prototypes	
Stereotypes	
Evaluative Formulations	
Differentiation	
Positive Evaluation of the Ingroup	A positive evaluation of Israel is only sustained within a largely devaluing context by the retelling of exodus with its two references to God's deliverance through Moses and Aaron (6, 8)
Devaluation of the "Other"	
Emotional Formulations	
Inter-Group Conflict	
Attachment and Belonging	
Interdependence	
Shared Fate	Verse 7 "you and your ancestors"—the present Israel's fate is bound to that of the exodus generation and their descendants

Verbal or Imaginal Representations	Definition or Example
Behavioral Formulations	
Identity Norms	Positive behavioral response in keeping with God's righteous acts in exodus was implicitly expected, as is indicated by 9a: "But they forgot the LORD their God"
Temporal Formulations	
Coherency Over Time	Present hearers are portrayed as witnesses to all the righteous acts of God done for them and their ancestors (7)
Possible Social Identities	(The context of 9–15 presents an implicit choice: returning to oppression or remembering and living in response to exodus)
Myths of Common Descent	
Genealogical	
Cultural-Ideological	The group gathered with Samuel traces her lineage in an unbroken line back to exodus
Shared Life Stories	
Obligation to Tell	The setting of the wheat harvest (Feast of Weeks) is an occasion to remember exodus
Actualization	

Jeremiah 32:20–23a

Verbal or Imaginal Representations	Definition or Example
Cognitive Formulations	
Categorization	
Named Group (group name or label)	"Your people Israel" (21)
Plural Pronouns	

Verbal or Imaginal Representations	Definition or Example
Boundaries	Israel defined by being brought out of Egypt.
Shared Beliefs	
Prototypes	
Stereotypes	
Evaluative Formulations	
Differentiation	Distinction between Israel and Egypt was powerfully wrought, not only with signs and wonders but with "great terror" (21)
Positive Evaluation of the Ingroup	Israel is portrayed as the object of God's attention (21). This implicit positive evaluation is muted by the explicit assertion in the literary context of v. 23b "they did not obey your voice or follow your law"
Devaluation of the "Other"	Decimation of Egypt is implied (21)
Emotional Formulations	
Inter-Group Conflict	
Attachment and Belonging	God acts on behalf of Israel are unprovoked, of God's own initiative
Interdependence	
Shared Fate	Generations are united by a shared fate both negatively and positively. Impending disaster in surrounding context is linked to the previous generation's lax attitude toward obedience. But the wonders perceived "to this day" in Israel are exodus-like
Behavioral Formulations	
Identity Norms	
Temporal Formulations	
Coherency Over Time	There are implied connections between Jeremiah's Israel (20) and the people whom God brought out of Egypt (21)

Verbal or Imaginal Representations	Definition or Example
Possible Social Identities	
Myths of Common Descent	
Genealogical	Ancestry is mentioned
Cultural-Ideological	Past and present generations, however, are unified by exodus
Shared Life Stories	
Obligation to Tell	
Actualization	

Nehemiah 9:9–12,36

Verbal or Imaginal Representations	Definition or Example
Cognitive Formulations	
Categorization	
Named Group (group name or label)	"Our ancestors" (9–10, 36). Pharaoh, his servants, and the people of the land (10)
Plural Pronouns	The outgroup is designated by the collective *they* (10) and the ingroup by *them* (the ancestors—11–12) and *we* (36)
Boundaries	
Shared Beliefs	
Prototypes	(Literary context: the prototypical member of Israel is insolent and unmindful of God's marvelous, exodus-like deeds—16–18, 26, 28–30, 33–35)
Stereotypes	Stereotypical Egyptian is also insolent (compare זיד here in 10 to 16 and 29)
Evaluative Formulations	
Differentiation	
Positive Evaluation of the Ingroup	

Verbal or Imaginal Representations	Definition or Example
Devaluation of the "Other"	The devaluation of Egypt is represented in images of mocking and fall (10–11). The comparative devaluation of Israel is expressed in the shared use of the term ידע for both Egypt and Israel

Emotional Formulations

Inter-Group Conflict	
Attachment and Belonging	God saw and heard Israel (9) and aligned himself with her by acting selectively on her behalf (10–11) and leading her (12). (Tender mercies and long-suffering are evident in the literary context—13–15, 17, 19–25, 27–33, 35)
Interdependence	
Shared Fate	

Behavioral Formulations

Identity Norms	

Temporal Formulations

Coherency Over Time	There is an image of an unbroken succession of ancestors and offspring from the time of suffering in Egypt onward (9, 16, 23, 24, 32, 34, 36). The sins of the past and present are intermingled in 33–37. The present status of slavery (36) is coherent with past experience
Possible Social Identities	
Myths of Common Descent	
Genealogical	
Cultural-Ideological	A relationship with Abram is shown, not primarily as a blood ancestor but as one who was "brought out" (7)
Shared Life Stories	
Obligation to Tell	
Actualization	

Psalm 78:11–14, 42–53

Verbal or Imaginal Representations	*Definition or Example*
Cognitive Formulations	
Categorization	
Named Group (group name or label)	Context: speaker identifies hearers as "my people" and then as Israel/Jacob (1–2)
	Ephraim—represents culpable Israel
Plural Pronouns	Context: Speaker switches to "we" (inclusive of speaker) in v. 3
	In vv. 42–53, two "theys"are interwoven: the typical Egyptian other and the "they" who was part of Israel but who was characterized by lawlessness, rebellion, unfaithfulness, and disloyalty.
Boundaries	Psalm 78 establishes Israel's unbroken chain and ideal boundary of "ones who remember exodus." This boundary excludes some who were once part of the ingroup but who forgot
Shared Beliefs	
Prototypes	Israel's prototypes consist of the ancestors (from the time of exodus forward) who either transmitted the stories of God's praiseworthy deeds or who were stubborn and rebellious and forgot them (1–11)
Stereotypes	
Evaluative Formulations	
Differentiation	
Positive Evaluation of the Ingroup	Israel's positive valuation by God is only implicit in God's orchestration of deliverance and his working of wonders on her behalf
Devaluation of the "Other"	Devaluation is explicit not only of Egypt as "other" but of the "other" within characterized by forgetfulness

APPENDIX 4: METHODOLOGY WORKSHEETS

Verbal or Imaginal Representations	*Definition or Example*
Emotional Formulations	
Inter-Group Conflict	
Attachment and Belonging	Belonging to the ingroup is inseparably linked to remembrance of God and his wonders. This is the core of covenantal relationship with God
Interdependence	
Shared Fate	
Behavioral Formulations	
Identity Norms	Psalm 78 implies that unfaithfulness can be avoided by hearing and telling the stories of God's great deeds. Remembering and telling the story is the behavioral norm that motivates covenant keeping
Temporal Formulations	
Coherency Over Time	There is a violation in the temporal sequencing of the story line. Verses 9–11 look backward to what was forgotten, then move forward again from Egypt to Canaan. Verses 43–72 look further back again to forgotten exodus. Hearers remember twice what "happened" once.
Possible Social Identities	Hearers must choose between joining the chain of "remembers" or of "forgetters"
Myths of Common Descent	
Genealogical	
Cultural-Ideological	The collective "we" is an unbroken line of those who remember and tell
Shared Life Stories	
Obligation to Tell	Literary context: hearers exhorted to heed and transmit the shared life-story of God's praiseworthy deeds (1–10). This is inclusive of the exodus
Actualization	The narrative sequencing strips the exodus of its particular historical context and invites hearers to participate

Psalm 105:23–39

Verbal or Imaginal Representations	*Definition or Example*
Cognitive Formulations	
Categorization	
Named Group (group name or label)	Hearers are addressed in the literary context of the retelling as "offspring of his servant Abraham, children of Jacob" (6), and as "my anointed ones" (15). Enveloping the exodus story, they are also labelled "his chosen ones" in vv. 6 and 43. In the exodus retelling the ingroup is addressed as "Israel" as they enter Egypt (23) and again as they are brought out (37). They are also addressed collectively as "his people" (24–25) and "his servants" (25)
Plural Pronouns	Context in vv. 1–5: Audience addressed anonymously by 10 plural imperatives
Boundaries	
Shared Beliefs	
Prototypes	
Stereotypes	
Evaluative Formulations	
Differentiation	In the literary context of the retelling, pro-Israel is differentiated from others as the recipient of divine favor and protection (12–15). Israel also is spatially differentiated in her being "brought out" from Egypt (37 and 43)
Positive Evaluation of the Ingroup	"And the LORD made his people very fruitful, and made them stronger than their foes" (24).
Devaluation of the "Other"	Egypt struck by decimating plagues emanating from Moses, Aaron, and God (26–36)

APPENDIX 4: METHODOLOGY WORKSHEETS

Verbal or Imaginal Representations	Definition or Example
Emotional Formulations	
Inter-Group Conflict	
Attachment and Belonging	God's covenant of land and its realization over time—with exodus at the center—is the shared fate of "a thousand generations" of Israel (8).
Interdependence	
Shared Fate	
Behavioral Formulations	
Identity Norms	The Psalm calls its hearers to make known, sing, tell, and remember God's wonders, and then it exemplifies these actions for them.
	Everything God has done for Israel (including exodus) is designed so that she might "keep his statutes and observe his laws" (45)
Temporal Formulations	
Coherency Over Time	The language and images of Psalm 105 resonate with the primary exodus story, linking hearers to the exodus generation
Possible Social Identities	
Myths of Common Descent	
Genealogical	
Cultural-Ideological	The landless Patriarchs anchor Israel's prior identity in a common condition
Shared Life Stories	
Obligation to Tell	
Actualization	Twofold "brought out" (37, 43) violates the temporal sequencing of the story line, removing it somewhat from a historical context. Such an atemporal deliverance is more inclusive

Psalm 106:7–12, 21–23

Verbal or Imaginal Representations	*Definition or Example*
Cognitive Formulations	
Categorization	
Named Group (group name or label)	Literary context: "Your people," "your chosen ones," "your nation," and "your heritage" (4–5)
Plural Pronouns	Literary context: "we" and "us" (6, 47)
Boundaries	
Shared Beliefs	
Prototypes	
Stereotypes	
Evaluative Formulations	
Differentiation	God saved and delivered Israel from the Sea and from their foe/enemy/adversary.
	Yet both the adversary and the exodus generation are referred to by the third person plural ("they")
Positive Evaluation of the Ingroup	
Devaluation of the "Other"	Waters covered Israel's adversaries so that not one of them was left (11)
Emotional Formulations	
Inter-Group Conflict	God overcomes unnamed adversaries and natural forces that resist his plans for Israel (9–11)
Attachment and Belonging	Above mentioned intervention asserts God's attachment to the exodus generation and her belonging to him
Interdependence	
Shared Fate	Appreciating exodus (8–11) leads to belief (12) and forgetting it (21–22) to incredulity (24)

APPENDIX 4: METHODOLOGY WORKSHEETS

Verbal or Imaginal Representations	Definition or Example
Behavioral Formulations	
Identity Norms	
Temporal Formulations	
Coherency Over Time	Literary context: Israel is portrayed as united with her forefathers in guilt (6), in cries of distress (44, 47), and the need for deliverance (47).
Possible Social Identities	Israel admits shared guilt with her ancestors (6), whose response to salvation was forgetfulness, rebelliousness, and iniquity. But as she now cries out for salvation anew it is with the proposed intention of responding discordantly with praise and gratitude (47–48)
Myths of Common Descent	
Genealogical	
Cultural-Ideological	
Shared Life Stories	
Obligation to Tell	
Actualization	

Psalm 136:10–15, 23–24

Verbal or Imaginal Representations	Definition or Example
Cognitive Formulations	
Categorization	
Named Group (group name or label)	Israel, Egypt, "Pharaoh and his army"
Plural Pronouns	"Us" (23–24)
Boundaries	
Shared Beliefs	

Verbal or Imaginal Representations	Definition or Example
Prototypes	
Stereotypes	
Evaluative Formulations	
Differentiation	Unbalanced partiality toward Israel: Egypt struck and Israel brought out (10–11); Israel made to pass through the Red Sea but Egypt overthrown in it (14–15)
Positive Evaluation of the Ingroup	God's "strong arm" favors Israel
Devaluation of the "Other"	See above
Emotional Formulations	
Inter-Group Conflict	Images of supernatural conflict
Attachment and Belonging	God's great wonders and steadfast love converge on Israel. She is evaluatively distinct, loved, and favored by God.
Interdependence	
Shared Fate	
Behavioral Formulations	
Identity Norms	(Give thanks—vv. 1 and 26)
Temporal Formulations	
Coherency Over Time	Psalm 136 links "Israel" in the story (10–15) to "us" (23–24)
Possible Social Identities	
Myths of Common Descent	
Genealogical	
Cultural-Ideological	
Shared Life Stories	
Obligation to Tell	
Actualization	

Bibliography

Abrams, Dominic, and Michael A Hogg. *Social Identity Theory: Constructive and Critical Advances*. New York: Harvester-Wheatsheaf, 1990.

Albertz, Rainer. "Exodus: Liberation History Against Charter Myth." In *Religious Identity and the Invention of Tradition: Papers read at a Noster Conference in Soesterberg, January 4-6, 1999*, edited by Jan Willem van Henten and Anton Houtenpen, 128-43. Studies in Theology and Religion 3. Assen: Royal Van Gorcum, 2001.

Alexander, T. Desmond. *From Eden to the New Jerusalem: An Introduction to Biblical Theology*. Nottingham: InterVarsity, 2008.

Allen, Leslie C. *Psalms 101-50*. Rev. ed. Word Biblical Commentary. Nashville: Nelson, 2002.

Alter, Robert. *The Art of Biblical Poetry*. New York: Basic, 1985.

———. *The Five Books of Moses: A Translation with Commentary*. New York: Norton, 2008.

———. *Genesis: Translation and Commentary*. New York: Norton, 1996.

Anderson, Bradford A. "Edom in the Book of Numbers: Some Literary Reflections." *ZAW* 124, no. 1 (2012) 38-51.

Arnold, Bill T. *Genesis*. New Cambridge Bible Commentary. Cambridge: Cambridge University Press, 2009.

Arnone, Anna. "Journeys to Exile: The Constitution of Eritrean Identity through Narratives and Experiences." *JEMS* 34, no. 2 (2008) 325-40.

Ashley, Timothy R. *The Book of Numbers*. New International Commentary on the Old Testament. Grand Rapids: Eerdmans, 1993.

Ashmore, Richard D., et al. "An Organizing Framework for Collective Identity: Articulation and Significance of Multidimensionality." *Psychological Bulletin* 130 (2004) 80-114.

Assmann, Jan. "Collective Memory and Cultural Identity." *New German Critique* 95, no. 65 (1995) 125-33.

———. *Das kulturelle Gedächtnis: Schrift, Erinnerung und politische Identität in frühen Hochkulturen*. Munich: Beck, 1992.

———. *Moses the Egyptian: The Memory of Egypt in Western Monotheism*. Cambridge, MA: Harvard University Press, 1997.

Baker, Coleman A. *Identity, Memory, and Narrative in early Christianity: Peter, Paul, and Recategorization in the Book of Acts*. Eugene, OR: Pickwick, 2011.

———. "New Covenant, New Identity: A Social Scientific Reading of Jeremiah 31:31–34." *The Bible and Critical Theory* 4, no. 1 (2008) 5.1–5.11.

———. "Social Identity Theory and Biblical Interpretation." *BTB* 42 (2012) 129–38.

Bal, Mieke. *Death & Dissymmetry: the Politics of Coherence in the Book of Judges*. Chicago: University of Chicago Press, 1988.

Ballinger, Pamela. *History in Exile: Memory and Identity at the Borders of the Balkans*. Princeton: Princeton University Press, 2003.

Bar, Shaul. "Who Were the 'Mixed Multitude'?" *Hebrew Studies* 49 (2008) 27–39.

Bar-Tal, Daniel. "Group Beliefs as an Expression of Social Identity." In *Social Identity: International Perspectives*, edited by Stephen Worchel et al., 93–113. London: Sage, 1998.

Barth, Fredrik. *Ethnic Groups and Boundaries: The Social Organization of Cultural Difference*. Prospect Heights, IL: Waveland, 1969.

Beer, Georg. *Exodus*. Handbuch zum Alten Testament. Tübingen: Mohr Siebeck, 1939.

Bell, Daniel. *The Cultural Contradictions of Capitalism*. 2nd ed. London: Heinemann, 1979.

Berquist, Jon L. "Identities and Empire: Historiographic Questions for the Deuteronomistic History in the Persian Period." In *Historiography and Identity (Re) Formulation in Second Temple Historiographical Literature*, edited by Louis Jonker, 3–13. LHBOTS 534. London: T. & T. Clark, 2010.

Bikmen, Nida. "History, Memory, and Identity: Remembering the Homeland in Exile." PhD diss., The City University of New York, 2007.

Blenkinsopp, Joseph. *David Remembered: Kingship and National Identity in Israel*. Grand Rapids: Eerdmans, 2013.

Boling, Robert G., and G. Ernest Wright. *Joshua: A New Translation with Notes and Commentary*. The Anchor Bible. Garden City, NY: Doubleday, 1982.

Bonnet, Hans. *Reallexikon der ägyptischen Religionsgeschichte*. Berlin: de Gruyter, 1952.

Bosman, Jan P. *Social Identity in Nahum: A Theological-Ethical Enquiry*. Piscataway, NJ: Gorgias, 2008.

Braulik, Georg. *Deuteronomium 1–16, 17*. Die neue Echter-Bibel Kommentar zum Alten Testament mit der Einheitsübersetzung. Würzburg: Echter, 1986.

Brettler, Marc Zvi. *The Creation of History in Ancient Israel*. New York: Routledge, 1995.

Bridge, Edward. "Polite Israel and Impolite Edom: Israel's Request to Travel through Edom in Numbers 20.14–21." *JSOT* 35, no. 1 (2010) 77–88.

Brodie, Thomas L. *Genesis as Dialogue: A Literary, Historical, and Theological Commentary*. Oxford: Oxford University Press, 2001.

———. "The Literary Unity of Numbers: Nineteen Atonement-Centered Diptychs as One Key Element." In *The Books of Leviticus and Numbers*, edited by Thomas Römer, 455–72. Leuven: Uitgeverij Peeters, 2008.

Brown, Rupert. *Group Processes: Dynamics within and between Groups*. Oxford: Blackwell, 2000.

Brown, Rupert, and Dora Capozza. "Motivational, Emotional, and Cultural Influences in Social Identity Processes." In *Social Identities: Motivational, Emotional and Cultural Influences*, edited by Rupert Brown and Dora Capozza, 3–29. New York: Psychology, 2006.

Bruckner, James K. *Exodus*. New International Biblical Commentary on the Old Testament. Peabody, MA: Hendrickson, 2008.

Brueggemann, Walter. "The Book of Exodus: Introduction, Commentary, and Reflections." In *NIB*, edited by Leander E. Keck et al., 1:677–981. Nashville: Abingdon, 1994.

———. "A 'Characteristic' Reflection on What Comes Next (Jeremiah 32.16–44)." In *Prophets and Paradigms: Essays in Honor of Gene M. Tucker*, edited by Stephen B. Reid, 15–32. Sheffield: Sheffield Academic, 1996.

———. *A Commentary on Jeremiah: Exile and Homecoming*. Grand Rapids: Eerdmans, 1991.

———. "Conversations among Exiles." *The Christian Century* (July 2–9, 1997) 630–32.

———. *Deuteronomy*. Abingdon Old Testament Commentary. Nashville: Abingdon, 2001.

———. *First and Second Samuel*. Interpretation: A Bible Commentary for Teaching and Preaching. Louisville: Knox, 1990.

———. "Psalms in Narrative Performance." In *Performing the Psalms*, edited by Dave Bland and David Fleer, 9–29. St Louis: Chalice, 2005.

———. "A Response to the 'Song of Miriam' by Bernhard Anderson." In *Directions in Biblical Hebrew* Poetry, edited by E. R. Follis, 297–302. Sheffield: JSOT, 1987.

———. *The Theology of the Book of Jeremiah*. New York: Cambridge University Press, 2007.

Brueggemann, Walter, and William H. Bellinger Jr. *Psalms*. New Cambridge Bible Commentary. New York: Cambridge University Press, 2014.

Bullock, C. Hassell. *Encountering the Book of Psalms: A Literary and Theological Introduction*. Grand Rapids: Baker Academic, 2001.

Butler, Trent C. *Joshua*. Word Biblical Commentary 7. Waco: Word, 1983.

Calvin, John. *Commentaries on The Four Last Books of Moses Arranged in the Form of a Harmony*. Translated by Rev. Charles William Bingham. Grand Rapids: Baker, 1979.

Carr, David. "Narrative and the Real World: an Argument for Continuity." *History and Theory* 25 (1986) 117–31.

Carr, David M. "What is Required to Identify the Pre-Priestly Narrative Connections between Genesis and Exodus? Some General Reflections and Specific Cases." In *A Farewell to the Yahwist? The Composition of the Pentateuch in Recent European Interpretation*, edited by Thomas B. Dozeman and Konrad Schmid, 159–80. Atlanta: SBL, 2006.

Carter, Warren. "Social Identities, Subgroups, and John's Gospel: Jesus the Prototype and Pontius Pilate (John 18.28—19.16)." In *T&T Clark Handbook to Social Identity in the New Testament*, edited by J. Brian Tucker and Coleman A. Baker, 235–51. New York: Bloomsbury T. & T. Clark, 2014.

Cassuto, Umberto. *A Commentary on the Book of Exodus*. Translated by Israel Abrahams. Jerusalem: Magnes, 1983.

———. *A Commentary on the Book of Genesis, Part II: From Noah to Abraham*. Jerusalem: Magnes, 1964.

Childs, Brevard S. *The Book of Exodus: A Critical, Theological Commentary*. Old Testament Library. Philadelphia: Westminster, 1974.

———. *Introduction to the Old Testament as Scripture*. Philadelphia: Fortress, 1979.

———. *Memory and Tradition in Israel*. London: SCM, 1962.

Choi, John H. *Traditions as Odds: The Reception of the Pentateuch in Biblical and Second Temple Period Literature*. London: T. & T. Clark, 2010.

Christensen, Duane L. *Deuteronomy 1:1—21:9*. Rev. ed. Word Biblical Commentary 6A. Nashville: Nelson, 2001.

Cinnirella, Marco. "Exploring Temporal Aspects of Social Identity: the Concept of Possible Social Identities." *EJSP* 28 (1998) 227–48.

Clements, Ronald E. "The Book of Deuteronomy: Introduction, Commentary, and Reflections." In *NIB*, edited by Leander E. Keck et al., 2:271–552. Nashville: Abingdon, 1998.

———. *Jeremiah. Interpretation: A Bible Commentary for Teaching and Preaching*. Atlanta: Knox, 1988.

Cole, Alan. *Exodus*. Tyndale Old Testament Commentaries. Downers Grove, IL: InterVarsity, 1973.

Condor, Susan. "Social Identity and Time." In *Social Groups and Identities: Developing the Legacy of Henri Tajfel*, edited by W. Peter Robinson, 285–315. Oxford: Butterworth-Heinemann, 1996.

Coogan, Michael D. "Exodus, The." In *The Oxford Companion to the Bible*, edited by Bruce M. Metzger and Michael D. Coogan, 9. New York: Oxford University Press, 1993.

Cornell, Stephen. "That's the Story of Our Life." In *We Are a People: Narrative and Multiplicity in Constructing Ethnic Identity*, edited by Paul Spickard and W. Jeffrey Burroughs, 41–53. Philadelphia: Temple University Press, 2000.

Cornell, Stephen, and Douglas Hartmann. *Ethnicity and Race: Making Identities in a Changing World*. Thousand Oaks, CA: Pine Forge, 2007.

Craigie, Peter C. *The Book of Deuteronomy*. New International Commentary on the Old Testament. Grand Rapids: Eerdmans, 1976.

———. *Psalms 1–50*. Biblical Commentary. Waco: Word, 1983.

Currid, John D. *A Study Commentary on Deuteronomy*. Darlington: Evangelical, 2006.

Curtis, Adrian. *Psalms*. Epworth Commentaries. Peterborough: Epworth, 2004.

Cushman, Philip. *Constructing the Self, Constructing America: A Cultural History of Psychotherapy*. Reading, MA: Addison-Wesley, 1995.

Davis, John J. *Moses and the Gods of Egypt: Studies in Exodus*. Old Testament Series. Grand Rapids: Baker, 1971.

De Fina, Anna. *Identity in Narrative: A Study of Immigrant Discourse*. Amsterdam: Benjamin's, 2003.

De Pury, Albert. "Le choix de l'ancêtre." *TZ* (2001) 105–14.

———. "Le cycle de Jacob comme légende autonome des origins d'Israël." In *Congress Volume*, edited by J.A. Emerton, 78–96. New York: Brill, 1991.

Deaux, Kay et al. "Parameters of Social Identity." *JPSP* 68, no. 2 (1995) 280–91.

Delumeau, Jean. *History of Paradise: The Garden of Eden in Myth and Tradition*. Chicago: University of Illinois Press, 2000.

Dozeman, Thomas B. *Exodus*. Eerdmans Critical Commentary. Grand Rapids: Eerdmans, 2009.

Driver, S. R. *A Critical and Exegetical Commentary on Deuteronomy*, 3rd ed. Edinburgh: T. & T. Clark, 1978.

Durham, John I. *Exodus*. Word Biblical Commentary. Waco: Word, 1987.

Edelman, Diana V. "YHWH's Othering of Israel." In *Imagining the Other and Constructing Israelite Identity in the Early Second Temple Period*, edited by Ehud Ben Zvi and Diane V. Edelman, 41–69. New York: Bloomsbury T. & T. Clark, 2014.

Edelman, Diana V., and Ehud B. Zvi, eds. *Remembering Biblical Figures in the Late Persian and Early Hellenistic Periods: Social Memory and Imagination*. Oxford: Oxford University Press: 2013.

Esler, Philip F. "Collective Memory and Hebrews 11: Outlining a New Investigative Framework." In *Memory, Tradition, and Text: Uses of the Past in Early Christianity*, edited by Alan Kirk and Tom Thatcher, 151–71. Society of Biblical Literature Semeia Studies 52. Atlanta: SBL, 2005.

———. *Conflict and Identity in Romans*. Minneapolis: Augsberg Fortress, 2003.

———. "Ezra-Nehemiah as a Narrative of (Re-invented) Israelite Identity." *BibInt* 11 (2003) 413–26.

———. *Galatians*. New York: Routledge, 1998.

———. "Group Boundaries and Intergroup Conflict in Galatians: A New Reading of Gal. 5:13—6:10." In *Ethnicity and the Bible*, edited by Mark G. Brett, 215–40. Leiden: Brill, 1996.

———. "Group Norms and Prototypes in Matthew 5.3–12: A Social Identity Interpretation of the Matthaean Beatitudes." In *T&T Clark Handbook to Social Identity in the New Testament*, edited by J. Brian Tucker and Coleman A. Baker, 147–71. New York: Bloomsbury T. & T. Clark, 2014.

———. "Jesus and the Reduction of Intergroup Conflict: The Parable of the Good Samaritan in the Light of Social Identity." *BibInt* 8, no. 4 (2000) 325–57.

———. "'Keeping it in the Family': Culture, Kinship and Identity in 1 Thessalonias and Galatians." In *Families and Family Relations as Represented in Early Judaisms and Early Christianities*, edited by Jan Willem van Henten and Athalya Brenner, 145–84. Leiden: Deo, 2000.

———. "An Outline of Social Identity Theory." In *T&T Clark Handbook to Social Identity in the New Testament*, edited by J. Brian Tucker and Coleman A. Baker, 13–39. New York: Bloomsbury T. & T. Clark, 2014.

———. "'Remember My Fetters': Memorialisation of Paul's Imprisonment." In *Explaining Christian Origins and Early Judaism: Contributions from Cognitive and Social Sciences*, edited by Petri Luomanen et al., 231–58. Biblical Interpretation Series 89. Boston: Brill, 2007.

———. "Social Identity, the Virtues, and the Good Life: A New Approach to Romans 12:1—15:13." *BTB* 33 (2003) 51–63.

Esler, Philip F., and Ronald A. Piper. *Lazarus, Mary and Martha: Social-Scientific Approaches to the Gospel of John*. Minneapolis: Fortress, 2006.

Finitsis, Antonios. "The Other in Haggai and Zechariah 1–8." In *The "Other" in Second Temple Judaism: Essays in Honor of John J. Collins*, edited by Daniel C. Harlow et al., 116–31. Grand Rapids: Eerdmans, 2011.

Fishbane, Michael. *Biblical Interpretation in Ancient Israel*. Oxford: Clarendon, 1985.

———. *Text and Texture: Close Readings of Selected Biblical Texts*. New York: Schocken, 1979.

Freedman, David N. "Moses and Miriam: The Song of the Sea (Exodus 15:1–18, 21)." In *Realia Dei: Essays in Archaeology and Biblical Interpretation in Honor of Edward F. Campbell, Jr. at His Retirement*, edited by P. H. William and T. Hiebert, 67–83. Atlanta: Scholars, 1999.

Freedman, David N., and B. E. Willoughby. "עברי" in *Theological Dictionary of the Old Testament*, edited by G. Johannes Botterweck, Helmer Ringgren, and Heinz-Josef Fabry, 10:431. Grand Rapids: Eerdmans, 1999.

Fretheim, Terence E. "The Book of Genesis: Introduction, Commentary, and Reflections." In *The New Interpreter's Bible: General Articles on the Old Testament; Genesis; Exodus; Leviticus*, edited by Leander E. Keck et al., 1:319–674. Nashville: Abingdon, 1994.

———. *Exodus*. Interpretation: A Biblical Commentary for Teaching and Preaching. Louisville: Knox, 1991.

Friedman, Jonathan. "The Past in the Future: History and the Politics of Identity." *AA* 94 (1992) 837–59.

Frisch, Amos. "The Exodus Motif in 1 Kings 1–14." *JSOT* 87 (2000) 3–21.

Gaebelian, Frank E., ed. *Genesis—Numbers*. Expositor's Bible Commentary 2. Grand Rapids: Regency Reference Library, 1990.

Gaertner, S. L., and J. F. Dovidio. *Reducing Intergroup Bias: The Common Ingroup Identity Model*. Philadelphia: Psychology, 2000.

Gerstenberger, Erhard S. *Psalms, Part 2, and Lamentations*. Forms of the Old Testament Literature 15. Grand Rapids: Eerdmans, 2001.

Greenstein, Edward L. "Mixing Memory and Design: Reading Psalm 78." *Prooftexts* 10 no. 2 (1990) 197–219.

Greifenhagen, F. V. *Egypt on the Pentateuch's Ideological Map: Constructing Biblical Israel's Identity*. London: Sheffield Academic, 2002.

Hakola, Raimo. "The Burden of Ambiguity: Nicodemus and the Social Identity of the Johannine Christians." *NTS* 55 (2009) 438–55.

———. "'Friendly' Pharisees and Social Identity in Acts." In *Contemporary Studies in Acts*, edited by T. E. Phillips, 181–200. Macon, GA: Mercer University Press, 2009.

———. *Reconsidering Johannine Christianity: A Social Identity Approach*. Hoboken, NJ: Taylor and Francis, 2015.

———. "Social Identity and a Stereotype in the Making: The Pharisees as Hypocrites in Matt 23." In *Identity Formation in the New Testament*, edited by Bengt Holmberg and Mikael Winninge, 123–39. Tübingen: Mohr/Siebeck, 2008.

———. "Social Identities and Group Phenomena in Second Temple Judaism." In *Explaining Christian Origins and Early Judaism: Contributions from Cognitive and Social Sciences*, edited by Petri Luomanen et al., 259–76. Biblical Interpretation Series 89. Boston: Brill, 2007.

Halbwachs, Maurice. *Les cadres sociaux de la mémoire*. New York: Arno, 1975.

———. *On Collective Memory*. Edited by Lewis A. Coser. Chicago: University of Chicago Press, 1992.

Hall, Stuart. "Cultural Identity and Diaspora." In *Theorizing Diaspora: A Reader*, edited by Jana Evans Braziel and Anita Manner, 233–46. Malden, MA: Blackwell, 2003.

Hamilton, Victor P. *The Book of Genesis: Chapters 1–17*. New International Commentary on the Old Testament 1. Grand Rapids: Eerdmans, 1990.

Hauser, Alan J. "Two Songs of Victory: A Comparison of Exodus 15 and Judges 5." In *Directions in Biblical Hebrew Poetry*, edited by Elaine R. Follis, 265–84. Sheffield: JSOT, 1987.

Hearon, Holly. "The Story of 'the Woman who Anointed Jesus' as Social Memory: A Methodological Proposal for the Study of Tradition as Memory." In *Memory, Tradition, and Text: Uses of the Past in Early Christianity*, edited by Alan Kirk and Tom Thatcher, 99–118. Semeia Studies. Atlanta: SBL, 2005.

Hendel, Ronald. "The Exodus in Biblical Memory." *JBL* 120, no. 4 (2001) 601–22.

Henry, Matthew. *Matthew Henry's Commentary on the Whole Bible, Complete and Unabridged in One Volume*. Peabody, MA: Hendrickson, 1991.

Hinkle, Steve, and Rupert Brown, "Intergroup Comparison and Social Identity: Some Links and Lacunae." In *Social Identity Theory: Constructive and Critical Advances*, edited by Dominic Abrams and Michael A. Hogg, 48–70. New York: Harvester-Wheatsheaf, 1990.

Hoffman, Yair. "A North Israelite Typological Myth and a Judaean Historical Tradition: The Exodus in Hosea and Amos." *VT* 39 (1989) 169–82.

Hoffmeier, James K. "The Arm of God Versus the Arm of Pharaoh in the Exodus Narrative." *Biblica* 67, no. 3 (1986) 378–87.

Hogg, Michael A. "Social Identity and Group Cohesiveness." In *Rediscovering the Social Group: A Self-Categorization Theory*, edited by John C. Turner with Michael A. Hogg et al., 89–116. New York: Blackwell, 1987.

———. "Social Identity Theory." In *The Blackwell Encyclopedia of Social Psychology*, edited by A. Manstead and M. Hewstone, 555–60. Oxford: Blackwell, 1995.

Hogg, Michael A., and Dominic Abrams. *Social identifications: A Social Psychology of Intergroup Relations and Group Processes*. London: Routledge, 1988.

Hood, Jared C. "I Appeared as El Shaddai: Intertextual Interplay in Exodus 6:3." *WTJ* 76 (2014) 167–88.

Hossfeld, Frank-Lothar. "Psalm 78." In *Psalms 2: A Commentary on Psalms 51–100*, edited by Klaus Baltzer, 282–301. Hermeneia—A Critical and Historical Commentary on the Bible. Minneapolis: Fortress, 2005.

House, Paul R. "Examining the Narratives of Old Testament Narrative: An Exploration in Biblical Theology." *WTJ* 67 (2005) 229–45.

Howard, David M., Jr. *Joshua*. New American Commentary. Nashville: Broadman & Holman, 1998.

Hyatt, J. Philip. *Exodus*. New Century Bible Commentary. Grand Rapids: Eerdmans, 1971.

Isbel, Charles David. *The Function of Exodus Motifs in Biblical Narratives: Theological Didactic Drama*. Lewiston, NY: Mellen, 2002.

Janzen, Waldemar. *Exodus*. Believers Church Bible Commentary. Scottdale, PA: Herald, 2000.

Japhet, Sara. *From the Rivers of Babylon to the Highlands of Judah: Collected Studies on the Restoration Period*. Winona Lake, IN: Eisenbrauns, 2006.

Johnstone, William. *Exodus*. Old Testament Guides. Sheffield: JSOT, 1990.

Jonker, Louis. "Reforming History: The Hermeneutical Significance of the Books of Chronicles." *VT* 57 (2007) 21–44.

———. "Textual Identities in the Books of Chronicles: The Case of Jehoram's History." In *Community Identity in Judean Historiography: Biblical and Comparative Perspectives*, edited by Gary N. Knoppers and Kenneth A. Ristau, 197–217. Winona Lake, IN: Eisenbrauns, 2009.

Kaiser, Walter C. "[922d] תושב [tôshāb] sojourner." In *Theological Wordbook of the Old Testament*, edited by R. Laird Harris et al., 1:411–12. Chicago: Moody, 1980.

Kaminsky, Joel S. "Israel's Election and the Other in Biblical, Second Temple, and Rabbinic Thought." In *The 'Other' in Second Temple Judaism: Essays in Honor of John J. Collins*, edited by Daniel C. Harlow et al., 17–30. Grand Rapids: Eerdmans, 2011.

Kirk, Alan K. "Social and Cultural Memory." In *Memory, Tradition, and Text: Uses of the Past in Early Christianity*, edited by Alan Kirk and Tom Thatcher, 1–24. Atlanta: SBL, 2005.

Klein, Ralph W. *1 Samuel*. Word Biblical Commentary. Waco: Word, 1983.

———. "The Books of Ezra & Nehemiah: Introduction, Commentary, and Reflections." In *The New Interpreter's Bible: 1 & 2 Kings, 1 & 2 Chronicles, Ezra, Nehemiah, Esther, Tobit, Judith*, edited by Leander E. Keck et al., 3:661–851. Nashville: Abingdon, 1999.

Knight, George A. *Theology as Narration: A Commentary on the Book of Exodus*. Grand Rapids: Eerdmans, 1976.

Korostelina, Karina V. Social *Identity and Conflict: Structures, Dynamics, and Implications*. New York: Palgrave Macmillan, 2007.

Kulp, Joshua. "'We Were Slaves': Rava's Babylonian Haggadah." *Conservative Judaism* 60, no. 3 (2008) 59–75.

Lamoreaux, Jason T. "Social Identity, Boundary Breaking, and Ritual: Saul's Recruitment on the Road to Damascus." *BTB* 38 (2008) 122–34.

Lau, Peter H. W. *Identity and Ethics in the Book of Ruth: A Social Identity Approach*. Beihefte zur Zeitschrift für die alttestamentliche Wissenschaft 416. Berlin: de Gruyter, 2011.

Lee, Archie C. "The Context and Function of the Plagues Tradition in Psalm 78." *JSOT* 48 (1990) 83–89.

Leibowitz, Nehama. *Studies in Bamidbar (Numbers)*. Translated and adapted from the Hebrew by Aryeh Newman. Jerusalem: World Zionist Organization, Dept. for Torah Education and Culture in the Diaspora, 1980.

Leonard, Jeffery M. "Identifying Inner-Biblical Allusions: Psalm 78 as a Test Case." *JBL* 127, no. 2 (2008) 241–65.

Leveen, Adriane. *Memory and Tradition in the Book of Numbers*. Cambridge: Cambridge University Press, 2008.

Lieu, Judith M. *Christian Identity in the Jewish and Graeco-Roman World*. New York: Oxford University Press, 2004.

Linde, Charlotte. *Working the Past: Narrative and Institutional Memory*. New York: Oxford University Press, 2009.

Lipschits, Oded, et al., eds. *Judah and the Judeans in the Achaemenid Period: Negotiating Identity in an International Context*. Winona Lake, IN: Eisenbrauns, 2011.

Lipschits, Oded, and Manfred Oeming, eds. *Judah and the Judeans in the Persian Period*. Winona Lake, IN: Eisenbrauns, 2006.

Longman III, Tremper. *How to Read Exodus*. Downers Grove, IL: InterVarsity, 2009.

Lucas, A. "The Number of Israelites at the Exodus." *PEQ* 76 (1944) 164–68.

Mann, Thomas W. *Deuteronomy*. Westminster Bible Companion. Louisville: Westminster John Knox, 1995.

Marcus, Hazel, and Paula Nurius. "Possible Selves." *American Psychologist* 41 (1986) 954–69.

Marohl, Matthew J. *Faithfulness and the Purpose of Hebrews: A Social Identity Approach*. Eugene, OR: Pickwick, 2008.

Martens, Karen. "'With a Strong Hand and an Outstretched Arm': The Meaning of the Expression byd ḥzqh wbzrwʻ nṭwyh." *Scandinavian Journal of the Old Testament: An International Journal of Nordic Theology* 15, no. 1 (2001) 123–41.

Mathews, Kenneth A. *Genesis 11:27—50:26*. New American Commentary. Nashville: Broadman & Holman, 2005.
Mayes, A. D. H. *Deuteronomy*. New Century Bible. Greenwood, CT: Attic, 1979.
Mays, James L. *Psalms*. Interpretation: A Bible Commentary for Teaching and Preaching. Louisville: Knox, 1994.
McCann, J. Clinton, Jr. "The Book of Psalms: Introduction, Commentary, and Reflections." In *The New Interpreter's Bible: 1 & 2 Maccabees; Introduction to Hebrew Poetry; Job; Psalms*, edited by Leander E. Keck et al., 4:639–1280. Nashville: Abingdon, 1996.
McConville, J. G. *Deuteronomy*. Apollos Old Testament Commentary. Leicester: Apollos, 2002.
Mendenhall, G.E. "The Census Lists of Numbers 1 and 26." *JBL* 77 (1958) 52–66.
Merrill, Eugene H. *Deuteronomy*. New American Commentary 4. Nashville: Broadman & Holman, 1994.
Meyers, Carol L. *Exodus*. Cambridge: Cambridge University Press, 2005.
———. "The Family in Early Israel." In *Families in Ancient Israel*, edited by Leo G. Perdue et al., 1–47. Louisville: Westminster John Knox, 1997.
Milgrom, Jacob. *Numbers*. JPS Torah Commentary. Philadelphia: Jewish Publication Society, 1990.
Miller, James. "Ethnicity and the Hebrew Bible: Problems and Prospects." *CBR* 6 (2008) 170–213.
Miller, Patrick D. *Deuteronomy*. Interpretation: A Bible Commentary for Teaching and Preaching. Louisville: Knox, 1990.
Moberly, R W L. *The Old Testament of the Old Testament: Patriarchal Narratives and Mosaic Yahwism*. Minneapolis: Fortress, 1992.
Nasuti, Harry P. "Historical Narrative and Identity in the Psalms." *HBT* 23 (2001) 132–53.
Nebreda, Sergio R. *Christ Identity: A Social-Scientific Reading of Philippians*. Forschungen Zur Religion Und Literatur Des Alten Und Neuen Testaments 240. Göttingen: Vandenhoeck & Ruprecht, 2011.
Nelson, Richard D. *Deuteronomy: A Commentary*. Old Testament Library. London: Westminster John Knox, 2002.
———. *Joshua: A Commentary*. Old Testament Library. Louisville: Westminster John Knox, 1997.
Newsom, Carol A. "God's Other: The Intractable Problem of the Gentile King in Judean and Early Jewish Literature." In *The "Other" in Second Temple Judaism*, edited by Daniel C. Harlow et al., 31–48. Grand Rapids: Eerdmans, 2011.
Niccacci, Alviero. "The Exodus Tradition in the Psalms, Isaiah and Ezekiel." *LA* 61 (2011) 9–35.
Noth, Martin. *Exodus: A Commentary*. Old Testament Library. London: SCM, 1962.
———. *Numbers: A Commentary*. Old Testament Library. Philadelphia: Westminster, 1969.
Olson, Dennis T. "Negotiating Boundaries: The Old and New Generation and the Theology of Numbers." *Interpretation* 51, no. 3 (1997) 229–40.
———. *Numbers*. IBC. Louisville: John Knox, 1996.
Peterson, Brent O. *Popular Narratives and Ethnic Identity: Literature and Community in Die Abendschule*. Ithaca: Cornell University Press, 1991.
Petrie, F. *Egypt and Israel*. London: SPCK, 1911.

Pilch, John J. "Individual? Or Stereotypes?" *Bible Today* 39 (2001) 171–76.
Pons, Jacques. "La référence au séjour en Égypte et à la sortie d'Égypte dans les codes de loi de l'Ancien Testament." *Études théologiques et religieuses* 63, no. 2 (1988) 169–82.
Rad, Gerhard von. *The Problem of the Hexateuch and Other Essays*. Translated by Rev. E. W. Trueman Dicken. 1st English ed. London: Oliver & Boyd, 1958.
Rendtorff, Rolf. *Das überlieferungsgeschichtliche Problem des Pentateuch*. Beiheft zur Zietschrift für die alttestamentliche Wissenschaft 147. Berlin: de Gruyter, 1976.
Ricoeur, Paul. *Time and Narrative*. 2 vols. Translated by Kathleen McLaughlin and David Pellauer. Chicago: University of Chicago Press, 1984–1985.
Roitto, Rikard. "Act as a Christ-Believer, as a Household Member or as Both?—A Cognitive Perspective on the Relationship between the Social Identity in Christ and Household Identities in Pauline and Deutero-Pauline Texts." In *Identity Formation in the New Testament*, edited by Bengt Holmberg and Mikael Winninge, 141–61. Tübingen: Mohr/Siebeck, 2008.
———. "Behaving like a Christ-Believer: A Cognitive Perspective on Identity and Behavior Norms in the Early Christ-Movement." In *Exploring Early Christian Identity*, edited by Bengt Holmberg, 93–114. Wissenschaftliche Untersuchungen zum Neuen Testament 226. Tübingen: Mohr/Siebeck, 2008.
Römer, Thomas. "Exode et Anti-Exode: La nostalgie de l'Egypte dans les traditions du desert." In *Lectio difficilior probabilior? L'exégèse comme experience de décloisonnement: mélanges offerts à Françoise Smyth-Florentin*, 155–72. Dielheimer Blätter zum Alten Testament und seiner Rezeption in der Alten Kirche 12. Heidelberg: Diebner and Nauerth, 1991.
———. "Exodusmotive und Exoduspolemik in den Erzvätererzählungen." In *Berührungspunkte: Studien zur Sozial- und Religionsgeschichte. Festschrift für Rainer Albertz zu seinem 65 Geburtstag*, edited by Rainer Albertz et al., 3–20. Alter Orient und Altes Testament: Veröffentlichungen zur Kultur und Geschichte des Alten Orients 350. Münster: Ugarit, 2008.
———. "Le cycle de Joseph." *Foi et Vie* 86, no. 3 (1987) 3–15.
Russell, Brian D. *The Song of the Sea: The Date of Composition and Influence of Exodus 15:1–21*. Society of Biblical Literature 101. New York: Lang, 2007.
Ryken, Leland. *Words of Delight: A Literary Introduction to the Bible*. Grand Rapids: Baker, 1987.
Saldarini, Anthony J. "Delegitimation of Leaders in Matthew 23," *CBQ* 54 (1992) 659–80.
Sarna, Nahum M. *Exodus*. JPS Torah Commentary. Philadelphia: Jewish Publication Society, 1991.
Scalise, Pamela J. "The End of the Old Testament: Reading Exile in the Hebrew Bible." *Perspectives in Religious Studies* 35, no. 2 (2008) 163–78.
Schmid, Konrad. Erzväter und Exodus: Untersuchungen zur doppelten Begründung der Ursprünge Israels innerhalb der Geschichtsbücher des Alten Testaments. Neukirchen-Vluyn: Neukirchener, 1999.
Schwartz, Barry. "Christian Origins: Historical Truth and Social Memory." In *Memory, Tradition, and Text: Uses of the Past in Early Christianity*, edited by Alan Kirk and Tom Thatcher, 43–56. SBL: Atlanta, 2005.
———. "Collective Memory and History: How Abraham Lincoln Became a Symbol of Racial Equality." *Sociol Q* 38 (1997) 469–96.
———. "Social Change and Collective Memory: The Democratization of George Washington." *Am Sociol Rev* 56 (1991) 221–36.

———. "Where There's Smoke, There's Fire: Memory and History." In *Memory and Identity in Ancient Judaism and Early Christianity: A Conversation with Barry Schwartz*, edited by Tom Thatcher, 7–37. Atlanta: SBL, 2014.

Scott, Jack B. "109a אלף, (°elep) thousand." In *TWOT*, edited by R. Laird Harris et al., 1:48. Chicago: Moody, 1980.

Sherif, M., et al. *Intergroup conflict and Cooperation: the Robbers Cave Experiment*. Norman: University of Oklahoma Book Exchange, 1961.

Shreckhise, Robert. "The Problem of Finite Verb Translation in Exodus 15.1–18." *JSOT* 32, no. 3 (2008) 287–310.

Singer, Karl H. *Die Metalle Gold, Silber, Bronze, Kupfer und Eisen im Alten Testament und ihre Symbolik*. Forschung zur Bibel 43. Würzburg: Echter, 1980.

Smith, Anthony D. *Myths and Memories of the Nation*. Oxford: Oxford University Press, 1999.

Smith, Eliot R., and Michael A. Zarate. "Exemplar and Prototype Use in Social Categorization." *Social Cognition* 8 (1990) 243–62.

Smith, Jonathan Z. "What a Difference a Difference Makes." In *To See Ourselves as Others See Us: Christians, Jews and Others in Late Antiquity*, edited by Jacob Neusner and Ernest S. Frerichs, 3–48. Chico, Calif.: Scholars, 1985.

Spaulding, Mary B. *Commemorative Identities: Jewish Social Memory and the Johannine Feast of Booths*. Library of New Testament Studies 396. London: T. & T. Clark, 2009.

Stigers, Harord G. "(330a) גר (gēr) sojourner." In *TWOT*, edited by R. Laird Harris et al., 1:155–56. Chicago: Moody, 1980.

Stuart, Douglas K. *Exodus*. New American Commentary 2. Nashville: Broadman & Holman, 2006.

Sumner, William G. *Folkways: a Study of the Sociological Importance of Usages, Manners, Customs, Mores, and Morals*. Boston: Ginn, 1906.

Tajfel, Henri. *Human Groups and Social Categories: Studies in Social Psychology*. Cambridge: Cambridge University Press, 1981.

———. *Social Identity and Intergroup Relations*. EJSP. New York: Cambridge University Press, 1982.

Tajfel, Henri, ed. *Differentiation between Social Groups: Studies in the Social Psychology of Intergroup Relations*. New York: Academic, 1978.

Tajfel, Henri, et al., eds. "Social Categorization and Intergroup Behavior." *EJSP* 1 (1971) 149–78.

Tellbe, Mikael. *Christ-Believers in Ephesus: A Textual Analysis of Early Christian Identity Formation in a Local Perspective*. Wissenschaftliche Untersuchungen zum Neuen Testament 242. Tübingen: Mohr/Siebeck, 2009.

Terrien, Samuel L. *The Psalms: Strophic Structure and Theological Commentary*. Eerdmans Critical Commentary. Grand Rapids: Eerdmans, 2003.

Thoits, P., and L. Virshup. "Me's and We's: Forms and Functions of Social Identities." In *Self and Identity: Fundamental Issues*, edited by R. D. Ashmore and L. Jussim, 106–33. New York: Oxford University Press, 1997.

Throntveit, Mark A. *Ezra-Nehemiah*. Interpretation: A Bible Commentary for Teaching and Preaching. Louisville: Knox, 1992.

Tigay, Jeffrey H. *Deuteronomy: The Traditional Hebrew Text with the New JPS Translation*. JPS Torah Commentary 5. Philadelphia: Jewish Publication Society, 1996.

Triandis, Harry C. "Individualism and Collectivism." In *The Handbook of Culture and Psychology*, edited by David R. Matsumoto, 36. Oxford: Oxford University Press, 2001.

Tucker, Dennis W. "Revisiting the Plagues in Psalm CV." *VT* 3 (2005) 401–11.
Turner, E. "Rites of Communitas." In *Encyclopedia of Religious Rites*, 97–101. New York: Routledge, 2004.
Turner, John C. "The Experimental Social Psychology of Intergroup Behavior." In *Intergroup Behavior*, edited by John C. Turner and Howard Giles, 66–101. Chicago: University of Chicago Press, 1981.
———. "Social Identity, Interdependence and the Social Group: A Reply to Rabbie et al." In *Social Groups and Identities: Developing the Legacy of Henri Tajfel*, edited by W. Peter Robinson, 25–63. Oxford: Butterworth-Heinemann, 1996.
———. "The Social Identity Perspective." In *Social Identity: Context, Commitment, Content*, edited by Naomi Ellemers et al., 8–34. Oxford: Blackwell, 1999.
Turner, John C., et al. *Rediscovering the Social Group: Self-Categorization Theory*. New York: Blackwell, 1987.
Ukwuegbu, Bernard O. "Paraenesis, Identity-defining Norms, or Both? Galatians 5:13—6:20 in the Light of Social Identity Theory." *CBQ* 70 (2008) 538–59.
Utzschneider, Helmut, and Wolfgang Oswald. *Exodus 1–15*. Edited by Walter Dietrich et al. Translated by Philip Sumpter. International Exegetical Commentary on the Old Testament. Stuttgart: Kohlmammer, 2015.
van der Toorn, Karel. "The Exodus as Charter Myth." In *Religious Identity and the Invention of Tradition: Papers Read at a Noster Conference in Soesterberg, January 4–6, 1999*, edited by Jan Willem van Henten and Anton Houtenpen, 113–27. Assen, Netherlands: Royal Van Gorcum, 2001.
van Seters, John. "The Patriarchs and the Exodus: Bridging the Gap between Two Origin Traditions." In *The Interpretation of Exodus: Studies in Honour of Cornelis Houtman*, edited by Riemer Roukema et al., 1–15. Dudley, MA: Peeters, 2006.
Vieweger, Dieter. "'. . . und führte euch heraus aus dem Eisenschmelzofen, aus Ägypten, . . .'. כור הברזל als Metapher fur die Knechtschaft in Agypten (Dtn 4,20; 1 Kon 8,51 und Jer 11,4)." In *Gottes Recht als Lebensraum: Festschrift für Hans Jochen Boecker*, edited by Peter Mommer et al., 265–76. Neukirchen-Vluyn: Neukirchener, 1993.
Watts, James. "Song and the Ancient Reader." *Perspectives in Religious Studies* 22, no. 2 (1995) 135–47.
Wenham, Gordon J. *Genesis 16–50*. Word Biblical Commentary 2. Dallas: Word, 1994.
Wood, Leon J. "(570a) זעקה cry, outcry." In *Theological Wordbook of the Old Testament*, edited by R. Laird Harris et al., 1:265–76. Chicago: Moody, 1980.
Zakovitch, Yair. *"And You Shall Tell Your Son . . . ": The Concept of the Exodus in the Bible*. Jerusalem: Magnes, 1991.
Zerubavel, Eviatar. *Time Maps: Collective Memory and the Social Shape of the Past*. Chicago: University of Chicago Press, 2003.
Zerubavel, Yael. *Recovered Roots: Collective Memory and the Making of Israeli National Tradition*. Chicago: University of Chicago Press, 1995.

www.ingramcontent.com/pod-product-compliance
Lightning Source LLC
Chambersburg PA
CBHW070253230426
43664CB00014B/2524